BREAKING RANKS

BREAKING RANKS

HOW THE RANKINGS INDUSTRY RULES
HIGHER EDUCATION AND WHAT TO DO ABOUT IT

COLIN DIVER

JOHNS HOPKINS UNIVERSITY PRESS

BALTIMORE

© 2022 Johns Hopkins University Press
All rights reserved. Published 2022
Printed in the United States of America on acid-free paper
2 4 6 8 9 7 5 3 1

Johns Hopkins University Press
2715 North Charles Street
Baltimore, Maryland 21218-4363
www.press.jhu.edu

Library of Congress Cataloging-in-Publication Data

Names: Diver, Colin S., author.
Title: Breaking ranks : how the rankings industry rules higher education
and what to do about it / Colin Diver.
Description: Baltimore : Johns Hopkins University Press, 2022. | Includes
bibliographical references and index.
Identifiers: LCCN 2021017977 | ISBN 9781421443058 (hardcover) | ISBN
9781421443065 (ebook)
Subjects: LCSH: Universities and colleges—Ratings and rankings—United
States. | Education, Higher—Social aspects—United States. | Education,
Higher—United States—Evaluation.
Classification: LCC LB2331.63 .D58 2022 | DDC 378.73—dc23
LC record available at https://lccn.loc.gov/2021017977

A catalog record for this book is available from the British Library.

Special discounts are available for bulk purchases of this book.
For more information, please contact Special Sales at specialsales@jh.edu.

To Joan, who has taught me everything important

Contents

PREFACE

My career as law-school dean, college trustee, and college president largely coin-
cided with the era in which college rankings emerged as a powerful force in American higher education. Like most educators, I know from firsthand experience what
it is like to live under their ominous, often oppressive, shadow. But I also know
what it is like to escape from their grip, thanks to my service as the president of a
school—Reed College—that famously refused to play the game.

Those diverse experiences provide the motivation for this book. As you might
expect, I am not a fan of college rankings. But this volume is not just an extended
diatribe against them or a futile call for their abolition. Rather, it is a sincere effort
to understand and explain, as well as critique, a phenomenon that seems to have
become a permanent feature of the higher educational landscape. I utilize personal
experiences as illustrations, but I draw much more heavily on the enormous body
of scholarship about higher education: its market structure, its financing and operation, its inputs and outputs, and the numerous methods available for evaluating
and comparing individual institutions.

Rankings have undoubtedly served useful purposes. Yet they have also seriously misled many college applicants and badly distorted the behavior of educators.
In my view, their costs have outweighed their benefits, and my primary advice to
both applicants and educators is to ignore them. Nonetheless, being a realist, I
know that these annual "best-college" lists continue to exert a magnetic pull on
higher education. Therefore, this book is dedicated to helping those who do pay
attention to this phenomenon—students and their families, precollege counselors,

higher-education faculty and administrators, alumni, donors, public funders, government regulators—to make the soundest possible use of the information such publications provide and to avoid falling into the traps that they so cleverly set for the unwary.

My focus in this volume is not, alas, on all of higher education but rather only on its most competitive segment. Of the 7,600 postsecondary institutions in America, only about 400 admit fewer than half of their applicants, and roughly 800 admit fewer than three-quarters. The remaining schools compose the vast ecology of "non-selective" institutions: two-year community colleges, for-profit institutions, some open-enrollment private nonprofits, and many non-flagship public universities.

In many ways this non-selective sector is the most important component of American higher education. For it is the schools in this segment that struggle, year in and year out, always underfunded and underappreciated, to educate America's most academically disadvantaged students. These are the institutions attended by most low-income students, students of color, children of immigrants, working-class kids, and older adults trying to earn a degree while juggling job and family. Yet this sector is not the realm of college rankings, which are aimed almost exclusively at students who aspire to attend selective schools and who seek guidance in choosing among them.

I focus primarily on undergraduate education because it is the entry point into the world of higher education that affects by far the largest number of rankings consumers. Given my background, I also discuss legal education as a source of comparison or an illustration of general points. Nevertheless, professional and graduate schools are so diverse in character and mission that I make no attempt to survey the distinctive systems that exist to evaluate all of them.

Following a brief prologue, I have divided my presentation into four parts. The first discusses the evolution of college rankings, from beguiling curiosities and occasional scorecards of a school's performance to a veritable ruling regime—what I sometimes call a "rankocracy." Chapter 1 situates the idea and wisdom of rating colleges within the overall phenomenon of product and service ratings in our society. Chapter 2 presents a brief history of the college-ranking industry and a more detailed description of its current landscape. The next chapter unpacks and critiques the formulas customarily used to construct those pervasive best-college lists. The following three chapters discuss the ways in which they have gradually shaped, and often distorted, the behavior of the participants in American higher education—including applicants, their parents, and counselors, as well as college administrators.

Part II explores the widely held view that the most influential college rankings, especially those published by U.S. News & World Report,* are fundamentally designed to measure—and perpetuate—prestige and wealth. Chapter 7 covers the increasingly common view of American higher education as a means of conferring pedigree, based on the relative prestige of the school that one has attended. The following three chapters examine the uses and abuses of three common proxies deployed in an attempt to measure prestige: "expert" (peer) opinion, institutional wealth, and spending per student.

Part III is devoted to investigating the curious practice of judging the quality of the "producers" (i.e., the colleges) in the educational industry by various characteristics of their "customers" (i.e., the students they do, or don't, admit). Chapter 11 introduces the general concept of student selectivity and then explores one approach to measuring it—namely, evaluating a college's incoming students by their prior academic performance in high school. In the next two chapters I turn to the more commonly used, and much more controversial, method of measuring student selectivity: the average scores of entering students on standardized admissions tests. Focusing primarily on the SAT, these chapters explore the practices and limitations of utilizing test scores to measure an individual student's academic potential, as well as the uses and abuses of relying on those results to evaluate the quality of entire institutions. Chapter 14 delves into yet a different approach for measuring student quality—namely, using metrics, such as acceptance rates and enrollment rates, as a scorecard for how well colleges perform in the highly competitive admissions game. I conclude part III by interrogating the curious failure of most ranking systems to give comparable weight to different schools' success in achieving racial and ethnic diversity.

---

* Because this publication and others that publish comprehensive college rankings are available both online and in print, I have decided not to use the italics that traditionally identify print material.

In contrast to the input measures canvassed in parts II and III, part IV addresses the factors that I consider most critical for judging a college's quality—namely, what a college actually does to serve the interests and needs of its students, and how much it contributes to the larger society. The first two chapters in this part address the elusive, but essential, issue of assessing how well various institutions succeed in teaching their students useful skills and knowledge. Chapter 18 discusses the importance of college completion and the use of graduation rates to evaluate a school's performance. In the next chapter I turn to the widespread practice of judging colleges and universities by their students' subsequent career success. Chapter 20 focuses on how well these schools serve lower-income students—by making their educational programs affordable to such students and helping them to move up the economic ladder. Part IV ends with a chapter asking whether, and how, we might compare colleges by their success in preparing their graduates to live truly fulfilling lives.

In the concluding chapter, I offer advice on how both college-going applicants and educational administrators can live in a world saturated with college rankings, while avoiding being trapped in their seductive embrace.

BREAKING RANKS

PROLOGUE

On July 1, 2002, I became president of Reed College in Portland, Oregon. As I began
to fill the shelves in my office with books and mementos from my previous life as a
law-school dean, I could feel the weight already lifting from my shoulders. "I'm no
longer subject to the tyranny of college rankings," I thought. "I don't need to worry
about some news magazine telling me what to do."

Seven years prior to my arrival at Reed, its then president, Steven Koblik, had
decreed that Reed would no longer cooperate with the annual U.S. News & World
Report "Best Colleges" rankings.[1] As a practical matter, this meant that college staff
would no longer have to invest hours in filling out the magazine's annual surveys
and questionnaires. Most importantly, it signaled that Reed would no longer be
complicit in an enterprise it viewed as antithetical to its core values. And it would
no longer be tempted to distort those values to satisfy some stranger's dubious
standards of excellence.

The fact that Reed had taken this rebellious stance was one of many features that attracted me to apply for its presidency. I took it to be a statement that
Reed viewed education as a path to a genuinely fulfilling life, not just a ticket to a
high-paying job. The college defined its goal as imparting learning, not just conferring credentials. It measured itself by internal standards of academic integrity, not
just external applause. Of course, Reed was a real-world institution, whose attainments often fell short of its ambitions. But it kept its aspirations front and center
in its daily life. And it decided that cooperating with U.S. News was incompatible
with those aspirations.

I soon began to understand that there was a growing cottage industry of college evaluators, many spurred by the commercial success of U.S. News. In the ensuing years, I came to view this industry as a "rankocracy"—a group of self-appointed, mostly profit-seeking journalists who had claimed for themselves the role of arbiters of educational excellence in our society. It wasn't just the U.S. News rankings that were incompatible with Reed's values. Virtually the whole enterprise of listing institutions in an ordinal hierarchy of quality, with its faux precision, dubious methodologies, and blaring best-college headlines, was deeply hostile to Reed's true mission.

Maintaining Reed's stance turned out to be more of a challenge than I had realized. Refusing to play the game didn't protect us from being included in the standings. U.S. News and its coterie of fellow "rankocrats" just went ahead and graded the college anyway, based on whatever data they could scrape up and "expert" opinions they could sample. Every once in a while, when I saw that U.S. News had once again assigned us a lower number, I would feel those old competitive juices flowing. In moments like that, I had to take a deep breath or go for a walk. And throw the magazine into the trash.

At the same time, I couldn't pick and choose which rankings to celebrate simply because they made Reed look good. We had to remain vigilant to avoid stumbling into complicity—or hypocrisy. I recall one morning early in my tenure, when I discovered a banner headline on the college's website, announcing that the Princeton Review had named Reed the number one undergraduate institution in all the land for "best classroom experience." I made a quick phone call to the vice president for college advancement, and the story vanished. Later, when I described the incident to a fellow college president, she laughed and said, "Being pure is tough, isn't it?"

Yes. But in our case, it was worth the effort. It enabled all of us at the college to do what we thought was most consistent with our mission, without looking over our shoulders to see how it might affect our alleged place on the status scale. It enabled us to keep focused—ferociously at times—on the pursuit of academic excellence without having our heads turned by the siren songs of pedigree and prestige.

I came by my sense of liberation honestly. In 1989, I had become dean of the University of Pennsylvania's Law School. The next year, U.S. News began to publish annual rankings of law schools. Over the next nine years of my deanship, its numerical pronouncements hovered over my head like a black cloud. During those years, for reasons that remained a complete mystery to me, Penn Law's national position would oscillate somewhere between 7th and 12th. Each upward movement would be a cause for momentary exultation; each downward movement, a cause for distress.

My admissions dean reported that prospective applicants were keenly attuned to every fluctuation in the annual pecking order. So were my alumni. If we dropped from 8th to 10th, alumni would ask what went wrong. If we moved up to 7th, they would ask why we weren't in the top five. At professional meetings, fellow deans would lament the absurdity of the assessment formula, even as their communications staff publicly celebrated every uptick in their standing. Stories would circulate about the latest clever trick employed by some law school to game the system. Each year, Penn's president would proudly present to the board of trustees a list of the university's schools whose ranking numbers had improved. And she'd make no mention of those whose numbers had slipped.

During that time, I also served as a trustee of my undergraduate alma mater, Amherst College. By the standards of the rest of the world, U.S. News treated Amherst very kindly, almost always placing it in the top two liberal arts colleges in the nation. Amherst was far too genteel to boast publicly. But the topic often arose at the fall meeting of the board of trustees, right after the release of the latest U.S. News "Best Colleges" edition. If Amherst came in second, someone would always ask, "Why is Williams College ahead of us again?" I came to understand that, in the world of college rankings, everyone thinks they are being treated unfairly, except during those fleeting moments when they sit at the top of the sand pile.

The feelings of resentment, frustration, and anxiety triggered by college rankings are truly pervasive in the world of higher education. And, as we shall see in the pages that follow, those feelings—even among those at the top—are thoroughly justified.

PART I

THE COLLEGE RANKING INDUSTRY

From Curiosity, to Scorekeeper, to Rankocracy

CHAPTER 1

APPLES, ORANGES, AND REFRIGERATORS

SHOULD COLLEGES BE RANKED?

Ours is a rankings-obsessed society. We assign ratings to virtually every product and service on the market: cars and tires; movies and television shows; restaurants and resorts; washing machines and laundry detergents; plumbing fixtures and toilet paper; refrigerators and, yes, even the apples and oranges that go inside them.

The reasons for this obsession are obvious. First, we want information that will help us make better purchases. We once thought we could rely on personal experience and word of mouth to make informed judgments about what to buy. Now those sources seem hopelessly overmatched by the staggeringly complex array of products and services we routinely encounter. As hard as it tries, product advertising cannot fill the void. The ceaseless barrage of targeted advertising, channeled by the internet into our mobile devices, may succeed in penetrating to our emotional core. But it affords us precious little information that is useful to our rational faculties. Amid this flood of self-serving, attention-grabbing appeals, we crave some neutral, objective, and blissfully simplifying advice.

Yet we want more than just good, reliable, unbiased information about the products and services we might buy. We seek comparative information. For most of our purchases, good enough is not good enough. We want better. And, truth be told, many of us want the best. In our consumer economy, shopping has become a form of recreation, almost like a game or a sport. As with real sports, this is one we want to win by choosing the superior product or service. Indeed, in our secular, individualistic society, consumption has become a source of identity. Some people seek to demonstrate their worth—to others and even to themselves—by pulling in to the company parking lot in the top-ranked electric sedan or by telling colleagues about their vacation at the number-one-rated Caribbean resort. For a website seeking to optimize the number of users' clicks for its advertisers, a sure-fire strategy is to offer a list of "top 20 cities for retirees" or "10 best keto restaurants." We instinctively believe in the myth of a free market in which unrestrained competition among producers and sellers yields not only the optimal mix of quality, price, innovation, and variety but also an ever-changing list of winners and losers.

So we crave ratings and rankings. Ratings are essentially grades. The units of measurement may be letters or adjectives or numbers, stars or chili peppers or tomatoes, but they reflect an ordinal ranking of quality. An A paper is better than a B paper, and a 5-star Uber driver is better than a 3-star driver. Ratings distill evaluations along multiple dimensions into an assessment into a single dimension. "Excellent argument, good organization, concise writing" equals an A on a term paper. "Safe driver, clean car, good conversation" equals a 5-star ranking for my Uber ride. And, once you have ratings, it is a very short step to rankings. Take a single rating, or an average of multiple ratings, for several students or Uber drivers, array them in a spreadsheet from best to worst, and . . . voila! . . . you have a ranking.

RANKING REFRIGERATORS

When people think about how to rate (and rank) various products, many view Consumer Reports as the gold standard. Consider, for example, how it evaluates refrigerators.[1] First, it surveys its members and asks them to rate their own refrigerators on reliability and satisfaction. Then CR purchases a wide array of models, brings them into its laboratory, and tests them. Based on these trials, it grades the performance of each refrigerator in five categories. It then combines those results into an overall score on a numerical scale.

What makes people think that Consumer Reports' rankings are trustworthy? Several things. First, CR appears to be unbiased. It is a nonprofit corporation that makes most of its money on subscriptions from its members, as well as contributions from foundations and individuals. It agrees to test and rate a product only if the seller of that item agrees not to use the CR rating in its advertising. It does not advertise rated products on its own website or in its literature.

Second, CR appears to be expert and objective. It actually tests the products it rates, using engineers, technicians, and scientific instruments. It divides a diverse product classification into subcategories—in the case of refrigerators, five different styles—reflecting the various preferences held by consumers. It makes pricing information readily available, so readers can compare relative quality with cost. And it typically accompanies its ratings with a lengthy article on the factors that go into its quality judgments, as well as on the attributes that consumers should consider in making an informed choice.

It makes perfectly good sense to rate refrigerators. They represent a reasonably large investment that consumers expect to last for several years. Refrigerators all perform essentially the same function, and there are well-accepted measures of how adequately they do so. To be sure, refrigerators are status symbols for some people (what might be called the "Sub-Zero set"), but for most buyers, their functional characteristics significantly outweigh their status-signifying role. So, sure, Consumer Reports—go ahead and rank them.

By contrast, rankings seem dubious, if not downright ridiculous, for many other products and services. What is the best apple? Is a Braeburn really better than a Granny Smith, as one website claims? What is the best painting in the world, or even in the Metropolitan Museum of Art? What is the best piece of classical music, or even the best string quartet? People do attempt to answer these questions, but taste predominates to such an extent that most of us take such pronouncements with a grain of salt. And there are some things that even our rankings-obsessed culture refuses to try to rank—at least seriously. Is there a "best" religion?

Which brings me to college rankings . . .

REASONS TO RANK COLLEGES

To what extent does it make sense to rank colleges? Where on my implicit rankability spectrum, running from refrigerators to religions, would I place colleges?

There are, to be sure, several good reasons why people would want to rank higher educational institutions. First, for many individuals, a college education is one of the most complex and expensive purchases they will ever make. Obtaining a baccalaureate degree (the primary focus of this book) typically requires four academic years' worth of full-time study, which means taking roughly 32 semester-long courses or course equivalents. Each of these courses requires (for students who make the effort) more than 50 hours of classroom or lab time and hundreds more hours in studying and completing assignments. In residential programs, the package includes housing and meals. And most colleges also offer a wide variety of counseling, health care, athletic, and community-life services and facilities.

All of this requires what is, for the majority of Americans, a huge investment. The College Board (which administers the SAT) tells us that the annual net cost of attendance for the average residential student enrolled in a public four-year university is about $19,500.[2] This includes required tuition and fees (minus scholarship grants), plus room and board, books, and living expenses. For students enrolled in private nonprofit colleges, the cost is $33,200. Multiply those yearly numbers by four. Of course, these are just averages. For those paying full tuition and fees at, say, Amherst, Penn, or Reed, the four-year cost of attendance can exceed $300,000.[3]

Second, college becomes a part of your long-term identity in a way that virtually no other purchase does. As I discuss in chapter 7, for many people in our so-called meritocratic society, a bachelor's degree is an essential signifier of pedigree. And colleges work very hard to preserve this lifelong association. They depend heavily on charitable contributions from their alumni, which means they continually reinforce the relationship between the school and its graduates. Whenever a graduate achieves professional success or reaches a personal milestone, the news appears on the institution's website and in its alumni magazine, and sometimes even in press releases. When you send in that first tuition deposit in the summer after your high-school graduation, you are making a huge investment in your personal development, as well as your lifetime opportunities and reputation. No wonder you want the best possible information about that choice before you make it.

Third, this is a purchase that most people make only once. It's true that approximately a third of college students transfer from the institution they entered as a freshman to another school, and a handful do so twice or more. When

Sarah Palin burst onto the national scene as the Republican vice presidential candidate in 2008, we learned that in the years from 1982 to 1987, she had attended five colleges (including one, the University of Idaho, twice). But even the Sarah Palins of the world can't really be described as knowledgeable repeat consumers, in the way that consumers of, say, apples, oranges, or even refrigerators are. I sometimes say that choosing a college—like buying an old house or having children—is something that is really difficult to understand fully until you are in it up to your neck. Still, before making that leap, you want all the advice you can get.

REASONS NOT TO RANK COLLEGES
The Complexity of the "Product"
There are also very good reasons why a college education cannot and should not be ranked. The first is the sheer complexity of what the consumer is buying. The educational component alone is staggeringly complex. In taking the roughly 32 courses required for a baccalaureate degree, students at most institutions can choose from hundreds of course offerings, organized into dozens of departments, varying by instructional style (lecture, seminar, or laboratory), learning objectives (substantive knowledge, technique, or theory), evaluative procedures (examinations, papers, original research, or creative works), location and environment (study on campus, in the surrounding community, or overseas), course size (huge lectures, small seminars, or independent studies), knowledge level (from introductory to advanced), and many other characteristics.

Beyond the formal educational program is what might be called an informal one. This includes the participants' emotional, moral, and social development, fed (intentionally or accidentally) by the ways in which the college has structured campus life, provided counseling and other support services, composed its student body for peer-effect learning, and situated itself within a larger community. Then there is the entire range of noneducational (or, at most, quasi-educational) benefits, providing students with opportunities for entertainment, building school spirit, physical exercise, religious or spiritual exploration, nutrition, housing, medical and counseling assistance, career advice, and on and on. College is not a product or even a service. It is a four-year life experience.

The Variety of Consumer Preferences

The enormous complexity of the "product" we call higher education reflects an even greater diversity in the needs and preferences and aspirations that its "consumers" seek to satisfy. Consider just a few examples. Chad is a conscientious student from a working-class family who is skilled at carpentry and craves the thrill of a packed football stadium. Tanya is the only African American student in her high-school class who took both physics and advanced calculus. The third child in a devoutly Catholic family, Maureen is the student government president and captain of her tennis team. Bored with high school, Jonah studied cryptography as a hobby while writing two graphic novels. Amanda was home schooled by her parents while helping to run the family farm. Carlos held down three part-time jobs while taking every social studies course available at his urban high school. During the summer after her junior year at a private boarding school, Sarah had an internship on Capitol Hill that inspired a passion for government service. Tyrell spent two years tracing his family's journey from Jim Crow Mississippi to his multicultural Oakland neighborhood.

In a world of such diverse stories, and so much human variety, is there a single "best" college? Are there even 500 best colleges?

The Consumer Is Also a Producer

A third obstacle in constructing any single or simple method of ranking colleges is the fact that the value of the primary service being provided—education, in both its formal and informal aspects—crucially depends on the amount of effort a person invests. Students are producers of their own education as much as consumers of it. Of course the value of many products depends in part on the effort put into utilizing them. Getting the most out of your Whirlpool refrigerator requires that you figure out how to adjust the temperature settings, where to store the fruits and vegetables, and perhaps how to operate the ice maker. But the purpose of a refrigerator is not self-improvement. Nor is that the purpose of even more-complex consumer products, such as laptop computers or automobiles, no matter how lengthy their instruction manuals may be. To be sure, there are aspects of a college experience that are solely or primarily about simple enjoyment—think of dorm parties, football games, Frisbee on the quad. But those are incidentals, sidelights, diversions.

The supposed reason why colleges exist and why the vast majority of their students attend them is self-development. This means two things relevant to my argument. First, you cannot rate a college based on its fundamental purpose without simultaneously assessing the effort made by its students to take advantage of what the school offers. Second, rankings cannot tell high-school seniors how they will be transformed by that experience.

College Is an Investment in Long-Term Outcomes

This leads to a fourth problem with college ratings. Unlike apples and oranges, or refrigerators and cars, college is not simply a short-term consumption activity. It is a long-term investment in human capacity—the ability to do financially, socially, emotionally, and even spiritually rewarding work; to teach oneself and others how to learn, adjust, and adapt; to analyze, reason, evaluate, and create; to appreciate beauty, ingenuity, order, complexity, and subtlety. The capacity, in short, to lead a fulfilling life. As we shall see, those things are brutally difficult to measure in any reliable way, and their attainment cannot be observed for many years, or even decades.

A Surfeit of Readily Available Information about Colleges

The editors at U.S. News like to brag that their publications have filled a void in the quantity and availability of comparative information about colleges. Robert Morse, the long-serving rankings czar at the company, has been quoted as saying, "We believe we've been driving transparency in higher education data."[4] As a description of its early best-college editions, Morse is correct, and his employer deserves credit for that fact. By now, however, that informational void has been filled to overflowing. An enormous quantity of evaluative information—both statistical and descriptive—is now readily available to anyone with even a speck of curiosity about higher education.

Start with the data reported by colleges to the US Department of Education and publicized on its National Center for Educational Statistics (NCES) website. The Center's Integrated Postsecondary Education Data System (IPEDS) is a veritable fountain of data on some 7,600 postsecondary institutions.[5] For each institution, the College Navigator site reports hundreds of bits of information on tuition, fees, financial aid, enrollment, admissions, retention and graduation rates, programs and majors, varsity athletics, student debt, and even campus crime.[6] The US Department of Education's College Scorecard site is a kind of official college guide that highlights specific measures of institutional character and performance.[7]

And its College Affordability and Transparency List enumerates the schools with the highest and lowest sticker prices and net prices.[8]

Another important source of institutional information is the Common Data Set (CDS). The CDS represents a collaboration among selective schools, the College Board, Peterson's college guides, and U.S. News. It was developed to relieve educators from the incessant demands for information from various publications. The CDS collects much of the information reported to IPEDS in one place, along with a great deal more detail. Most colleges report these data on their websites. Many other private organizations and publishers have collected some or all of the publicly available data from IPEDS, CDS, and college web pages and packaged it for consumption by their readers. This group includes not only popular guides, such as Fiske's and Barron's, but also websites, such as collegeresults.org and ucan-network.org.

The huge variety of publicly accessible data gives potential applicants the freedom to compare colleges according to virtually any criterion they consider important. Thanks to CDS, for example, they can evaluate institutions based on the percentage of undergraduate men in fraternities, or the percentage of freshmen with SAT math scores in the 600–699 range, or the number of class sessions with enrollments below 10. Thanks to College Navigator, they can readily distinguish among schools by, say, the number of women on their varsity lacrosse teams, the proportion of their student body disciplined for drug abuse, or the average cost of books and supplies for commuting students.

In other words, applicants no longer need to be told by a mediocre news magazine what criteria matter for them in choosing a college, and how much each factor should be weighted. With a few clicks on a computer keyboard or mobile device, they can find virtually everything they need to know to satisfy their particular interests, tastes, and desires. If U.S. News wants to take credit for helping to unleash this flood of information, it should declare victory, take a bow, and move on. Its work is done.

THE PROCRUSTEAN BED: THE HOMOGENIZING EFFECT OF RANKINGS

At the heart of my objection to college rankings is their unfortunate tendency to homogenize a sector historically characterized by immense institutional variety, one that seeks to satisfy the equally huge variations in students' needs and preferences. Unlike the government-mandated educational systems of other nations, American higher education features a glorious proliferation of institutional forms, goals, structures, practices, and missions. That diversity is a national treasure. And it should be preserved.

The Difficulty of Classifying Higher Educational Institutions

In an attempt to organize the unruly mass of American higher education, the Carnegie Foundation has a long-established system for categorizing colleges and universities. It identifies seven basic classifications: doctoral universities master's-degree colleges and universities, baccalaureate-degree colleges, associate-degree colleges, special-focus two-year schools, special-focus four-year schools, and tribal colleges.[8]

Carnegie then subdivides these categories by a host of factors, such as type of control (public, private nonprofit, private for-profit); level of research activity; enrollment size; admissions selectivity; arts-and-sciences versus professional focus; relative concentrations of full-time and part-time students; numbers of undergraduate and graduate students; proportion of students living on campus; and so on. The result is that the Carnegie scheme yields hundreds of distinct categories.

Even so, the Carnegie classification system barely scratches the surface of organizational diversity. Throughout our colonial and national history, thousands of reformers, entrepreneurs, religious leaders, philanthropists, and public officials have founded and nurtured institutions designed to appeal to virtually every conceivable type of educational predilection. There are religious schools; military academies; work colleges; single-sex colleges; minority-serving institutions; universities that excel at research or athletic competition; schools with structured curricula or with open curricula; institutions that specialize in engineering, art, or music; colleges that perpetuate privilege and others that promote the American dream.

EIGHT PROFILE SCHOOLS

I refer to many of those schools in the pages to follow. In particular, I use eight colleges and universities as exemplars of the rich diversity of American higher education. I confess that my choice is skewed toward the highly selective tiers of higher education, for the simple reason that this is the primary domain of most college ranking systems. I discuss the eight schools very briefly here and provide more-detailed descriptions in the appendix.

Four of my profile institutions illustrate that unique American contribution to the world of higher education, the liberal arts college: Amherst, Berea, Reed, and Spelman. All share a common passion for student-centered, multidisciplinary undergraduate instruction in a supportive residential setting. Yet they differ enormously. Amherst is the quintessential New England college, aspiring to, and usually achieving, excellence in every dimension—instruction, research, demographic diversity, residential life, and even intercollegiate athletic competition. Berea is a zero-tuition work college, devoted almost entirely to educating the economically disadvantaged children of Appalachia. Reed is a hothouse for intellectual exploration, a kind of undergraduate graduate school for brainy freethinkers. And Spelman is one of the most prominent and respected historically Black colleges, one of only two that exclusively serve women.

The other four of my profile schools are large universities: City College of New York (itself part of the City University of New York consortium), the University of Michigan, the University of Notre Dame, and the University of Pennsylvania. They all provide a wide range of undergraduate, graduate, and professional degree programs, combined with a heavy emphasis on research, which reflects their debt to the nineteenth-century German university model. Yet they, too, differ markedly from one another. City College—a bona fide university, notwithstanding its college label—exemplifies the urban public university, committed to providing a world-class, inexpensive education to the children of immigrants and the working class. Michigan is a prototypical flagship state university, competing at the highest levels of scholastic and athletic achievement, while gradually shifting from dependence on state appropriations to the private sector's high-tuition/high-donations model. To many, Notre Dame is the consummate Catholic university, combining a nationally prominent research and academic profile with a deep devotion to its religious roots. And Penn is a member of the Ivy League that traces a continuous path from its founding in the colonial era to national and international distinction in teaching and research.

The institutional variety of American higher education is reflected in the multiple labels—such as college, university, academy, school, and institute—used to describe the entities that populate the sector. For expositional convenience in the discussion that follows, I use the unmodified terms college, school, and institution to refer to all of those entities collectively. Where the context involves a distinct subset, I use phrases such as liberal arts college, research university, or law school. Likewise, when I intend to refer to pre-collegiate schools, I so indicate by using the labels high school or secondary school.

THE IMPACT OF COMPREHENSIVE
RANKINGS ON INSTITUTIONAL DIVERSITY

The eight schools that I profile throughout this book stand in for the many hundreds of selective colleges and universities scattered across the American landscape, each with its unique history, mission, and character. Trying to squeeze all that variety into the procrustean bed of a single ordinal scale threatens to occlude those differences, to the manifest disadvantage of both prospective applicants and educational administrators. In choosing which schools to apply to or to enroll in, high-school seniors are pressured to undervalue and overlook important distinctions not captured in the rankers' formulas. And in setting institutional priorities, educators are tempted to distort their practices and policies, even at the expense of altering their culture and character, in a mad scramble to accommodate some stranger's monolithic definition of quality.

One commentator used the fancy term "pernicious isomorphism" to describe the homogenizing effect of rankings.[10] Proving that they have had such an effect is difficult, given the multiple forces that buffet higher education. Nonetheless, suggestions abound in the literature. For example, consider what Yale law professor Henry Hansmann said about the impact of rankings on the competition between Harvard's and Yale's law schools.[11] Prior to the advent of law-school rankings in 1990, about half of the applicants admitted by Yale chose to attend that school, and most of the rest went to Harvard. According to Hansmann, applicants sorted themselves by "interest": those seeking an "academic" law-school experience chose Yale, he said, while those seeking a more "commercial" focus chose Harvard. After the rankings proclaimed that Yale was the number one law school in all the land, its matriculation rate shot up to 80 percent. Applicants stopped sorting themselves by interest and began making choices primarily based on their scores on the LSAT (Law School Admission Test) and college grade-point averages (GPAs). As a result, Hansmann concludes, rankings have been a "mixed blessing" for Yale.

Or consider the undergraduate program at the University of Chicago. For a long time, Chicago was justly regarded as a self-selection school. Among students with strong academic credentials, those with distinctively intellectual interests—the "brainy nerds," in common parlance—were drawn to Chicago. As a result, it received far fewer applications than its Ivy League counterparts and had to admit a higher proportion of those individuals to fill its entering class. Despite the acknowledged fact that Chicago had a faculty almost without peer in American higher education, it chronically lagged behind the Ivies in U.S. News. One of the principal culprits was its higher acceptance rate.

In 2006, when Chicago was ranked 15th, the university's new president, Robert Zimmer, launched a series of steps designed to raise its comparative position by increasing the applicant pool and thereby reducing the acceptance rate. He succeeded admirably, attracting an applicant pool that ballooned from 9,100 in 2006 to 34,600 in 2020. As a result, Chicago's acceptance rate plummeted from 40 percent to 6 percent. U.S. News rewarded his efforts that year with a number three ranking. But many observers, especially among Chicago's "old guard," have grumbled that this accomplishment came at the sacrifice of the university's uncompromising intellectual standards. One emeritus professor recently accused Chicago of succumbing to "the false coin of academic glory doled out by the U.S. News and World Report."[12]

Curmudgeons abound in the academic world, and we should be leery of taking such grumblings as the gospel truth. But, as I point out repeatedly in the chapters to come, there is ample evidence showing that college rankings have powerful impacts on higher education, many of which have had the unfortunate effect of punishing the individualism that has been the very lifeblood of our system.

CHAPTER 2

MEET THE RANKING INDUSTRY'S 800-POUND GORILLA —AND ITS COUSINS

I began my academic career back in 1975, with joint faculty appointments at Boston University's schools of law and management. In both of those settings, we were well aware of our competitive environment, although most of our information was anecdotal. We knew, for example, which of our peers tended to prevail in the competition for new faculty prospects. As active scholars, we had a pretty good idea of which departments were producing the best research. Sometimes we learned where our most promising admitted applicants ended up going. And, at least for undergraduate programs, there were some published college guides, such as Barron's and Peterson's, that contained both qualitative descriptions and statistical data. But the notion of compiling a unitary, comprehensive ranking of colleges or professional schools was almost completely foreign to us.

About the only example with which we were familiar was a series of books that a Cal State professor named Jack Gourman self-published, beginning in 1967. His "Gourman Reports" purported to rank entire schools, as well as individual academic departments, in exquisite arithmetical detail, on a scale of 2.01 to 4.99. Because Gourman gave his readers no information about how he compiled his ratings, and no one in higher education seemed to recall having been interviewed by him, most professional educators dismissed his assessments as completely inconsequential.[1]

Well, perhaps Professor Gourman's reports were regarded as unimportant, but the idea of ranking colleges was hardly inconsequential. Over the next couple of decades, that idea bore fruit far beyond what he, or most of us, could have foreseen.

THE EARLY HISTORY OF COLLEGE RANKINGS

The idea actually goes back to the turn of the last century, with the publication of occasional lists that rated colleges by the numbers of their graduates whom the authors considered to be especially distinguished or successful.[2] The US Bureau of Education, the precursor to today's Department of Education, once classified women's colleges into two categories, marked as "A" (including the highly selective Seven Sisters) and "B" (200 others). In 1910, the Bureau was asked by the Association of American Universities to rank a broader spectrum of colleges, in order to provide the AAU's members with an "objective" measure of undergraduates' preparation for graduate study. In response, the Bureau prepared a list of 344 institutions, sorted into five levels of quality. Its inadvertent release to the public prompted a huge outcry from the higher-education industry. President Taft responded by issuing an executive order banning its distribution!

After that, private rankings popped up from time to time. Some were based on outcomes, such as the number of a school's alumni appearing in *Who's Who in America*. More frequently, they were based on reputational surveys sent to educators. Examples included a review of institutions published by the

North Central Association of Schools and Colleges in 1924, and a top 10 listing of national universities and colleges published by the *Chicago Sunday Tribune*. And then there were the "Gourman Reports," based on who knows what.

U.S. NEWS & WORLD REPORT ENTERS THE FIELD

The watershed event in the history of rankings occurred in 1983, when a struggling weekly news magazine, U.S. News & World Report, first published a set of "best-colleges" lists, based on a peer-reputation survey sent to 1,308 college presidents. The questionnaire asked them to select up to 10 schools that "did the best job of providing an undergraduate education" within their respective institutional categories (national universities, national liberal arts colleges, and seven regional categories).[3] About half of the presidents responded. Based on their votes, U.S. News ranked 25 national universities, 25 national liberal arts colleges, and 10 schools, each in the other categories. It declared that Stanford was the best national university and Amherst the best national liberal arts college.

Many readers at the time viewed the publication as a curiosity, an entertaining feature story to be read and then quickly discarded. But at least one man saw it as the future, not only for U.S. News, but also for the higher-education industry. That man was Mortimer Zuckerman, a successful real estate developer and magazine publisher who acquired the magazine in 1984. Under the leadership of Zuckerman and his editor, Mel Elfin, it again published best-college lists, based on peer evaluations, in 1985 and 1987. The following year, seeking to cloak their obvious subjectivity in a garb of scientific objectivity, it introduced the statistical component that has come to dominate its rankings—and those of its subsequent competitors—ever since.

This component was based on the results of a detailed

questionnaire sent to colleges and universities, asking them to report information on matters such as their acceptance rates (percentage of applicants admitted) and yield rates (percentage of admitted applicants enrolled), the average scores of their entering class on standardized admissions tests (the SAT or the ACT), the ratio of students to faculty, dollars spent on instruction, and so on. By 1988, the U.S. News listings had already achieved sufficient influence that most institutions were willing to invest considerable staff time in assembling the data and filling out the forms.

The shift in emphasis from peer reputational ranking to statistical measures of performance fell especially hard on some of the highly regarded public flagship universities. Between 1983 and 1989, the University of California, Berkeley, saw its purported national ranking drop from 5th to 24th; the University of Michigan sank from 7th to 25th. Apparently either the experts were wrong, or the statistics were. Or perhaps both. Meanwhile, the "expanded Ivies" (the Ivy League universities plus MIT, Chicago, Duke, and Stanford) settled securely into the top dozen spots.[4]

In 1990, U.S. News began publishing comparative assessments of professional schools in business, education, engineering, law, and medicine. The following year, its editors disclosed information about the weights they assigned to the various elements of their formula, inaugurating a gradual process of providing greater transparency about their methodology. In subsequent decades, U.S. News has tirelessly tinkered with its rating procedures. It has added new measures of performance, dropped others, and repeatedly altered the weights assigned to the factors. For example, in 1996 it added output measures, including first-year retention and graduation rates. In 2004 it ceased using yield rate in its student selectivity metric. In 2018, it included a measure of social mobility and, in 2021, student debt. Over the years, U.S. News has steadily reduced the weight assigned to measures of student selectivity, such as acceptance rates and entering students' average SAT scores. Likewise, it has fiddled with the category of persons solicited for its reputational surveys. In 1988, it added faculty deans and admissions deans to its earlier roster of presidents. For a period of time, U.S. News even sought the opinion of high-school college counselors, only to drop them in 2020.

In 1997, the magazine first published its rankings online, making it possible to present vastly more data than could fit into the print edition and to display specialized assessments based on such criteria as affordability, social mobility, or teaching quality. Its website now permits potential applicants, who pay for a "College Compass" service, to generate individualized listings of schools, based on personal qualifications (e.g., high-school GPAs and SAT scores) and institutional preferences (e.g., state locations, sizes, or religious affiliations).

COPYCAT BEST-COLLEGE RANKINGS

U.S. News spawned a stampede of copycats seeking to distill the profusion of college characteristics into a single measure of quality. In 1990, Money magazine issued its first edition of "America's Best College Buys," attempting, as the title suggests, to measure the financial payoff from attending different institutions. In 2005, Washington Monthly began ranking colleges based on "what they do for the country," with an emphasis on social mobility, research output, and community service.

That same year, the United Kingdom's Times Higher Education began to rate global universities. Later it teamed up with the Wall Street Journal to publish a comprehensive (WSJ/ THE) ranking of American colleges, based on measures of institutional resources, student engagement, outcomes, and campus environment. In 2008, Forbes magazine published a

TABLE 2.1.

Positions of profile schools in six best-college rankings (2019–2021)

College	Forbes	Money	Niche	U.S. News	WSJ/THE	WM
Amherst	28	80	37	2[a]	21	1[a]
Berea	464	243	33	33[a]	144	3[a]
City College	411	113	494	176[b]	229	154[b]
Michigan	20	4	23	24[b]	23	29[b]
Notre Dame	18	60	16	19[b]	28	23[b]
Penn	6	30	10	8[b]	13	7[b]
Reed	105	551	81	63[a]	86	78[a]
Spelman	468	498	308	54[a]	138	92[a]

Sources: Forbes (2019); Money (2020); Niche (2021); U.S. News (2021B); Wall Street Journal (2021); Washington Monthly (2020).
[a] Ranking among national liberal arts colleges.
[b] Ranking among national universities.

comparative appraisal of 569 colleges, based heavily on outcome measures, such as post-graduate earnings and career distinctions. Comprehensive, ordinal rankings popped up in many other places, mostly on the web. Examples included Kiplinger's "Best College Values," College Choice's "100 Best Colleges and Universities," Niche's "Best Colleges," College Factual's "Best Colleges," and College Raptor's "Best Colleges."

Despite their different focuses and methodologies, most of these publications have regularly given highest billing to the same cast of Ivy-plus characters. For example, if you look at the top five universities in each of the assessments released in 2019–2020 by Forbes, Money, Niche, U.S. News, WJS/THE, and Washington Monthly, MIT appears in all six lists; Harvard, Stanford, and Yale in five; and Princeton in four. Yet when you move further down the listings, the ordering of schools begins to change, reflecting variations in the methods and formulas used by different organizations.

Table 2.1 illustrates this phenomenon by displaying how our eight profile schools fared in those six comprehensive rankings.

Direct comparisons of the schools in this table are difficult, for two reasons. The first is that U.S. News and Washington Monthly separate universities from liberal arts colleges, while the other four lump them all together. The second is that the six publications use somewhat different measures of institutional excellence. For example, Money seems to produce the most divergent results, because it rewards schools that combine low costs of attendance with high post-graduate earnings. Forbes relies more heavily on measures of post-graduate success than on college affordability. Niche differs sharply from others because it gives more weight to environmental factors, such as campus quality, safety, and surrounding amenities. Washington Monthly has tried to position itself as the "answer to U.S. News & World Report"[5] by focusing on the ways in which colleges contribute to the public good, both directly and through their graduates. Although its numerical orderings do indeed deviate significantly from those published by its rival, for our eight schools, they are remarkably similar. Table 2.1 suggests that those with particularly distinctive missions, such as Berea, City College, Reed, and Spelman, are more likely to have wildly disparate rankings, depending on the methodology used.

SPECIALIZED RANKINGS

In addition to the comprehensive rankings, a host of more-specialized ones has emerged, many of them discussed in greater detail in subsequent chapters. For example, the Princeton Review, a test-preparation company, annually publishes a book containing multiple top 25 lists, based on the results of a survey sent to thousands of college students.[6]

Its categories famously range from the serious (e.g., "best classroom experience") to the whimsical (e.g., "Birkenstock-wearing, tree-hugging, clove-smoking vegetarians"). An outfit called Parchment publishes "student choice" rankings, derived from a survey asking college students to report the schools to which they were admitted and the one at which they matriculated. CollegeNET produces a "Social Mobility Index" that seeks to measure the degree to which institutions of higher education help their students progress from economically disadvantaged backgrounds to high-paying post-baccalaureate careers.

Numerous outlets, including PayScale and Money, purport to grade colleges by financial return on investment, based on the career earnings of graduates and the average net cost of attendance. The website RateMyProfessors.com uses student survey–based ratings of individual teachers to compile an assessment of colleges by overall instructional quality. The Center for Measuring University Performance at the University of Massachusetts, Amherst, ranks institutions by various measures of research productivity, as well as total endowment.

All of the publishers of comprehensive best-college rankings discussed in the previous section of this chapter now offer additional specialized listings, derived from data vacuumed up and fed into their computational machines. For example, the U.S. News website offers categories such as "A-Plus Schools for B Students," "Most Debt," "Top Universities for International Students," and the like. The WSJ/THE website permits its viewers to compile separate lists of schools based on each of its subsidiary factors (outcomes, resources, etc.). And Niche, the maestro of college-related data-vacuumers, offers dozens of assessments by individual institutional characteristics and dimensions.

Finally, scholarly researchers have issued occasional or one-time rankings, typically based on a specific variable. A prominent example discussed at several places in this book is a social-mobility metric, published by economist Raj Chetty and his colleagues at a Harvard think tank called "Opportunity Insights." Other examples include a revealed-preference ranking produced by Christopher Avery and his coauthors, return-on-investment listings compiled by scholars at Georgetown University's Center on Education and the Workforce, and a financial value-added assessment published by the Brookings Institution.

GLOBAL UNIVERSITY RANKINGS

The success of the U.S. News listings has spawned a host of national rankings in other countries—"league tables," as they are generally known. These systems are used mostly by central governments to judge and reward the performance of their publicly funded universities. In addition, a host of "global" rankings has sprung up to compare leading institutions of higher education from around the planet. Given their aspiration to assess these schools by relative academic prestige, most global ranking formulas give heavy weight to measures of research output and faculty distinction. The most influential include the Shanghai Ranking, the Times Higher Education World University Rankings, and the Quacquarelli Symonds (QS) World University Rankings.[7] Not to be left behind, U.S. News itself recently began publishing ratings of world universities.[8]

I have not focused on global rankings in this book, primarily because they are of limited interest to prospective American college students. They are most relevant to foreign students weighing whether to attend a leading American or British institution or stay closer to home. Also, as a burgeoning literature attests,[9] they raise almost all of the same methodological and behavioral issues canvassed throughout this book.

Despite the proliferation of single-variable grading systems, by far the most prominent and influential ones remain the comprehensive, multiple-variable models. Among them, there is no question that U.S. News continues to sit atop the pyramid. As its number-cruncher-in-chief, Robert Morse, admitted (perhaps pridefully), the U.S. News college rankings have become "what some consider the 800-pound gorilla of American higher education."[10]

He's right. In a sector increasingly populated by chimpanzees, bonobos, and the occasional orangutan, U.S. News is still the 800-pound gorilla.

CHAPTER 3

MAKING "BEST-COLLEGE STEW"

A RECIPE FOR DISASTER?

Like many members of my generation, my education in gourmet cooking began by watching Julia Child's syndicated TV show, *The French Chef*. Judging by my occasional attempts at haute cuisine, I was not a very good student. Perhaps I was distracted by Julia's nonstop, effervescent chatter or the occasional culinary mishaps that made her unedited cooking classes so entertaining. But I do remember one important lesson: when you combine a lot of ingredients into a stew, you want to make sure you bring out the flavor of each one. You should still be able to taste the bacon and the porcini mushrooms in the beef bourguignon.

In my later life as an educational administrator, I sometimes thought that the art of composing a college ranking was the equivalent of preparing a stew. You select a group of ingredients, measure each one carefully, combine them in a strict sequence, stir, cook, and serve. If you do it just right, you might end up with a delicious, classic French dish. If you do it badly, you end up with gruel.

In my experience, the efforts of U.S. News and its followers to produce best-college rankings have typically wound up with the equivalent of gruel. A careful look at the "recipes" for preparing these dishes gives us a pretty clear picture of why that has happened.

BEST-COLLEGE RANKING RECIPES

To create its 2021 listings, U.S. News combined 16 different ingredients, grouped under seven headings (outcomes, expert opinion, faculty resources, financial resources, student excellence, alumni giving, and graduate debt) to produce an overall score for each ranked school, on a scale of 1 to 100.[1] The data fed into this recipe derive from replies to the magazine's annual statistical questionnaires and peer-evaluation surveys. Most of the quantitative information is also available from the US Department of Education, but some (such as the alumni-giving rate) is not. Since there is often a time lag in federal reports, U.S. News takes some pride in publishing data that are, in at least some instances, more current.

In a practice begun back in 1997, U.S. News adjusts some of the metrics in its formula, in an attempt to measure institutional value added. These calculations use proprietary algorithms to estimate the extent to which a school's performance on a particular criterion is higher or lower than one might expect, given the distinctive characteristics of the institution and its student body. For example, in addition to calibrating the raw overall graduation rate, U.S. News also includes something called "graduation-rate performance," to reward schools, such as Berea College, that achieve a higher graduation rate than might be expected, given the level of academic preparation reflected in their student populations.

Other leading comprehensive rankings have used formulas that are broadly similar to those utilized by U.S. News. For its 2021 edition, the WSJ/THE employed 15 measures, grouped under four headings (resources, engagement, outcomes, and environment).[2] Some of its factors—including graduation rate, educational expenses per student, and student/faculty ratio—were also used by U.S. News. Several others, such as various survey-based ratings of student engagement and post-graduate salaries, were different. Forbes used approximately 13 factors in its formula, and Washington Monthly, 21. Niche surely won the prize by somehow managing to incorporate over 200 separate ingredients into a single ordinal list of best colleges.[3]

Taken individually, most of the factors that are employed seem plausibly relevant to an evaluation of higher educational institutions. But one can readily see that any process purporting to produce a single comprehensive ranking of best colleges rests on a very shaky foundation.

PROBLEM #1: SELECTION OF VARIABLES

The first problem involves the choice of variables to include or leave out in the ranking formula. As I have pointed out in chapter 1, the immensely complex product we call "college education" has literally hundreds of dimensions that could potentially be examined. While there is widespread agreement about the general purposes of higher education, when it comes to rankings, that consensus quickly dissolves into arguments about the choice of qualities to include and metrics to use.

Why, for example, does U.S. News look at spending per student, but not endowment per student? Why does it measure faculty salaries, but not faculty research output? Why does it calculate graduation rate but not post-graduate earnings in its outcome measures? Why has it ceased to employ yield rates for admissions, while still factoring in acceptance rates? Why do some rankings include racial and ethnic diversity, while most ignore it? Indeed, why do some formulas use just a handful of variables, while others incorporate dozens or even hundreds? At best, the rankers give vague replies to such questions, offering no supporting evidence for their choice of particular variables. Very rarely do they explain why they have left out others, including those that their competitors use.

PROBLEM #2: ASSIGNING WEIGHTS TO VARIABLES

Equally arbitrary is the process of determining what weights to assign to the variables. The pseudoscientific precision of the mathematical formulas used in the most popular rankings is really quite comical. For 2021, U.S. News decreed that the six-year graduation-rate factor was worth precisely 17.6 percent in its overall formula, and the freshman-to-sophomore-year retention rate, exactly 4.4 percent. As another example, Washington Monthly somehow divined that its Pell graduation-gap measure (comparing the graduation rate of lower-income Pell grant recipients with non-Pell recipients) factored in at 5.56 percent of its overall rating, while a college's number of first-generation students deserved a measly 0.92 percent.

U.S. News has long been well aware of the arbitrariness of the weights assigned to variables used in its formulas. In 1997, it commissioned a study to evaluate its methodology. According to Alvin Sanoff, the managing editor of the rankings issue at that time, its consultant concluded: "The weight used to combine the various measures into an overall ranking lacks any defensible empirical or theoretical basis."[4] The magazine evidently just shrugged its shoulders and kept right on using its "indefensible" weighting scheme. As have all the other formulaic rankers, one strongly suspects.

PROBLEM #3: OVERLAP AMONG VARIABLES

A third problem is the degree of overlap among variables—a condition statisticians call "multicollinearity." In statistical terms, the ranking formulas purport to use multiple independent variables (such as SAT scores, graduation rate, class size, and spending per student) to predict a single dependent variable (numerical rank). It turns out, however, that most of the so-called independent variables are, in fact, dependent on each other. A 2001 analysis found "pervasive" multicollinearity in the formula then used by U.S. News, with most pairs of variables overlapping by over 70 percent.[5] For example, a college's average SAT score (for its entering students) and its graduation rate were almost perfectly correlated.

Why is this a problem? When factors such as SAT scores and graduation rates are collinear, the true impact of either on colleges' overall rankings can be quite different from the weighting percentage nominally assigned by the formula. For example, the 2001 study found that a school's average SAT score actually explained about 12 percent of its ranking, even though the U.S. News formula nominally assigned that factor a weight of only 6 percent. The SAT statistic had this outsized influence because it directly, and strongly, affected 7 of the 14 other variables. For this reason, researchers such as Robert Zemsky and Susan Shaman argued quite persuasively that it takes only a tiny handful of variables to explain almost all of the differences in the U.S. News rankings.[6] In other words, many of the factors so carefully measured and prominently featured by the magazine are just window dressing.

Furthermore, as I explain more fully in chapter 9, most of the criteria explicitly used by U.S. News (and, by extension, most of the other comprehensive rankers) turn out to be heavily dependent on an unidentified background element: namely, institutional wealth. This should be intuitively obvious for the faculty-resources and financial-resources measures. As studies have repeatedly shown, however, the degree of institutional wealth also corresponds directly with the level of entering students' SAT scores, freshman retention rates, graduation rates, alumni giving, and even peer reputation. So a ranking that gives separate weights to each of those factors ends up largely measuring the same thing.

PROBLEM #4: THE SALIENCE OF NUMBERS

A further problem with the evaluative systems illustrated by U.S. News is the outsized impact exerted by the numerical scores that those systems produce. Scholars call this quality "salience"—that is, the tendency of one measure to dominate all the others, simply because of its greater visibility. Taking an example from the 2021 U.S. News edition, we can ask whether Berkeley (ranked 22nd among national universities) was really better than its downstate neighbor, USC (24th). These two numbers said yes. Yet, when you look at the underlying data (to say nothing of all the qualitative factors ignored by the formula), the only plausible conclusion is that the two schools, while very different, were equivalent in overall quality. Their total scores on U.S. News's magic 100-point scorecard (82 and 80) were also almost identical. Berkeley seemed to be superior on some measures (e.g., peer evaluation and student excellence), and USC on others (e.g., faculty resources and financial resources). Yet there it was, in neon lights: number 22 versus number 24.

As one moves further down the ladder, the numerical differences among the schools—and surely the real quality differences—shrink to the vanishing point. Wheaton College (Massachusetts) and Hendrix College, two very fine small liberal arts colleges, received overall raw scores of 61 and 60 from U.S. News. Yet Wheaton was ranked 84th (in a tie) and Hendrix 93rd (also in a tie). The notion that, in this case, a student should choose Wheaton over Hendrix simply because of this one difference is ludicrous. But, as many scholars have documented, ranking numbers speak loudly, often drowning out other, more edifying ways of assessing an institution's strengths and weaknesses.

In a study of the enrollment decisions made by high-achieving students who attended Colgate University between 1995 and 2004, Amanda Griffiths and Kevin Rask noted that over half of the surveyed students chose Colgate merely because it was ranked higher than the other schools to which they were admitted.[7] This deciding factor, they observed, was independent of other measures of academic quality, such as student/faculty ratio or expenditures per student. Another investigation examined the impact of a 1995 decision by U.S. News to increase the number of institutions that were ordinally ranked.[8] Prior to 1995, schools that received raw scores between 26th and 50th in its formula were merely listed alphabetically in a "second tier." The researchers found that when the magazine began assigning a specific number to those additional schools, they experienced a statistically significant increase in applications, wholly independent of any changes in the underlying quantitative measures of their academic quality.

PROBLEM #5: FIDDLING WITH THE FORMULA

Compounding the inherent arbitrariness of the ranking methodology, rankocrats keep changing it, so as to render comparisons from one year to the next essentially meaningless. Ever since 1983, U.S. News has made repeated alterations in the variables used in its formula, the weights assigned to those factors, the procedures for measuring them, and the number of colleges listed.

Why does U.S. News keep changing its recipe? Many observers accuse the publisher of instituting changes just for the purpose of shaking things up, to generate enough drama to keep readers coming back year after year. Its editors firmly deny that charge. Instead, they typically give rather vacuous explanations for the changes, often citing "expert" opinion. But, unlike academic experts, the magazine's editors don't cite the results of peer-reviewed studies to substantiate their assertions.

In fact, it's not difficult to guess the reasons for at least some of the changes. One can readily explain several adjustments—for example, the belated inclusion of social mobility and college affordability—as responses to widespread criticism of the formula's blatant wealth bias. Other revisions reflect efforts to discourage cheating. As I describe in chapter 6 and subsequently, U.S. News has been engaged in an ongoing whack-a-mole exercise with institutions bent on gaming their system. Find a loophole, close it. Find another loophole, close that one. Ad infinitum.

Additional alterations may have been made to avoid the embarrassment of implausible results. In the magazine's first ranking of law schools, Yale finished 1st, and Harvard wound up an ignominious 5th. U.S. News quickly fixed that. Until quite recently (when Stanford inched into the second spot), it's been Yale (1st) and Harvard (2nd) at the top. A more celebrated example involves the ranking of the undergraduate program at the California Institute of Technology. In 1999, the U.S. News statisticians made an obscure change in the way the magazine plugged spending per student into its overall score computation. As a result, Caltech (which spends much more per student than its peers) vaulted from 9th place in 1999 to 1st place in 2000. Oops! The editors made short work of that statistical adjustment, and Caltech settled back to its "proper" position in the pecking order, below the perennial top dogs (Princeton, Harvard, Yale, and Stanford).

The Caltech episode illustrates a related problem: buyer's

remorse. Since a school's numerical position in the hierarchy can bounce around from year to year, often for reasons that bear no relation to changes in its underlying quality, applicants who rely on those numbers to make college choices can get unpleasant surprises. Imagine an applicant who, in 2000, chose Caltech because it was ranked 1st in U.S. News, in preference to, say, Princeton (then 4th). A year later, that person wakes up to discover that the two schools have traded places. By graduation time, Princeton is still 1st, while Caltech has sunk to 8th.

PROBLEM #6: ONE SIZE DOESN'T FIT ALL; THE "BEST-COLLEGE" ILLUSION

Just as there is no single best stew, there can be no single best-college ranking, given the enormous complexity of a college education and the variability in student preferences discussed in chapter 1. It takes real chutzpah to claim that a formula, composed of arbitrarily chosen factors and weights that keep changing from year to year, can produce a single, all-purpose measure of institutional quality. Of course, all of the rankocrats concede this fact and take pains to advise readers to use their numerical listings only as a starting point in the search, not as an absolute method for making decisions. In service to that advice, most publications offer multiple single-dimension assessments in addition to their comprehensive best-colleges lists. And many of them supply tools to help prospective applicants construct even more-personalized interschool matchups. U.S. News, for instance, encourages readers (for a subscription fee) to compare institutions of their choice along various prescribed dimensions, such as graduation rate or affordability. The WSJ/THE version invites online users to manipulate the default weightings of its four factors—institutional resources, student engagement, outcomes, and campus environment—according to their individual preferences.

Despite these largely commendable refinements, all of the rankers use their best-colleges lists as the public relations bait to hook their audiences. And powerful bait it is. By the time curious readers get to the underlying information and the specialized rankings, they have been told by a seemingly authoritative organization what *the* correct ordering of colleges is, from best to worst. The unstated message comes through loud and clear: "Berkeley is better than USC. Ignore that relative assessment at your peril."

What we have, in sum, is a group of popular rankings that simplify the complexity of evaluating a college's performance by arbitrarily selecting a collection of measures, many of which overlap substantially, and then assigning equally arbitrary weights in order to purée them together into a single offering. The result is a tasteless mush. All the distinctive flavors of these wonderful schools get reduced to gruel.

As Malcolm Gladwell has written, "It's an act of real audacity when a ranking system tries to be comprehensive and heterogeneous."[9] He quotes Robert Morse in explaining why the U.S. News formula is the way it is: "We're just saying, we've made a judgment." In other words, "Trust us."

And, as we shall see in the following chapters, the implication extends further: "Trust us so much that you will fundamentally change your behavior as consumers and producers of higher education in America."

CHAPTER 4

WHO CARES ABOUT COLLEGE RANKINGS ANYWAY?

APPLICANTS DO!

When U.S. News began ranking colleges and universities in the mid-1980s, many of us in the higher-education establishment dismissed its annual issue as "the U.S. News swimsuit edition." The reference, of course, was to the annual *Sports Illustrated* feature edition, published since 1964 and filled with glossy images of models wearing skimpy bathing suits. I thought to myself, "The U.S. News college rankings have about as much to do with 'news' as the nearly naked models of *Sports Illustrated* have to do with 'sports.' No one will take these rankings seriously."

How wrong I was. When U.S. News named Amherst as the number one liberal arts college in 1983, the school's staff purchased 25,000 copies of the magazine and sent them to potential applicants nationwide.[1] In my college-saturated hometown of Boston, the media trumpeted stories every fall about where each local institution appeared in the latest editions. While presidents and deans of these schools made suitably dismissive statements about suspect methodologies and unreliable data, their public relations officers were celebrating each uptick in their standing.

The U.S. News rankings issues became instant best sellers. The publisher sold 485,000 reprints of its first stand-alone college guide. By 1998 it was selling 2.3 million copies of its annual rankings magazine and about 700,000 copies of its freestanding guide.[2] Readership numbers exploded once the rankings moved to the internet. Within 72 hours of the release of its 2007 "Best Colleges" report, the U.S. News website received 10 million page views, compared with its normal count of 500,000 page views *per month*. And its 2009 edition received 15.3 million page views.[3]

Still, back at the dawn of the rankings era, one could reasonably ask, Is this really any different from the *Sports Illustrated* swimsuit issue? These annual collegiate beauty contests may be a popular vehicle for curiosity and amusement, or even alumni bragging rights, but do they really have any substantive impact on the behavior of applicants or of those who advise them, such as parents and college counselors?

As we all know by now from personal experience, the answer is emphatically yes. And a generation of research confirms that conclusion. The college rankings have spawned a cottage industry of popular and academic studies that attempt to determine their true impact on applicant behavior. Although the methods and results of these investigations vary, the overall pattern is quite clear. With each passing decade, rankings have become steadily more influential for college-bound students.

APPLICANTS' INTEREST IN RANKINGS

One obvious way to gauge the impact of these rankings on college-bound applicants is simply to ask them. A prominent example is the "American Freshman" survey, conducted annually by the Cooperative Institutional Research Program (CIRP) at UCLA's Higher Education Research Institute (HERI).[4] CIRP is a collaborative effort among a large number of academic institutions that, each fall, administer a lengthy survey to their incoming first-year students. Although survey data from individual schools are highly confidential, HERI compiles the results from its member institutions and publishes the cumulative results annually.

One of the many questions on the CIRP survey asks respondents to identify, from a list of options, what reasons they considered "very important" in deciding which college to attend. In 1995, when CIRP first added the category "rankings in national magazines," 10 percent of the respondents cited that reason. By 2005, the proportion had grown to 17 percent, and by 2015, to 20 percent. To be sure, there were other options that received a greater number of positive answers. For example, on the 2015 survey, 70 percent of the respondents noted that "the college has a very good academic reputation." And 61 percent mentioned that "the college's graduates get good jobs." Indeed, 9 of the 20 possibilities received higher percentages than the one regarding rankings. But many of those options, such as the "academic reputation" and "good jobs" reasons, were probably shaped indirectly by impressions gleaned from reading the rankings.

Another useful source consists of "Student Poll" surveys, conducted periodically by the Baltimore-based market research firm Art & Science Group.[5] Although the methodology varies from survey to survey, Student Polls generally focus on college-bound high-school seniors with relatively high standardized test scores. The first two polls, reported in 1995 and 2002, suggested that magazine rankings were a relatively weak influence on students' choices of where to apply and where to matriculate. But by 2013, that picture had clearly changed when 66 percent of the respondents said they considered them—a number that increased to 72 percent in 2016.

Applicants not only pay attention to such publications, but they also talk about them. In the 2016 Student Poll, 56 percent of the respondents reported that they discussed rankings with their parents, 51 percent with friends, 30 percent with high-school college counselors, and even 29 percent with high-school teachers. Significantly, a 1997 Art & Science poll showed that applicants' *parents* were paying closer attention than their children. For example, 42 percent of surveyed parents said they were "very familiar" with rankings, compared with only 27 percent of students. Parents also felt that these listings had a higher "impact" and were more "reliable" than students did. Since applicants consistently mention their parents as an important source of information on colleges, it seems highly likely that rankings' direct influence on prospective students is magnified through the indirect channel of parental advice.

Student Poll surveys have also attempted to identify the relative importance of various magazine rankings and college guides. Over the past 25 years, U.S. News has continued to be the one most widely read, although the range of sources consulted has expanded as the number of its competitors has proliferated. In the 1995 poll, 26 percent of student respondents said they were "very familiar" with the U.S. News publications, compared with 20 percent for Barron's, 16 percent for Peterson's, and 16 percent for Money magazine. By 2016, the top five sources were U.S. News (35 percent), Forbes (27 percent), the Princeton Review (27 percent), Niche (21 percent), and Money (21 percent). The Student Poll results also reveal the relative degrees of credibility assigned by college applicants to different sources. In 1995, respondents listed Barron's and Peterson's college guides as more "reliable" than U.S. News. But by 2013, U.S. News was listed as "most influential" by fully 58 percent of the respondents, with the Princeton

Review trailing at 21 percent, Forbes at 9 percent, and others even further behind.

In an analysis of the 1995 CIRP data, Patricia McDonough and her colleagues concluded that the students who said rankings were "very important" in their choice of college were more likely to come from families with high incomes and college-educated parents, have higher GPAs, and have submitted a larger number of college applications.[6] They also had a greater probability of attending a residential private college or university and aspiring to a professional career. More-recent studies demonstrate that this pattern still persists. For example, the Student Poll surveys have consistently shown that these sources of information receive more attention from, and carry more weight with, students who have high SAT or ACT scores and come from higher-income households. On the 2016 survey, 81 percent of the respondents agreed with the statement that "students who care about prestige and status care about rankings."

IMPACTS ON APPLICANTS' BEHAVIOR

If students and their parents regard rankings as an important and reliable source of information about college quality, one would expect that they would have an impact on students' actual application and matriculation decisions. And indeed they do. In a veritable cascade of studies, scholars have documented their influence on applicant behavior. Many investigations have found that, after an improvement in a college's standing on the U.S. News listing, the institution tends to experience measurable increases in the numbers of applications it receives, the yield rate on its offers of admission, and the average SAT or ACT scores of its entering class. Likewise, a decline in its position seems to correlate with decreases in those measurements.[7]

The impact of ranking changes depends, of course, on their magnitude. According to most researchers, the typically small movements in institutional positions produce comparably modest effects on students' application and enrollment decisions.[8] But the research literature also shows that large, visible movements produce greater effects on applicant behavior. An example is a study of national universities by Marc Meredith, focusing on the 1991-2000 period, during which U.S. News assigned numerical ranks to only the top 25 or 50 schools and placed all others in quartile tiers, listed alphabetically.[9] He showed that movements between tiers had a substantial impact on admissions outcomes, with the biggest changes being experienced by public universities. Likewise, Nicholas Bowman and Michael Bastedo used data from the 1998–2005 U.S. News editions to show that moving onto what was then its "front page" produced a "substantial boost in the following year's admissions indicators for all institutions."[10]

Conversely, in a recent paper, Andrew Meyer and his coauthors found a 2 to 6 percent decline in applicant volume when a college dropped below the top 50.[11] While these investigations are merely suggestive, they certainly accord with our intuition that large shifts in a college's reputed standing will call forth comparable changes in its applicant pool and, probably, its matriculation rate as well. The findings are also consistent with our intuition that the *visibility* of rankings (for example, appearing on the "first page") may well matter as much as their *content*.

After two generations' worth of experience, the verdict is in. The applicant "marketplace" has spoken. Loudly. College rankings get applicants' attention and affect their behavior. And, as we shall see in the next two chapters, when applicants alter their behavior, so do educators.

CHAPTER 5

RESIST OR EMBRACE

EDUCATORS' RESPONSES TO RANKINGS

One can understand why college-bound high schoolers might pay attention to the rankings. And even take them seriously. To most prospective applicants, higher education is a vast mystery, filled with literally thousands of choices, each one bewilderingly complex—exciting and terrifying in equal measure. Young people in their mid-to-late teens often find themselves overwhelmed by hormonal, emotional, and social changes. Of course they might grasp at any straw in the wind.

But professional educators? Surely they wouldn't fall for some journalists' best-colleges hype. As Leon Botstein, long-serving president of Bard College, famously described the U.S. News rankings in a 2001 *New York Times* interview: "It is the most successful journalistic scam I have seen in my entire adult lifetime. A catastrophic fraud. Corrupt, intellectually bankrupt, and revolting."[1]

WHY EDUCATORS SHOULD REJECT RANKINGS

One doesn't need to be as outspoken as Botstein to agree with the sentiment he so pithily expressed. At first blush, there are at least three good reasons why those who run our nation's colleges and universities might be expected to ignore this entire genre of institutional evaluation. First, as accomplished scholars, most academic administrators are well aware of the methodological flaws, if not to say utter vapidity, of the popular rankings. Even if these educators let down their scholarly guard for a moment, they will be constantly reminded by the steady diet of journalistic critiques.[2]

Second, most changes in ranking numbers are small and short lived—down a notch this year, up a notch the next.[3] As scholars have repeatedly shown, most of the movement from year to year is statistical noise, not reflecting real changes in underlying institutional quality, but, rather, the accidental impact of small variations in methodology or the reporting practices of individual schools.[4]

Third, and perhaps most importantly, it is really difficult, and very expensive, to make more than a trivial move up the ladder. Educators know this intuitively, and a growing body of scholarship has reinforced that understanding.[5] In one often-cited study based on data from the 2012 U.S. News edition, Shari Gnolek and her colleagues asked what changes a school such as the University of Rochester would have had to make in order to move from a position in the mid-30s to one in the top 20.[6]

The answer was that it would have taken significant improvements in virtually every one of the 16 variables utilized in the U.S. News formula that year. Just the increases in faculty compensation and per-student expenditures alone would have cost the university an additional $112 million a year. According to the authors, even moving up one rung on the U.S. News ladder would have cost Rochester about $7,400 per student. Given the fact that the academic reputation measure (assigned a 22.5 percent weight in 2012) changes very little from year to year, it would have been practically impossible for Rochester to reach the top 20, even with that kind of investment. Finally, all of this assumed that Rochester's competitors would have made no adjustments of their own in response, but would have simply sat by and watched Rochester scramble toward the big time.

RESISTING THE RANKINGS

Faced with all of these reasons to ignore the rankings, would it be surprising if rational college administrators threw up their hands and said, "To hell with it"? Well, it turns out that a few have. But only a few.

The Resistance Movement

The most widely celebrated act of institutional rebellion was the 1995 decision by Steven Koblik, then president of Reed College, to cease cooperating with U.S. News. After Reed's act of defiance attracted national attention, it appeared for a moment that Stanford University would throw its formidable weight behind the movement.[7] Gerhard Casper, Stanford's president, announced that he would stop filling out the U.S. News annual reputational survey.[8] A group of Stanford students formed an organization dubbed FUNC (Forget U.S. News Coalition) and called on their counterparts at other universities to spread the anti-rankings gospel.[9] That same year, the president of Alma College sent a letter to 480 of his peers, urging them to boycott the annual U.S. News peer-assessment survey.[10]

The resistance movement seemed to gain some momentum in 2007, thanks to the efforts of a self-styled educational reformer named Lloyd Thacker, the founder of an organization called the Education Conservancy. In May of that year, Thacker sent a letter to hundreds of college and university presidents asking them not to participate in the annual reputational survey and to release only data "collected in accord with clear, shared professional standards."[11] The letter became the focus for discussion at the June 2007 meeting of the

Annapolis Group, a national association of liberal arts colleges. A majority of the 80 college presidents in attendance voted in support of a statement pledging not to fill out the survey and to develop an alternative system for collecting and reporting data on institutional quality and performance.[12]

These repeated calls for rebellion produced almost no tangible results. Casper's statement sparked plenty of talk but virtually no action. Several months after the issuance of Thacker's letter, only 62 schools had signed it.[13] The brand-name elite institutions were noticeably absent from that list. In response to the Annapolis Group's statement, 19 top-ranked liberal arts colleges, including the likes of Amherst, Williams, and Swarthmore, issued a collective promise to publish on their websites all of the data they supply to U.S. News and refrain from mentioning its rankings in their "new promotional materials."[14] But the signatories made no promise to refuse to cooperate with U.S. News altogether, despite acknowledging the "inevitable biases" of its methodology. Although I had attended the June 2007 Annapolis Group meeting, I declined to sign Thacker's letter, because I predicted that anything less than a complete boycott would be an empty gesture. And it was.

The Price of Resistance

During my tenure as president of Reed, I had countless conversations about U.S. News with my counterparts. Almost without exception, they said two things: they hated its rankings, and they were terrified of resisting. Everyone, it seemed, was familiar with the price Reed had paid for its 1995 act of defiance. Alvin Sanoff later explained what his fellow editors at U.S. News did in response. Instead of simply dropping Reed from the listings, they arbitrarily assigned it "the equivalent of the lowest score among National Liberal Arts Colleges for each piece of objective data in the magazine's methodology."[15] As a result, in 1996, Reed—which had once appeared as high as 9th on the national liberal arts college list—found itself dumped into the bottom quartile. Just in case anyone in higher education might not have noticed what had happened to a small college out in Portland, Oregon, the *Wall Street Journal* published an article in its national edition describing the event.[16]

Looking back on the episode, Sanoff conceded that the magazine's response to Reed's decision was "more punitive than logical." His choice of words is instructive: punishment is a treatment ordinarily dispensed by someone in authority. By 1995, U.S. News already saw itself as an authority figure—a rankocrat, in my coinage—empowered to dispense retribution for noncompliance with its edicts. Even today, there is good evidence that U.S. News continues to penalize Reed. In 2019, a group of its students performed an analysis for their statistics course. With faculty supervision, they reverse engineered the U.S. News formula, plugged in Reed's actual data, and concluded that the college should have received a ranking in the mid-30s, rather than its actual 68th-place position that year.[17]

A further reminder of the price of resistance was provided in a 2007 *Washington Post* column, penned by Michele Tolela Myers, president of Sarah Lawrence College.[18] She reported having been told by representatives of U.S. News that, if a school failed to submit data that wasn't otherwise publicly available, the magazine would assume a value for the missing item equal to one standard deviation below the average for comparable schools. Since Sarah Lawrence did not ask applicants for their SAT scores—and therefore did not submit test-score data to U.S. News—this meant that U.S. News would arbitrarily assign an average SAT score value about 200 points below the mean for Sarah Lawrence's peer institutions.

St. John's College provides yet another grim reminder of the price that holdouts can pay for having the temerity to ignore the rankings machine.[19] Famed for its demanding, four-year "great books" curriculum, St. John's is about as distinctive an animal as you'll find in today's higher-education menagerie. Reflecting its singularity—and intellectual intensity—the college's Annapolis campus refused to cooperate with U.S. News. The magazine, of course, included it anyway, typically placing it somewhere in the mid-100s among national liberal arts colleges. In frustration, Christopher Nelson, its president, finally gave in and grudgingly submitted the requested data. The next year its ranking shot up from 123rd to 56th. Its price for having resisted—or, to put it another way, its reward for finally toeing the line—was 67 places in the pecking order!

The U.S. News Holdouts

The failure of occasional acts of, and calls for, non-cooperation can be seen in the numbers. U.S. News reported that only 9 percent of the institutions listed in their 2020 edition declined to return its questionnaire. The name of each non-responding school was accompanied by a very inconspicuous footnote, signifying the school's refusal to submit data. Intriguingly, the number of abstainers rose to 15 percent in the 2021 issue, perhaps portending a growing disenchantment with rule-by-rankings. But a quick check confirms that the holdouts tended to be clustered at the bottom of the hierarchy. For example, the magazine footnoted only 24 (11 percent) of the 221 national liberal arts colleges. The highest of these were Whitman College (47th) and Reed College (63rd). All the others were in the bottom half. In the listings for national research universities, one had to go all the way down to 153rd (Quinnipiac University) to find a footnoted resister. City College, at 176th, was the next non-respondent on the list.

EMBRACING THE RANKINGS

The reality is that the vast majority of higher educational institutions cooperate with, and indeed embrace, the U.S. News grading system. The literature, both journalistic and scholarly, is full of stories about how competition for the best-college label has changed institutional behavior. Academic leaders have reshaped staff incentive and reward structures, altered admissions procedures and criteria, reordered expenditure priorities, and even rewritten strategic plans. A 2001 survey of college presidents by the Association of Governing Boards found that 76 percent of the respondents said that U.S. News rankings were "somewhat" or "very" important for their institutions; 50 percent had used them as internal benchmarks; 35 percent had publicized at least some results on their websites or in press releases; and 51 percent admitted that they had tried to raise their position in the published standings.[20]

The Case of Legal Education

As I well know from personal experience, rankings have had an especially potent impact on those who administer America's law schools. Sociologists Wendy Nelson Espeland and Michael Sauder painstakingly documented the influence exerted by U.S. News on legal educators in their appropriately titled book *Engines of Anxiety*.[21] The picture they painted isn't pretty. They stated that the magazine's rating system had dramatically distorted legal education, most especially impacting admissions and career services practices, but also affecting the allocation of resources, programmatic priorities, and even the job satisfaction and longevity of deans and associate deans.

Observers have offered several explanations why U.S. News has had such a powerful impact on legal education. First, and probably most importantly, the publication has enjoyed an effective monopoly on law-school rankings. It is true that various specialized evaluations pop up in other places from time to time,[22] but there is only one annual, comprehensive listing. By comparison with law schools, business schools have long been subject to assessments by multiple reputable sources. When I was dean of the Penn Law School, I envied the fact that my colleague, the dean of the Wharton School, would simply publicize Wharton's standing in *Business Week* when he felt the school had been shortchanged by U.S. News. I had nowhere else to turn—and nowhere to hide.

Second, because legal education is so homogeneous, rankings loom especially large in applicants' choices. There are only about 200 institutions serving a national or regional audience, all accredited by one entity (the American Bar Association's Section of Legal Education and Admission to the Bar). As a consequence of powerful professional and cultural forces, almost all law schools offer pretty much the same educational experience, aimed at the primary goal of preparing graduates to be able to pass a bar exam and take a job as a practicing attorney. Despite law schools' heroic efforts to differentiate themselves, prospective law students tend to view legal education as the relatively uniform product that it is. The one thing that most visibly differentiates law schools is their position on the U.S. News ladder. Applicants therefore pay almost slavish attention to those numbers. Knowing this, many law schools bestow an equally slavish fixation on trying to improve their rankings by whatever means possible.

The Case of Undergraduate Education

In the world of undergraduate education, academic administrators vary somewhat more in their obsession with rankings. But the vast majority take them with deadly seriousness and act accordingly. A poster child for embracing the U.S.

News system—and winning—is Northeastern University. As described in a 2014 *Boston Magazine* article by Max Kutner, Northeastern's remarkable ascendancy in the world of higher education can be attributed to a rankings-centered strategy instituted by its former president, Richard Freeland, and aggressively maintained by his successor, Joseph Aoun.[23]

When Freeland took over in 1996, the university was in a tailspin from financial pressures and programmatic cutbacks, reflected in its position at 162nd in the U.S. News list of national universities. Freeland determined that the salvation of Northeastern depended on its breaking into the top 100, a goal that he pursued publicly, relentlessly, and successfully. Taken together, the list of Freeland's techniques, as described in the *Boston Magazine* article, compose a how-to manual for like-minded administrators.

Start by directing your institutional research staff to reverse-engineer the U.S. News formula, so you can measure the impact of every possible tactic you might employ. Then adopt policies and practices calculated to raise your score on each of these factors. In order to improve your score on the small-class-size metric, set student enrollment caps of 19 for classes during the fall semester, shifting large classes to the spring. As a way of inflating the size of your applicant pool (and thus reducing your acceptance rate), adopt the Common Application and dramatically expand admissions recruiting. Continuously glad-hand fellow presidents who fill out the annual peer-assessment reputation survey. House more students on campus, in an effort to decrease dropout rates. Artificially raise your student selectivity numbers (based on fall enrollments) by instituting a spring matriculation for admitted applicants with low SAT scores and low high-school GPAs. Aggressively recruit overseas, but don't report SAT scores for foreign enrollees. Eliminate students doing co-op work projects from the FTE (full-time-equivalent) counts employed in the spending-per-student measure.

All of the techniques listed in Kutner's article—except for the last, which is unique to the handful of schools such as Northeastern that have formal co-op programs—are available to other institutions. And most of them have, in fact, been used by many colleges and universities for precisely the same purpose. Yet Northeastern stands out in terms of its success in playing this particular game. Between 1996 and 2020, its U.S. News position steadily soared, from 162nd to 40th. (In 2021, however, its ranking sagged to 49th. *Sic transit gloria!*)

Given the well-documented fact that most of the movement in the standings is just statistical noise, Northeastern's magical ascent might be written off as a quirk. But there are just enough other schools that have made significant upward progress to inspire copycat efforts. Examples of impressive numerical improvements over the 2010-2020 decade could include the University of Florida (from 48th to 30th) and Boston University (from 56th to 42nd). Significant upticks are very rare in the top echelons, of course, but even in that lofty realm, there are a few examples to encourage institutional striving. In chapter 1, I cited the University of Chicago, which managed to increase its position from 15th in 2006 to 3rd in 2020. Also consider the University of Pennsylvania. Penn had been stuck in the midteens until the arrival of Judith Rodin as its president in 1996. As documented by Robert Zemsky—and as I experienced first hand—her laserlike focus on improving Penn's standing paid off, as it jumped from 13th in 1997, to 7th in 1998, and eventually as high as 4th in 2005.[24]

Perhaps an even greater motivator than the desire to rise is the fear of falling. In the zero-sum world of ordinal rankings, college administrators everywhere are looking over their shoulders at the Northeasterns and Chicagos nipping at their heels. Anyone who pays attention to the annual U.S. News beauty contest—which is to say, every higher-education administrator—knows about schools such as Yeshiva University, which, during the 2010–2020 decade, slipped from 50th to 76th, or the University of Washington, going from 41st to 58th. There are many reasons for declines like these, undoubtedly most of them wholly beyond the institution's control, but numbers have a way of speaking for themselves.

RANKINGS' IMPACTS ON EDUCATORS' BEHAVIOR
Self-Promotion

The most visible, but in some ways least consequential impact of rankings on institutional behavior is their prominence in self-promotion. Think of all the free advertising U.S. News has received over the years from college public relations staffers touting the magazine's numerical judgments about their schools on their websites and in promotional literature. As Alvin Sanoff observed about his era as the magazine's rankings editor: "In fact, U.S. News itself did very little marketing. Why spend money when others do it for you?"[25]

Every year, the release of the U.S. News undergraduate listings in September triggers a veritable tsunami of self-congratulatory stories on college websites. Within days of the 2020 publication's release, for example, a Google search would have revealed dozens of stories from university news offices with headlines such as "Northwestern Climbs to No. 9 in US News 2020 Best Colleges Rankings" or "UCLA Named No. 1 in U.S. Public Institutions by U.S. News and World Report for Third Consecutive Year."

As Michael Luca points out in his study of business schools, there is also evidence of a "countersignaling" phenomenon among some top-ranked schools.[26] Despite the examples from Northwestern and UCLA cited above, most of the upper-tier institutions have become somewhat leery of boasting too openly about their successes. Most Ivy League universities and their elite cousins are content to reap the benefits of their high standings without lowering themselves to crow about them.

Incidentally, the countersignaling phenomenon does not appear to have deterred *student* publications at elite institutions from obsessing over their school's numbers. A Google search for responses to the release of the 2020 U.S. News edition reveals this morose headline from the *Chicago Maroon*, "UChicago's U.S. News Ranking Slips to No. 6, after Three Years at No. 3." Meanwhile, the *Daily Pennsylvanian* gleefully reported, "Penn Rises to No. 6 in U.S. News and World Report University Rankings." There is obviously a world of difference between slipping to number six and rising to number six.

Distortion of Priorities

Leaving aside the use of rankings as both stimulus and fodder for shameless self-promotion, by far their most consequential impact has been their distortion of institutional priorities and programs. Northeastern's Richard Freeland was hardly alone in shaping his administrative agenda around improving his school's U.S. News numbers. Similar measurements have insinuated themselves into the strategic planning process at many universities, often quite explicitly. For example, the 2005 strategic plan at Texas Tech University cited rankings 12 times and used them as a measure for achieving three of its nine "academic excellence" goals.[27] In its 2005 strategic plan, the University of Illinois Law School set a goal to move from the mid-20s to the top 20 in the U.S. News pecking order and identified specific steps to achieve that aim.

Rankings have been influential in the design of performance-funding schemes for state public university systems. The University of Florida's impressive rise in the U.S. News assessments provides a particularly vivid illustration.[28] Bernie Machen was hired as Florida's president in 2003, with the stated objective of propelling the school into the U.S. News list of top 10 public universities. (It was then 17th in that category.) Late in his tenure, Machen convinced the governor and the legislature to adopt a performance-funding formula for the state's public universities that would financially reward schools for improvement on several of the U.S. News metrics. Over the period from 2013 to 2019, this system generated an additional $62 million in funding, which the university used to achieve its top 10 goal . . . and then some! In 2021, U.S. News ranked Florida 6th among public universities.

In addition to these schemes, we know that improvements in a school's ranking position have been employed as measures of the performance of presidents, deans, and other administrators. In some reported cases, the linkage has been quite explicit. For example, the president of Arizona State University was reported to have been promised a salary bonus if he increased ASU's standing in U.S. News.[29] At the other extreme, slippage can cause heads to roll. In their study of law-school rankings, Espeland and Sauder reported that several career services directors were fired after their post-graduate employment statistics sagged.[30]

In most cases, the linkage between movement in a school's published ranking and assessment of an administrator's job performance is probably implicit, rather than explicit. During my tenure as dean of the Penn Law School, neither the president nor the provost ever told me that our standing in U.S. News was a factor in my performance evaluation. But the frequent public celebration of the schools whose numbers had improved brought home that message with perfect clarity. Indeed, for almost all higher educational administrators, it matters very little whether strategic plans or performance evaluations make overt mention of college rankings. They constantly lurk in your consciousness. And every time you think about changing admissions policies, or reallocating financial-aid funds, or capping class sizes, or altering budgetary priorities, they whisper in your ear. Often, they shout.

Gaming the Rankings

Critics often use the phrase "gaming the rankings" to describe the ways in which administrators respond to those whispers—or shouts—to alter institutional practices. But the term "gaming" covers a wide range of behaviors, not all of which are sinister. Some of the things colleges and universities do to move up one or two rungs on the ladder actually improve their educational programs. Of course, one might reasonably ask why professional administrators need such an artificial stimulus to do what is, after all, their job. But we all know that real human beings are prone to myopia, laziness, and even self-dealing. They need externally imposed standards of performance. Rankings, at their best, provide such standards.

The problem, as I argue at length in the pages that follow, is that the headline-grabbing best-college listings often supply perverse incentives that can actually harm the quality of the product being produced. They cause institutions to focus more on attracting students with impressive SAT scores than on educating them once they arrive on campus. They prompt schools to pour scarce resources into recruiting scads of surplus applications, so they can lower their acceptance rates and overburden their admissions staff, who are tasked with "holistically" reviewing every applicant. They encourage shifting financial-aid dollars from talented needy students to sometimes less-talented wealthy ones. They put an artificial constraint on the willingness of admissions officers to take chances on applicants with compelling personal stories but low test scores. They reward early-decision admissions policies that disadvantage low-income applicants. They encourage selectively scrapping standardized tests in favor of equally suspect admissions criteria.

And, as I discuss in the following chapter, rankings seem to have inspired a large number of otherwise honorable academic professionals to lie.

CHAPTER 6

GARBAGE IN?

THE MISREPORTING OF RANKINGS DATA

Throughout their history, the U.S. News rankings have been plagued by reports of institutions submitting incorrect data. In a 1995 *Wall Street Journal* story tellingly titled "Cheat Sheets," several educators conceded that they had submitted falsified (or at least "massaged") data to U.S. News and, in some cases, to college guidebooks as well.[1] The article noted almost 50 instances in which a school reported a higher number for its graduation rate or median SAT score to U.S. News than the corresponding figure it submitted to its bond-rating agency.

More recently, in 2012, Stephen Joel Trachtenberg, who had served as president of George Washington University from 1988 to 2007, wrote, "Just as athletes use steroids . . . colleges and universities succumb to their own set of pressures, including the desire to be top in the rankings. . . . Schools game the system by slicing and dicing their numbers."[2] How did Trachtenberg know this? Well . . . perhaps because, in that same year, his own university was found to have submitted inflated information about the high-school class standings of its incoming students for at least the previous decade.[3]

We all know the wisecrack about statistical measures: "Garbage in, garbage out." If the data on which the leading college rankings depend are garbage, are the rankings themselves garbage?

MASSAGING THE NUMBERS

Claremont McKenna, a highly regarded national liberal arts college, was caught having submitted false data to U.S. News and the US Department of Education from 2004 to 2012. The misinformation concerned enrollees' test scores, acceptance rates, freshman-retention rates, student/faculty ratios, graduation rates, and alumni-giving percentages.[4] According to Forbes magazine, the dean of admissions "developed a novel way to meet the school president's demands to improve the quality of the incoming class. He would simply lie."[5] As a penalty, Forbes (whose formula depended on data reported to the federal government) dropped Claremont McKenna from its college listings for a two-year period.

The literature is filled with similar accounts of misreporting, mostly to U.S. News, but sometimes to others, as well. Clemson University "manipulated" class-size data and "artificially boosted" data on its average faculty salaries.[6] From 2006 to 2012, Bucknell University submitted doctored SAT scores. Emory University furnished test-score data for admitted students, rather than actually enrolled ones, for over a decade.[7] For nine years, Iona College reported invented statistics about its acceptance rate, yield rate, SAT scores, student/faculty ratios, graduation rates, and alumni giving.[8] Not to be outdone, the University of Oklahoma supplied erroneous data to US. News for twenty years! Its falsified submission for 2019 finally enabled it to break into the top 100 among national universities.[9] Two years after the revelations, however, it slid back to 133rd.

In most years, U.S. News discloses information on schools that have been caught providing incorrect information. Its 2018 issue, for example, reported eight colleges whose submitted data were found by the magazine to be materially inaccurate.[10] Its 2019 issue listed five more, including

Johnson & Wales University, which "for many years" had misreported (by 62 percent) its financial expenditures per student; the University of California, Berkeley, which had "incorrectly included pledges in alumni-giving data since 2014"; and Scripps College, which had provided inaccurate alumni-giving rates.[11]

Law schools, those would-be bastions of professional ethics, have been particularly prone to engaging in questionable practices. In *Failing Law Schools*, Brian Tamanaha recounted several examples of outright false reporting.[12] In 2011, the University of Illinois admitted that its law school sent inaccurate admissions data to U.S. News that significantly inflated the median LSAT scores and undergraduate GPAs for classes entering in 2008, 2009, and 2010. (You may recall from chapter 5 that this law school's 2005 strategic plan had committed the school to achieving a top 20 ranking.) Also in 2011, the Villanova Law School was discovered to have supplied fraudulent LSAT scores and GPA figures for its entering classes at least as far back as 2002. Repeated allegations of law schools reporting phony graduate-employment data, discussed in chapter 19, led to lawsuits and a crackdown by the American Bar Association (ABA).

Other professional schools are hardly immune to the temptation to dissemble. In 2012, for example, Tulane's Business School was found to have submitted false data to U.S. News on its number of applicants and the test scores of its matriculants.[13] In 2018, the Fox Business School at Temple University was caught having provided erroneous information about its online MBA program. A further investigation by the university revealed falsifications involving six of the Fox School's other degree programs.[14] One can find similar accounts about professional schools as diverse as Sam Houston State University's education school, Texas Christian

University's business school, and the University of Florida's nursing school.[15]

CAN MISREPORTING BE PREVENTED?

Many observers think that the known incidents of misreporting are just the tip of a very large iceberg. In a 2012 survey of admissions directors, 91 percent said they believed other schools submitted false data—though only 1 percent of them admitted having done so themselves.[16] Rumors of too-good-to-be-true data swirled in meetings of law-school deans and college presidents that I regularly attended. On the other hand, U.S. News claims that "misreporting is rare."[17] In a truly charming invocation of humanity's better angels, Brian Kelly, editor and chief content officer at U.S. News, was reported to have said, "These are institutions that teach ethics. I find it incredible to contemplate that institutions based on ethical behavior would be doing this."[18] This statement stands in somewhat curious contrast to the magazine's annual list of cheaters.

To be sure, *publicly revealed* misreporting is indeed only a very small percentage of the total. But is *actual* misreporting rare? U.S. News claims that it checks for misrepresentation by "flagging year-over-year discrepancies, comparing data against federal government sources when available, and asking a school official to sign off on the school's data."[19] But this assertion only serves to send a clear signal to a college administrator intent on falsifying data: ratchet up bogus numbers slowly over time, doctor only the data not submitted to the federal government (or lie to the feds as well as to U.S. News), and keep the provost or the president in the dark (wink, wink).

The Prospect of Auditing Rankings Data

If U.S. News were serious about assuring users that its data were reliable, it could require respondents to obtain an independent audit of the information they submit. Why not? After all, colleges and universities are not permitted to apply for loans or issue bonds without having a financial audit by an independent accounting firm. Organizations such as Moody's and Standard & Poor's give such entities bond ratings (essentially a financial ranking), based solely on audited financial statements. And the US Department of Education requires institutions participating in federal postsecondary grant or loan programs to submit audited financial statements.

For the same reason, one might argue, colleges should not be permitted to "apply" for a favorable academic rating, in an attempt to attract tuition-paying students, without having an academic audit. If investors or the US government need audit-based protections against unduly rosy financial statements, surely applicants and their families need safeguards against exaggerated academic claims before they shell out thousands of their hard-earned dollars.

After the 1995 *Wall Street Journal* article about widespread cheating, U.S. News briefly considered requiring colleges to audit the data they submitted. But they dropped the idea.[20] I can easily imagine their thinking. Audits are expensive, and too many institutions would probably have balked at paying such a price to play the magazine's numbers game. Better to just keep on publishing rankings based on suspect disclosures!

Imposing Penalties for Misreporting Rankings Data

Another thing U.S. News could do is impose a harsh penalty on schools that report false information. As I mentioned in chapter 5, when Reed very publicly refused to submit *any* data, the magazine condemned the college to the purgatory of its bottom tier.[21] You'd think it should do at least that much to a school that submits *false* data. But no. In this latter case, the actual sanction imposed by U.S. News is a slap on the wrist. Usually it merely declares that the offender will be unranked for one year. Occasionally, it specifically asks the highest-placed officer of the college or university to certify the accuracy of future submissions. Forbes at least booted Claremont McKenna and Iona for two years. Why not drop such schools for 10 years?

But a moment's reflection suggests why rankers would never consider exacting such a steep price. A magazine does not want to make the penalty so severe as to discourage schools from participating in the first place. Nor does it want to impair the credibility of its assessments by eliminating name-brand schools from its lists. Imagine what would happen to the credibility of the U.S. News national colleges rankings if Claremont McKenna—perennially a top 10 school (8th in 2021)—were nowhere to be found for a decade?

Other Disincentives to Falsify Data

Higher-education officials found to have falsified data sometimes pay with their jobs. The dean of admissions at Claremont McKenna resigned after discovery of the school's nine-year stint of misreporting.[22] The dean of admissions at the Villanova Law School, along with three other admissions officers, quietly disappeared from the payroll.[23] Still, one can imagine that administrative staff who are tempted to cheat have to juggle competing pressures. Fail to improve your school's numbers, and you might lose your job. Cheat and get caught, and you could still lose your job. Not a pleasant choice.

One might reasonably ask, What about the higher-ups who push their subordinates to manufacture positive numbers? Why don't we read about boards of trustees firing more presidents or provosts? Occasionally, the top-level officer of an offending school does pay the price. For example, we are told that the dean of Temple's Fox Business School was "forced out." But we also learn that he turned right around and brought a $25 million defamation lawsuit against the university and its president.[24] Surely the most ominous news for would-be data manipulators, however, was a report in April 2021 that this same dean had been indicted on charges of fraud and conspiracy by the US Attorney for Pennsylvania.[25]

Misreporting can also lead to legal and regulatory troubles for the institution itself. For example, the ABA publicly censured the Villanova Law School in 2011 and required it to post a link about that censure on its website for two years. The revelations about Temple's business school triggered investigations by Pennsylvania's attorney general and the US Department of Education. They also spawned a class action lawsuit by the school's alumni, who claimed that the value of their degrees had been cheapened by the disclosures. The university is reported to have settled that lawsuit for over $5 million.[26] But let's face it, the odds of an institution's paying such a price are very low. Despite the attention-grabbing accounts of Temple's misfortunes, it's hard to imagine that most administrators intent on "massaging" data submitted to U.S. News would take the possibility of such consequences into account.

HOW TRUSTWORTHY ARE RANKINGS DATA?

Over time, the various college rankers, including U.S. News, have come to depend more and more on statistics that are publicly available or collected by third parties. Many listings now rely heavily on information reported by the US Department of Education. For example, in its 2020 issue, U.S. News stated that, if a school failed to submit information on such matters as standardized test scores, first-year retention rate, educational expenditures per student, faculty salaries, or graduation rate, the magazine would obtain the data from IPEDS or College Scorecard. Altogether, these categories compose approximately 60 percent of the weightings in its formula.

Of course, all of this information—just like the data on the U.S. News questionnaire—comes from the institutions themselves. Still, you might assume that rankings-obsessed educators would be less likely to submit false information to the government than to a private magazine. But it's been known to happen. The enterprising folks at Iona College, for example, were found to have provided identical false data, not only to U.S. News, but also to the US Department of Education, two New York State agencies, the Middle States Commission on Higher Education (Iona's accrediting agency), the College Board, the Council of Independent Colleges, and the National Collegiate Athletic Association.[27] As seventeenth-century political philosopher Algernon Sydney once quipped, "Liars need to have good memories." And, I would add, a good "copy" function on their computers!

An even better protection against data falsification is to rely on information from third parties not under the control of the institution or subject to its influence. Many publications rely at least partially on surveys by independent third parties. For example, the WSJ/THE relies on an annual Times Higher Education "Student Survey" to form the basis for its measures of student engagement. The Princeton Review bases its varied assessments of the quality of students' experiences entirely on the results of student surveys. Several others, including Forbes and Money, utilize earnings data compiled by PayScale from surveys of college graduates.

To the extent that statistics come from sources other than the institution itself or, if so, are independently verified by a third party, they should at least be immune from manipulation by the school being evaluated. Whether these sources are a reliable measure of a college's quality, however, is a much different question, one that I explore in detail in subsequent chapters. For example, one obvious problem with survey-based data is that students or graduates may have an interest in making their college look good—or perhaps may have a grudge against it.

So, what is the bottom line? Are most rankings poisoned by intentional or even careless misreporting? Probably not. But information is power, and the pressures to look good in the competitive world of higher education are relentless. At least until we have a system of independently audited academic-performance equivalents to financial statements, users of best-college lists will be well advised to take them with a grain of salt.

Looking back, I have to smile. How wrong I was in thinking that the U.S. News annual swimsuit issue would get tossed on the shelf, or into the trash, along with its *Sports Illustrated* counterpart. I don't know how the latter has affected the behavior of its audience. But I do know that the U.S. News rankings— and, by now, the entire industry they have spawned—have changed the attitudes, decision making, and even the lives of countless college administrators, as well as the entire higher-education ecosystem.

There are many explanations for this sorry state of affairs.

But, as I discuss in part II, most of them add up to this: post-secondary education has become a competition for prestige. And, in our popular culture, rankings have become the primary signifiers of prestige.

THE PRESTIGE
TREADMILL

REPUTATION, WEALTH, AND RANKINGS

CHAPTER 7

CONFERRING PEDIGREE

THE EDUCATIONAL ARISTOCRACY

Growing up in 1950s Boston, I quickly learned about pedigree. Who had it, and who didn't.

Pedigree in mid-century Boston was perhaps best captured in the sardonic toast said to have been given at a 1910 Holy Cross College alumni dinner by one of its graduates, John Collins Bossidy:

> And this is to good old Boston,
> The home of the bean and the cod,
> Where the Lowells talk only to Cabots,
> And the Cabots talk only to God.[1]

I sometimes heard that refrain repeated with other names inserted—Coolidge, Gardner, Lodge, Peabody, Saltonstall, Winthrop. This, I learned, referred to Boston's Brahmin caste. These were the families whose names appeared on museums, Harvard houses, and memorial plaques in Symphony Hall and Trinity Episcopal Church.

My parents lacked such a pedigree. My mother, Ethleen Diver, was the daughter of German and Swedish immigrants who grew up in a working-class section of Boston called Mission Hill. After her father died of tuberculosis, she put herself through Simmons College and landed a job as a legal secretary at Choate, Hall & Stewart, one of Boston's crustiest and WASPiest law firms, virtually all of whose lawyers had graduated from Harvard. While working full time, she studied law part-time at Northeastern University. It took her 24 years after passing the bar to convince the firm's partners that they could allow a woman—much less a second-generation American with a law degree from a "night school"—to practice law in their esteemed midst. But only as an employee of the firm, never as a partner.

My father, Benjamin Diver, had grown up in turn-of-the-century London. His father was a transplanted Irishman who worked in a shop mixing pipe tobacco for London's gentry, and his mother was an Englishwoman who served as a maid in their townhouses. Having finished high school in the city schools at the outbreak of World War I, he volunteered for the Queen Victoria's Rifles regiment. After 18 horrific months in the trenches of Belgium and France, he received a medical discharge for shell shock suffered in the Battle of the Somme. Upon his recovery, with the English economy in tatters and most of his comrades dead, he took a one-way passage to Canada and supported himself through odd jobs, such as laying track for the Canadian Pacific Railway.

A chance apprenticeship at a Montreal photographer's shop launched him on a career that would eventually lead to a staff appointment at the Massachusetts Institute of Technology, where he provided photographic support services for its research faculty. Just as Harvard was home to Boston's social elite, MIT was home to its scientific elite. During World War II, my father accompanied members of his department to war-torn England to work on the development of radar, enabling him, as he sometimes put it, to help "defeat the Germans a second time."

So my parents, first- and second-generation Americans who lived in a modest two-bedroom home, were exposed on a daily basis to Boston's version of social and educational aristocracy. And, by some form of osmosis, their experiences seeped into my consciousness.

THE AMERICAN ARISTOCRACY

The founders of the United States proudly renounced the patrician roots of their European forebears. In eighteenth-century Britain, aristocrats were the peerage, the class of wealthy landowners who traced their titles and privileges to dispensations conferred by monarchs dating back to William the Conqueror. Through the centuries, English society became structured into a rigid hierarchy. Titles and lands were passed down through the eldest male heir. Male children of aristocrats were groomed at Oxford and Cambridge for leadership roles in commerce, government, and the professions. Commoners learned their trades through apprenticeships.

Thomas Jefferson famously decreed that our nation would be led by a "natural aristocracy," based not on lineage and landholding, but on "virtue and talents."[2] Easy for him to say, with his 5,000-acre plantation staffed by a conscripted workforce of 130 slaves! In Jefferson's view, this natural aristocracy would consist of a small handful of Americans prepared for stewardship in the youthful Republic by rigorous instruction in moral philosophy, natural history, Greek and Latin, and religious (i.e., Protestant) studies. Leadership in the United States would depend not on the accident of birth—on one's family pedigree—but on native ability and personal effort.

Yet America has never quite cured itself of the craving for pedigree. The tight association of Boston's Brahmin class with Harvard, and its scientific elite with MIT, attests to the fact that, for many in our country, a college degree has supplanted family name as the dominant marker of social status. As Harvard philosopher Michael Sandel states, "credentialism," based largely on one's educational attainments, is "the last acceptable prejudice."[3] When you attend a lecture, the person introducing the speaker almost always mentions that individual's college degrees as a way of impressing the audience. Walk into a doctor's or lawyer's office and what do you see on the wall? College and graduate school diplomas. Recently, driving around suburban Boston, I spied an SUV with stickers reading "St. Paul's School," "Williams College," and "Harvard Law School." In other words, "I've made it. How about you?"

THE MERITOCRACY
Higher Education as the Measure of Merit
In modern parlance, Jefferson wanted to replace the aristocracy with a meritocracy. We sometimes forget that the latter term was originally used satirically. In a 1958 book, British sociologist and Labour Party activist Michael Dunlop Young coined the word to describe an education-based credentialing system that perpetuated class inequality while clothing it in the trappings of fairness.[4] With his bastardized Latin-Greek coinage—merit-o-cracy—Young described an aristocracy hiding under a thin veneer of merit.

In succeeding decades, however, the term lost its ironic connotation and settled into widespread use as a descriptor for a morally attractive system of governance. People occupying positions of influence and leadership in America earned those posts by talent and hard work. And the path to them ran straight through merit-selecting and merit-rewarding institutions of higher education.

Attacks on the Meritocratic Ideal
In recent years, however, a phalanx of scholars has launched

attacks on the idea of meritocracy. One set of complaints emphasizes the dehumanizing consequences of worshipping at the altar of merit. For example, Daniel Markovits has argued that the meritocratic myth "devours the elite" by "making them entirely dependent on their human capital, thus pushing them to train and work extra hard all the time, and to lose any sense of personal identity."[5] In this respect, today's meritocrats present a striking contrast to late-nineteenth century American aristocrats—Thorstein Veblen's "leisure class," whose members displayed their status not only by "conspicuous consumption," but also by "conspicuous leisure."[6]

In a similar vein, Markovits's Yale Law School colleague, Anthony Kronman, has railed against the increasing vocationalism of higher education and the abandonment of its earlier aspiration to equip students "for a life of responsible and enjoyable observation, judgment, and action."[7] Kronman even dared to resurrect the "A" word, arguing that colleges should seek to foster an "aristocratic ideal of character."

A second category of critiques echoes Young's assault on meritocracy's thinly concealed classism. My one-time Penn Law colleague (and now Harvard Law professor) Lani Guinier attacked the "tyranny" of meritocracy as a cover for perpetuating class-based and race-based privilege.[8] Likewise, Markovits argued that the beneficiaries of this system receive a "meritocratic inheritance that transmits privilege and excludes the middle class from opportunity."[9] A related critique from Michael Sandel has focused on the deep social divisions caused by our uncritical faith in meritocracy.[10] The winners in this type of competition, he argues, are filled with the hubris of thinking they made it entirely on their own—that good luck and community support had nothing to do with their success. This, in turn, inspires feelings of humiliation and contempt among the losers, breeding the deep divisions in twenty-first-century America.

Much of the contemporary attack on educational meritocracy is driven by the consistent linkage between standardized-test performance and the idea of merit, a subject I address in chapter 12. For now, it is enough to observe that the concept of merit, however ethically fraught, has become synonymous with educational attainment. And, as Lauren Rivera explains in her 2015 book, *Pedigree*, a prime marker of status has become possession of a degree from an elite educational institution.[11] In today's America, John Collins Bossidy might say, "The graduates of Yale talk only to the graduates of Harvard, and the graduates of Harvard talk only to God."

Status, Position, and Education

One plausible reason for the link between merit and educational attainment is the argument, made by many economists, that education is a "positional good." A positional good is one whose value to the user is at least partly a function of the status that its consumption conveys. And status is usually communicated by exclusivity—the fewer the number of people who are able to possess something, the more valuable it is.[12] By this thinking, getting admitted to a flagship state university is good, but acceptance by an Ivy League school is better, precisely because the latter is so much more difficult to attain.

Some aspects of education are obviously positional. Consider GPAs. A 3.50 GPA has no intrinsic meaning apart from relative performance. Does it place the student in the top 10 percent? The top 25 percent? A GPA of 3.50 used to connote outstanding academic performance. But in today's grade-inflated environment, as I discuss in chapter 11, that distinction is not so clear. To many students, the same would be said of the college they attended. Its value depends on its relative prestige. Is going to, say, USC a sign of educational success? Well, it depends on where USC is located in the prestige pecking order.

Most economists think higher education is positional, because income is.[13] In this view, many people jockey for higher-paying jobs as a way of signaling their superior self-worth. And they compete for greater-prestige college degrees because they see them as pathways to the best-paying positions.[14] There is surely some truth to this. But I think there is more at work here. There is a deep psychological yearning to be perceived as a winner, not only financially, but also socially. At least since Thorstein Veblen, sociologists have reminded us that we are status-seeking animals, in both our personal and organizational behaviors. And status is inherently relative. A status-seeker never really "makes it." One either rises or falls, occupying a position either above or below one's competitors. And so it is in the world of higher education, which is, after all, filled with status-seeking institutions catering to applicants with a similar bent.[15]

RANKINGS AND PEDIGREE

In the United Kingdom, you know where you stand because of your title. A duke is superior to an earl, and a viscountess to a baroness. The Duke of Cornwall ranks higher than the Duke of Sussex. The hierarchy and the conferring of titles are strictly top-down operations: they come from the sovereign. In America, no similar system of honorifics has existed. Until rankings. From 1983 onward, U.S. News assumed for itself the role of the British Crown. You don't have to refer to *Debrett's Peerage and Baronetage*.[16] You simply have to consult U.S. News's "Best Colleges" issue. Or, more recently, the best-colleges lists published by Money magazine, or Forbes, or the WSJ/THE, or Niche, or Washington Monthly. In their distinctive ways, they all seek to confer prestige.

But how can any of these would-be monarchs determine relative status? In some ways, it was much easier for U.S. News when it had a near-monopoly on college rankings. Like the Crown, its decisions were subjective and arbitrary, but they were the law. Once the field became more crowded, however, each of the rankers needed to find indicators that it could claim were better than those used by its competitors. The search for prestige-signifying proxies was on. In the following three chapters, I discuss the uses and abuses of the most widely employed surrogates: the expert opinion of educators, institutional wealth, and educational spending per student.

CHAPTER 8

MEASURING PRESTIGE BY POPULARITY POLL

THE OPINIONS OF "EXPERTS"

Like clockwork, every year during my tenure as dean of the Penn Law School, a peer-assessment questionnaire would arrive in my inbox from my "friends" at U.S. News. The survey asked me to assign each of 185 nationally accredited law schools to one of five quintiles, from best to worst, based on a school's "academic quality." So, shortly after I arrived at Reed in 2002, I was not surprised to receive a similar survey, this time asking me to rate 215 national liberal arts colleges. Since Reed refused to participate in the U.S. News rankings, I had the luxury of viewing the whole exercise from a more detached, shall I say "academic," perspective.

HOW "EXPERT" IS EXPERT OPINION?

Reading down the list of colleges that U.S. News had asked me to rate, I thought, How could I possibly know about the overall academic quality of even a handful of these schools? Oh, there were a few that I could confidently locate in the quintiles of prestige (or of disgrace). There, near the top of the alphabetical list, was Amherst College, my alma mater. Of course it belonged in the uppermost quintile. As an Amherst trustee, I had learned a fair amount about many of the schools in its peer group and athletic conference, such as Bowdoin and Middlebury and Williams. So I figured they all probably belonged up there, as well.

But what next? Looking down the U.S. News list, what did I know about, say, Albion College or Allegheny College or Augustana College? I realized that almost the only thing I could tell you about 80 percent of the schools was where they appeared in the previous year's U.S. News rankings. To be sure, over time I learned more about many of them. From the annual meetings of the Annapolis Group, I became acquainted with a number of presidents and a few provosts. They all seemed to be well-educated and well-meaning people. Some were especially personable or profound or downright irreverent. But did the fact that I liked the presidents of, say, Allegheny and Augustana tell me anything about what quintile their schools belonged in?

No. Not even close. For example, in order to place Allegheny in the second quintile—at least with any integrity—I would have had to know enough about all, or at least most, of the 215 colleges to conclude that 43 of them were better than Allegheny and 129 were worse. Unless I devoted every waking hour to studying, visiting, and evaluating all of those schools—or hired someone like Consumer Reports to do those things—how could I possibly figure that out?

Perhaps recognizing the folly of expecting raters to have enough knowledge to assign schools to five quality quintiles, U.S. News more recently has asked respondents simply to rank them on a Likert scale of 1 (marginal) to 5 (distinguished). We all know about this form of rating from our experience with almost every purchase we make, from buying shoes on Amazon to dining at restaurants to riding with Uber drivers. Today, everyone wants your opinion! So does U.S. News. Now, at least in theory, I wouldn't have to determine whether Allegheny is superior to 129 other colleges. I would just need to have a gut feeling that it's worth, say, a 4. The same way my hunch was that my last Uber ride deserved a 4.

Except there is one rather significant difference: I actually bought those shoes from Amazon, ate at that restaurant, rode with that Uber driver. I have never been a student or faculty member at Allegheny. Or even visited its campus, sad to say.

OPINION ABOUT WHAT?

When I was dutifully filling out the law-school peer-assessment forms back in the 1990s, I would occasionally ask myself, What standard am I supposed to be applying here? U.S. News wanted me to rank schools by "academic quality." But what is that? Best classroom teaching? Best skills training? Most sophisticated faculty research? Smartest students? Most famous alumni? Biggest endowment or budget? Upon honest reflection, I realized that I was rating other law schools by how much they resembled Penn, by whether they measured up to what we excelled at. But deans at other schools probably did the same thing, all of them applying a standard compatible with their distinctive experiences and preferences. Some of them might look at Penn and say, "too theoretical, too small, too corporate, too full of itself"—and dump it into a lower quintile.

However broad the range of standards applied by law-school deans, the variance of those used by undergraduate college presidents and deans is bound to be even larger. The various categories into which U.S. News classifies institutions encompass a wide range of types, sizes, cultures, and missions. Reflecting their schools' distinctive characters, survey respondents will probably apply many different standards of excellence. Furthermore, raters will undoubtedly vary in their degree of evaluative stringency. "Tough-guys" will award plenty of 1s and 2s and only a handful of 5s, while "nice-guys" may award every school either a 4 or a 5. Is a B from a notoriously stringent evaluator equivalent to the same grade from a soft touch?

One might respond by saying that variations in reviewer standards will just cancel each other out, leaving an overall score that is fair and representative. Perhaps. But there is always a danger that a peer-rating system will be distorted by systematic biases among the responding population. For example, one study found a bias against religious schools in the U.S. News peer evaluations.[1] If so, was Notre Dame penalized in 2021 by having received only a 4.2 peer rating (on a scale of 1 to 5) or Brigham Young University's Provo campus by having garnered only a 3.2? Hard to tell, but plausible. Likewise, what about possible systematic geographical favoritism toward institutions in the Northeast and against those in the Midwest or South? Or prejudices against schools thought to be politically conservative or against minority-serving colleges?

WHOSE OPINION COUNTS, AND WHOSE IS COUNTED?

The obvious flaws in peer-assessment ratings have led to repeated calls to boycott them, as I discussed in chapter 5. These attempts have fizzled, but the actual rate of response has steadily declined over the years. At the time of the 2007 boycott proposal, the response rate to the U.S. News peer-reputation survey was approximately 60 percent. By 2020, it had dropped to 43 percent, and by 2021, to 36 percent. Can a response rate of 36 percent produce an adequate sample size? U.S. News reports that it received 1,753 responses for its 2021 survey. But that was for 1,452 schools ranked in its 10 institutional categories. We aren't told how the replies were distributed across those categories. Nor is anything offered about their frequency and content. How many ratings did the name-brand elite schools receive, as compared with lesser-known schools? How often did respondents check the "don't know" box when asked to rank any particular school? How many ratings came from presidents, how many from provosts, and how many from admissions deans?

Whatever the actual numbers, it seems likely that the fate of most postsecondary institutions is in the hands of a pretty small number of anonymous—and not very well informed—respondents. True, U.S. News averages their reputational ratings over two years, but that barely diminishes the arbitrary nature of the process. The magazine boasts that its judgments rest solely on "thoroughly vetted" and "reliable" data. In the methodology statement, the editors proudly proclaim: "We do not conduct unscientific straw polls for use in our computations."[2] Oh yes they do!

THE WEIGHT OF OPINION

To say that a school's fate depends on a small number of anonymous evaluators is, of course, an overstatement, but not much of one. Historically, the peer-evaluation factor has received the most weight of all those used in the U.S. News formula. It was the sole basis for the magazine's first three rankings, but at least those issues purported to list only the top 25 national schools and the top 10 regional schools. That was arbitrary enough, but to use this procedure to assess hundreds of schools makes no sense. Even after adopting a statistically based methodology in 1989, U.S. News has continued to give the reputation factor prime importance. In 2021, it counted for 20 percent in the rating formula for undergraduate programs and 25 percent for law schools.

From the perspective of a ranking magazine, one advantage of assigning heavy weight to peer assessments is their "anchoring effect."[3] That is, reputational ratings tend to exercise a stabilizing influence on listings that might otherwise fluctuate dramatically from year to year. Of course, publications eager to maintain their readership want numerical orderings to change enough over time to supply a little drama—often produced by altering their formulas, if nothing else. But they don't want *too* much drama. Frequent wild swings in the annual ratings would undermine their credibility. The nice thing about peer evaluations is their stability, as numerous scholars have demonstrated. For instance, one study found very little variation in the peer evaluations of schools in the U.S. News survey over the period 2002–2010, regardless of where the school was located in its hierarchy.[4]

An obvious reason for the stabilizing effect of peer evaluations is the relatively static nature of the institutions being evaluated. Colleges are, after all, engineered for stability. Unlike commercial enterprises that make breakthrough discoveries, launch new product lines, or acquire competitors, most institutions of higher education trundle along year after year on exactly the same campus, with a largely life-tenured faculty, offering pretty much the same academic program, majors, and even courses. But another important reason that peer evaluations remain steady over time is their notorious echo effect. As scholars have repeatedly demonstrated, published rankings have a strong impact on peer assessments, which, in turn, have a significant effect on future rankings.[5] If college presidents, provosts, and admissions deans pay close attention to these annual beauty contests—as they emphatically do—there is no way that their view of other institutions in their market segment will not be heavily influenced by those schools' prior positions on the ladder.

The theory behind using peer assessments is straightforward. The quality of the pedigree conferred by a college depends on its prestige. This, in turn, is based on its reputation. If you want to know which are the most prestigious colleges, ask the experts—that is, the individuals who actually run them. But it turns out that these people are not, in fact, experts! College leaders may be well versed in their academic specialties; they are surely very knowledgeable about their own institutions and, probably, a handful of others in which they have worked or with which they compete. But, with rare exceptions, they are simply not experts on the hundreds of institutions in their Carnegie classification that U.S. News asks them to rate.

Further, the administrators asked to express their opinions have an obvious bias to give their own institutions high ratings and their would-be competitors low ones. And, once they have become beguiled by, or beholden to, the published rankings, they will mask their lack of expertise by relying on the very numerical orderings that their considered opinions are supposed to help influence.

Institutional peer assessments are popularity polls, pure and simple. They are not good measures of genuine academic quality. In fact, they are not even very good yardsticks of institutional prestige. They should not be used to rank colleges.

CHAPTER 9

THE WEALTH OF INSTITUTIONS

WHAT IS A COLLEGE WORTH?

In our materialistic culture, we are mesmerized by money. It becomes, for many of us, an essential measure of relative importance or prominence. We often reflexively equate personal prestige with material success. The best athlete has the highest salary. So, too, for corporate CEOs, lawyers, physicians, actors, musicians, and even university presidents. We gobble up lists of people ranked by total income or wealth, such as the annual "Forbes 400."

In the same spirit, we often judge institutions by their economic heft. The Gates Foundation is the most potent philanthropic entity because it's the richest, or so we might think. JPMorgan Chase, with its roughly $3 trillion in assets, reigns supreme over Bank of America and Wells Fargo. Apple has a larger market capitalization than Microsoft. Poor old Amazon can't seem to catch up.

So perhaps we should judge colleges in the same way. The best ones are simply the richest.

But what is a college or university worth? What is the equivalent of market capitalization for institutions lacking shares that are traded on open markets? In an accounting sense, one could add up the value of their easily quantifiable assets, such as real estate, physical plant and equipment, cash, and investments. But then there is the intangible value of a school's brand name. The corporations known as "Amherst College" and "Notre Dame University" are surely worth way more than their land, buildings, and marketable securities. Can you measure that? Let's see . . .

ENDOWMENT PER STUDENT AS A MEASURE OF WEALTH

Early in my presidency at Reed, I presented my plan for a $200 million fundraising campaign to the board of trustees. As I ticked off the various priorities that it would fund—financial aid, new dormitories, an environmental studies program, a performing arts building—heads nodded in apparent approval. Until I said: "And two-thirds of the total will go straight into the endowment!"

Pause. "Why do we need to increase the endowment?" asked one of my favorite trustees, a perennial devil's advocate. "Why don't we just spend what we raise? Let your successors take care of the future."

I could feel my East Coast competitive juices start flowing. "Because Amherst has a bigger endowment. Bowdoin has a bigger endowment. Wesleyan . . ." I suppressed the thought. "Because . . . we need a cushion to protect us from future shocks," I stammered.

In the back of my mind, I wondered, Do we really need to increase the endowment? Is this just about bragging rights?

It seems obvious that an endowment is a good measure of a college's wealth and, not surprisingly, its bragging rights. Everyone seems to want to know how big a school's endowment is—the US Department of Education, accrediting agencies, bond-rating agencies, college guides. And, yes, at least some of the organizations that rank institutions of higher education.

TABLE 9.1.

Endowment value per student (academic year 2018–2019)

College	Endowment per FTE student
Amherst	$1,223,642
Berea	$683,139
City College	$24,050
Michigan	$249,867
Notre Dame	$837,184
Penn	$562,092
Reed	$406,436
Spelman	$175,884

Source: IPEDS.

Significantly, however, U.S. News does not use endowment figures in its best-colleges formula, though it does, like many other news organizations, occasionally publish top 10 endowment lists. In 2020 Harvard was number one, at $41 billion, followed by Yale ($30 billion), Stanford ($28 billion), and Princeton ($26 billion).[1] Absolute numbers like these may be eye catching, but they convey little useful information to potential applicants, given the widely disparate size and activities of various institutions. For this reason, several college rankers and guides use endowment-per-student data. For example, a website called College Raptor bases its annual ratings on that measure.[2] In 2021, Princeton led the field, with a jaw-dropping $2.86 million in endowment funds per student. Amherst came in 10th, Reed 46th.

Most published endowment figures rely on IPEDS data from the US Department of Education. Table 9.1 presents its 2018 endowment-per-student figures for our eight profile schools. These figures showcase the huge inequalities in this particular measure of institutional wealth. The wide variations in these dollar amounts reflect many factors, such as institutional history and mission, alumni loyalty and wealth, fundraising effectiveness, and endowment investment strategy.

I was constantly reminded of these differences during my simultaneous service as Reed's president and a member of Amherst's board of trustees. Compared with Reed, Amherst enjoyed not only a larger cadre of very wealthy and supportive alumni but also a much deeper bench of investment professionals among its graduates who could be called upon to serve on its investment committee. Amherst was an early adopter of the endowment management philosophy most often associated with the late David Swensen, who served for over 35 years as Yale's chief investment officer. Like Swenson, Amherst's endowment managers built a portfolio filled with alternative investments—such as hedge funds, venture capital, private equity, and real assets—that consistently beat the indexes. Early in my tenure on Amherst's board, near the end of the tech bubble in the late 1990s, the college earned a return on its investment assets of nearly 50 percent in a single year. That performance increased its endowment by more than the school had just raised in a seven-year fundraising campaign!

Notre Dame is another successful practitioner of the Swenson investment philosophy. Employing a variant that it naturally called the "Notre Dame model," its investment committee earned a stunning 58 percent return in 2000. The university claims that it was the highest annual return for any higher-education endowment on record.[3] Berea's large endowment-per-student figure is also impressive, given its distinctive niche in the world of higher education. Its success appears to testify to the old-fashioned virtues of thrift, discipline, and long-term thinking, as well as the blessing of having a mission that appeals to many non-alumni philanthropists.

Yet endowment-per-student numbers, such as those presented in table 9.1, mask numerous variations that make interschool comparisons problematic. For example, IPEDS reports the total endowment figure for an entire institution, rather than for subsidiary schools or academic programs within that institution. As a result, one cannot fairly conclude that the University of Pennsylvania is superior to, say, Reed College just because the former's reported endowment per student (ca. $562,000) was higher than the latter's (ca. $406,000). A high-school student applying to Penn's College of Arts and Sciences might be more interested in the extent of endowment support for undergraduate education than for the entire university, including its graduate and professional schools, museums, research institutes, and hospitals.

As table 9.1 illustrates, public universities generally have much smaller endowments than their private-sector counterparts. Schools like City College and Michigan have historically relied heavily on public funding and only recently have begun to build investment portfolios. In a sense one could say that a portion of New York's and Michigan's state budgets are part of those schools' "endowments." For example, in recent years. City College has received about $11,800 per student in state and local appropriations, which is the rough equivalent of having an extra endowment per student of $295,000 (assuming a typical 4 percent annual spending rate from the endowment). Likewise, Michigan's approximately $6,600 state appropriation per student would be about the same as having $165,000 in additional investment funds per student.

If you add those amounts to the true numbers shown on table 9.1, you get a hypothetical total endowment-per-student figure of $319,050 for City College and $414,867 for Michigan. This technique provides a somewhat more meaningful—and more generous—comparison with the private schools. But there are obvious problems with using such an approach for public universities. Unlike true endowments, which are managed by the institutions themselves, per-student subsidies to public universities are subject to the shifting winds of state politics and priorities. Actual endowments, of course, are affected by fluctuations in the securities markets, but over the past half century, they have grown at an impressive average rate. By contrast, during that same period, subsidies for public universities have experienced a steady decline, as states have shifted their budgetary resources to health care, prisons, K–12 education, and other expensive priorities.

DONATIVE WEALTH

Another important source of an institution's value is the revenue-producing potential of its most important constituencies: namely, its alumni and the parents of its current and future students. Economist Gordon Winston calls this "donative wealth."[4] A school that has richer alumni is better positioned to raise more money per capita in charitable gifts. And an institution that draws its enrollment from more-prosperous families is likely to have not only more full-pay students who don't need financial aid, but also a cadre of parents able to make charitable gifts beyond tuition payments. The ability of a school to produce affluent alumni and attract children from monied families is thus a significant factor in its brand value and, hence, an important part of its overall corporate value.

Of course, this form of wealth is reflected in the size of an institution's endowment, discussed above, insofar as alumni and students' parents have made generous financial contributions in the past. But donative wealth also includes the capacity to attract gifts for other purposes, including capital funds for buildings and annual support for operating expenses. It will come as no surprise that these forms of donative wealth correlate very well with the size of a school's endowment and its financial health, as well as with its national ranking.

Measuring Fundraising Capacity

There are various ways to estimate a college's relative donative wealth. The most direct method is from data on annual fundraising revenue, collected by the Voluntary Support of Education (VSE) survey, administered by the Council for Advancement and Support of Education (CASE).[5] The college-by-college data are available from CASE, for a fee, and provide fodder for the annual press stories listing the top gift-receiving institutions. Nowadays Harvard and Stanford almost always lead the pack, with annual gift receipts over $1 billion, followed by the usual suspects. Once in a while another school will break into the billion-dollar club, as Johns Hopkins did in 2019, thanks to a $1.8 billion gift from alumnus Michael Bloomberg.

The US Department of Education's IPEDS database provides another, more publicly accessible source of fundraising data, which can be found in a line item labeled "private gifts, grants, and contracts revenue per FTE student." Using such information to compare institutions, however, is plagued by several problems. IPEDS data lumps gifts for annual operating expenses together with capital gifts for endowment or buildings. Also, like the IPEDS figures for endowment per student, both IPEDS and the VSE survey report gift income for an entire institution, rather than just those portions likely to be of greatest interest to undergraduate students. A further problem is that private-gift revenues tend to fluctuate, sometimes wildly, from year to year, depending on whether the school is in the midst of a fundraising campaign or happens to have received a few large capital gifts.

Ranking by Alumni-Giving Rate

Perhaps for the reasons described above, none of the popular comprehensive rankings use direct measures of fundraising success (or capacity) in their formulas. U.S. News does, however, give a small amount of weight to a metric it calls "alumni giving," which is based on the percentage of a school's graduates who made any gift to the school within the previous two years. The magazine justifies using this criterion as an indicator of alumni satisfaction with their school. Giving money back to one's alma mater is presumably an expression of both appreciation for the education one received in the past and confidence in the institution's prospects for the future. By implication, "better" colleges and universities are those that elicit higher levels of appreciation and confidence from their graduates.

One problem with the alumni-giving-rate factor is its susceptibility to gaming. Since institutions are not required to report these rates to the federal government, many people believe that the numbers submitted to U.S. News are especially unreliable. This concern may be illustrated by the recent cases of "misreporting" by Berkeley and Scripps recounted in chapter 6. Aside from outright falsification, one common form of manipulation involves removing the names of chronic non-givers from the college's alumni database, thereby handily reducing the denominator in the donors-per-capita calculation. Sometimes these statistically extinguished alumni experience a magical resurrection when they appear at a 25th or 50th reunion, check in hand. Other scams involve counting unfulfilled pledges as if they were gifts, attributing a single large sum to multiple non-donors, or shifting contributions that arrived near the beginning of one fiscal year to the previous year when needed to boost the numbers.

Another basis for objection to the alumni-giving metric is that it doesn't reflect the relative size of the donations that were made. Some observers question whether the level of alumni satisfaction would be better measured by average dollar amounts donated, rather than merely the number of donors. As an analogy, economists often claim that the best way to quantify the intensity of consumers' preferences is by the prices they pay, rather than the volume of sales transactions. They might therefore argue that a "better" college will attract a larger dollar volume of gifts, not just a greater number of them.

Forbes magazine periodically publishes a specialized "Grateful Grads" ranking, based on this view.[6] Its formula uses two factors: a seven-year average of total alumni donations per enrolled student, and a three-year average of the proportion of alumni who made any gift at all. Reflecting Forbes' characteristic celebration of wealth and prestige, it gives twice as much weight to the giving-per-student measure as to the participation-rate measure. In its 2019 listing, the top three institutions were Dartmouth, Williams, and Princeton. Virtually all of its top schools were the usual wealthy, elite institutions.

In this case, I would side with the choice made by U.S. News. Forbes' decision to use the magnitude of average gifts disadvantages schools whose graduates have lower incomes and less wealth but might have the same—or perhaps even more—appreciation for the education they received. In that sense, the giving-participation metric utilized by U.S. News could be viewed as a welcome exception to its general pro-wealth bias.

Tapping into Parental Wealth

As I mentioned earlier, the ability of a college to attract academically well-prepared applicants from high-income families is plausibly a component of that school's brand value and, hence, an additional form of institutional wealth. Affluent parents have become a rapidly growing segment of college developmental programs. In its 2019–2020 VSE fundraising report, CASE disclosed that colleges received almost as much money from "non-alumni individuals" as from their alumni.[7] A large number of those benefactors were parents of *current* or *former* students.

In fact, some of these donors were undoubtedly parents of would-be *future* students. A prominent illustration is Daniel Golden's oft-repeated account of how Donald Trump's son-in-law, Jared Kushner, got into Harvard in 1999 after his father donated $2.5 million to the university in 1998.[8] As we know from the 2019 affirmative action lawsuit against Harvard University, its admissions office still gives a sizable competitive edge to children of past or prospective donors, those whom it calls "dean's-interest" candidates.[9] Rick Singer, the mastermind behind the 2019 Operation Varsity Blues admissions scandal discussed below, used a different term, referring to this category as "back-door" admissions.[10]

I have sometimes kiddingly suggested that elite colleges should just capture their parental wealth more directly and openly—by auctioning off, say, 10 percent of the places in their entering classes. After all, if that is the best way to sell rare and valuable works of art, such as Van Gogh paintings, why isn't it also the best way to allocate rare and valuable seats in elite colleges? Not only would this method enable these institutions to avoid the subterfuge of dean's-interest admissions decisions, but it would also establish a true market price for seats in various schools. And then, perhaps, U.S. News—or better yet, Forbes—could use those market prices to rank colleges!

Of course, I'm being facetious. No self-respecting public or nonprofit institution would have the chutzpah—or risk its governmental subvention or tax exemption—to adopt such a scheme openly. But the Varsity Blues admissions scandal actually gave us a small taste of how my hypothetical auction system might work. Since the affair was first revealed in March 2019, more than 55 wealthy parents have been criminally charged with—and most have been convicted of—paying bribes to Rick Singer to get their children admitted to such universities as Georgetown, USC, or Yale.[11]

In some instances, Singer secured admission by hiring someone to take the SAT test in the applicant's place. In other cases, he bribed college athletic coaches in low-visibility sports—such as sailing, crew, water polo, or tennis—to certify to the admissions office that the candidate was a star athlete. The reported amounts give us a hint of what at least some parents would be willing to bid in an open auction to get their child admitted to an elite school. The highest reported bribe—a cool $1.2 million—was paid to obtain a seat in the entering class at Yale. Admission to USC and Georgetown, by contrast, reportedly fetched payments of "only" $400,000 each.[12] That's a ranking, of sorts.

Given obvious confidentiality concerns, measures of parental wealth or incomes are not used in any popular rankings. There have, however, been occasional studies that reveal school-by-school variations in parental earnings. A leading example is the "intergenerational mobility" data gathered by Raj Chetty and his colleagues at Harvard's Opportunity Insights think tank, which I discuss more fully in chapter 20.[13] These researchers obtained data on the family incomes (expressed in 2015 dollars) of virtually every student who attended college in roughly the years 1996-2014. Thanks to an interactive presentation on the *New York Times* website, anyone can conveniently access the data for any of the institutions surveyed.[14] Table 9.2 shows figures for seven (all but Berea) of our eight profile schools.

As one can readily see, and as the data from Chetty and

TABLE 9.2.
Selective parental income data (circa 2013)

College	Median income[a]	Top 1%[b]	Top 20%[c]	Bottom 20%[d]
Amherst	$158,200	21	60	5
Berea	N/A	N/A	N/A	N/A
City College	$40,200	<1	15	23
Michigan	$154,000	9	66	4
Notre Dame	$191,400	15	75	2
Penn	$195,500	19	71	3
Reed	$157,800	8	65	3
Spelman	$58,700	1	26	11

Source: Chetty et al. (2017), accessed in Upshot (2017).
Note: N/A = not available.
[a] Median family income of all enrolled students. Income data are for the families of students attending college in the years 1996 to 2014, expressed in 2015 dollars.
[b] Percentage of enrolled students from families with incomes in the top 1 percent of national incomes.
[c] Percentage of enrolled students from families with incomes in the top 20 percent of national incomes.
[d] Percentage of enrolled students from families with incomes in the bottom 20 percent of national incomes.

his coauthors glaringly demonstrate, institutional wealth and parental affluence generally go hand in hand. Indeed, by every measure—endowment per student, fundraising capacity and success, alumni wealth, and parental incomes—the elite institutions mostly float to the top, and everyone else struggles to keep from sinking.

FINANCIAL-HEALTH MEASURES

A final wealth-related indicator of institutional prestige is a set of measures used by various rankers and raters of colleges to assess their overall financial health. A particularly robust example is the "financial-health grades" published annually by Forbes magazine.[15] Mimicking bond-rating agencies such as Moody's and Standard & Poor's, Forbes dispenses ratings designed to measure the financial resiliency of individual colleges and universities. For the 2021 edition, its formula included such factors as endowment, spendable assets, annual expenditures, debt load, operating profit or loss, and investment return.

Applying the formula to data available from IPEDS, Forbes assigned both numerical and letter grades to 921 private four-year institutions. (It was unable to rate public institutions, since their finances are backed by the revenue-generating capacity of their states.) Sixty schools (including Amherst, Berea, Penn, and Notre Dame) received A+ scores. Reed and Spelman each earned an A. As an indication that grade inflation has not yet contaminated the Forbes magazine ratings—or as evidence of the fiscally perilous condition of private, nonprofit higher education—over 60 percent of the schools received Cs and Ds.

The US Department of Education also publishes financial-health grades for private educational institutions.[16] Federal legislation requires colleges or universities seeking to participate in federal-funding or federal-loan programs (known as Title IV institutions) to demonstrate their "financial responsibility" by submitting annual audited statements to the DOE. The department computes and publishes a composite score for each Title IV school, on a scale ranging from –1 (for financially troubled schools) to +3.0 (for fiscally healthy ones). That score is based on factors similar to those used by Forbes. In the DOE's latest report, all of the private institutions in our profile group received the highest number of points. Indeed, the prevalence of 3.0 scores makes it impractical to use this index to rank selective schools.

There are various other resources for assessing organizations' financial health. For example, in a recent book called *The College Stress Test*,[17] Robert Zemsky and his coauthors measured the fiscal stress of both private and public colleges on a scale of zero (minimum stress) to 12 (maximum stress). By their estimate, 60 percent of the schools were healthy, 30 percent were "struggling," and 10 percent were "deeply troubled." Not surprisingly, both the authors and the publisher have been loath to name the "deeply troubled" institutions. No school, regardless how fragile its finances may be, wants prospective applicants to think it is about to fold. Significantly, this fact doesn't prevent Forbes from publishing a list of colleges to which it assigns grades of C, C–, and even D. But there are no Fs on its list. Those, presumably, are the schools that have already gone out of business.

As another example, a financial-aid advisory firm called Edmit has devised a formula to assess the probability that a college could run out of money in the near future.[18] Like Forbes, it assesses only private institutions. Its 2019 rankings gave 485 schools a "high" grade (for good fiscal health), 215 a "medium," and 235 a "low." In 2020, however, after plugging in estimates of the impact of the COVID-19 pandemic, the number of "high" grades dropped by 100, while the number of "low" ones increased by 110. Although the long-term impacts of the pandemic are impossible to predict,[19] one thing is certain: it will widen the already staggering inequality in institutional wealth that characterizes American higher education.

All of the direct measures of institutional wealth canvased in this chapter make regular appearances in college guidebooks, governmental databases, news stories, and specialty listings. But most of the popular comprehensive rankings rely instead on surrogates for wealth, including the amounts that schools spend per student, and, necessarily, the revenues that they have to generate in order to support those outlays— topics to which we now turn.

CHAPTER 10

THE SPENDING RAT RACE

MAXIMIZING PER-STUDENT SUBSIDY

From 2001 to 2020, the average tuition at American institutions of higher education increased by 159 percent.[1] That is almost exactly three times as fast as the rate of inflation, measured by the consumer price index (CPI). What in the world is going on?

During my tenure as a college president, I confess to having been complicit in raising tuition at a higher rate than the CPI. Even so, it seemed as though we never had enough money. Every year the cost of running the college kept rising. It would have been one thing if we were educating more students, I thought. But we weren't. Each year it appeared to cost more to serve the same number of students. Much more.

I knew that our production function was intrinsically expensive. Like most selective colleges and universities, we were providing what I often called an "artisanal" form of education. Instruction was high touch, face to face, interactive. It was led by full-time educational craftspeople. We supported their efforts with an array of other resources affording equally personalized attention, including a library and information technology, science laboratories, and visual and performing arts facilities. As a residential school, we surrounded all of these educational offerings with equally high-touch student-life services, such as housing, nutrition, counseling, health care, and fitness.

So it was obvious to me why our expenditure levels were so high, at least compared with the mass-produced, internet-based instruction offered by some for-profit universities. But what was less obvious to me was why the cost of higher education—not just at Reed, but apparently at most colleges and universities—kept rising faster than the CPI.

THE SPENDING TREADMILL
What Drives College Spending?

In looking for answers, I was initially attracted to a theory suggested by economist William Baumol. According to his explanation, artisanal undertakings, such as performing a string quartet or providing a college education, are afflicted with what he called a "cost disease."[2] The producers of such services, he said, face ever-rising labor costs to attract highly trained professionals (e.g., violinists or philosophy professors). But, unlike manufacturers or financial institutions, colleges and universities can't offset the rising costs of their professional labor with technology-driven productivity gains. People today produce string quartets and philosophy seminars in pretty much the same way as they did back in Haydn's time.

Baumol's theory finds some support in a special inflation index called the higher-education price index (HEPI). HEPI is calculated each year by Commonfund, a nonprofit organization that manages many college endowments. It attempts to measure the rate of increase in the price of the particular inputs used to produce higher education, such as faculty and professional salaries, academic buildings, library books, computers, and so on. As a college president, I took some solace in the fact that HEPI was almost always higher than the CPI. For example, from 2001 to 2020, HEPI increased by 69 percent, while the CPI rose by only 47 percent.[3]

As that comparison of inflation rates demonstrates, it turns out that Baumol's cost-disease theory explains only a relatively small portion of the observed escalation in postsecondary educational expenditures. As several researchers have shown, most of the cost inflation has less to do with involuntary factors, such as increases in faculty and professional salaries, and much more to do with voluntary ones, such as added administrative staff and expanded programming.[4] In other words, academic budgets are growing so fast, not because inflation is pulling them, but because administrators are pushing them. Why?

Howard R. Bowen, former president of both the University of Iowa and Grinnell College, offered an alternative explanation, sometimes called "Bowen's Rule."[5] His theory is essentially a prestige-driven explanation of spending. Since colleges and universities strive for the intrinsically unlimited (and unmeasurable) objective of higher status, they are trapped on a treadmill, endlessly raising money so they can spend every nickel in the quest for greater bragging rights. Bowen's argument bears a kinship relation to the theory, discussed in chapter 7, that education is a positional good whose value to individual students depends on the fact that only a few other people are able to consume it (i.e., attend and graduate from that particular school). As economists have repeatedly observed, positional-good markets are characterized by winner-take-all arms races.[6]

The arms-race analogy, however, may be somewhat misleading. For example, in the 1970s and 1980s, the United States and the Soviet Union were deliberately seeking to outspend each other on weaponry. But their goal was to have *more missiles*, not to *spend more per missile*. The goal of the educational arms race is not to educate more students, but to spend more on each student. That, after all, is the grim logic of positional goods: make them more and more exclusive—that is, prestigious—by limiting the number of consumers!

Maximizing Subsidy per Student

Organizational economists like to ask what it is that different kinds of organizations seek to maximize. In the for-profit world, the answer usually given is shareholder value—that is, the total value of a company's equity shares, as priced by the stock market. What is it, I sometimes wondered, that colleges seek to maximize? Williams College economist Gordon Winston suggested that the answer is "subsidy per student."[7] Prestige-driven colleges, he argued, seek to signal their relative status in the marketplace by providing their students with a product that costs much more to produce than the price they charge. Perhaps it's no coincidence that Winston would come up with such a formulation, teaching, as he did, at a spectacularly well-endowed, high-subsidy institution.

As one can see from the data on our eight profile schools in table 10.1, most selective institutions do, in fact, spend more per student than they charge in their posted sticker-price tuition and fees (shown in the first and second columns). During my service on Amherst's board of trustees, whenever someone talked about full-pay students, one of my fellow trustees would protest. "No one pays the full cost of an Amherst education," he would say. "Everyone is getting subsidized." To him, that was a point of pride. As you can see from table 10.1, he was absolutely right. In 2018, even those students able to pay the full posted tuition were receiving, on average, the equivalent of a $32,509 subsidy per year, or roughly about $130,000 over their four-year residency. Not bad.

The effective subsidy is even greater when you compare spending per student with what the *average* student pays, shown in table 10.1 as net tuition (sticker price less average

TABLE 10.1.
Per-student spending, tuition, and subsidy (academic year 2018–2019)

College	Spending/FTE[a]	Posted tuition[b]	Net tuition/FTE[c]	Subsidy/FTE[d]
Amherst	$88,935	$56,426	$27,541	$61,394
Berea	$41,399	$39,900	$2,751	$38,648
City College	$35,971	$7,140/14,810	$4,047	$31,924
Michigan	$70,234	$15,262/49,350	$24,489	$45,745
Notre Dame	$73,625	$53,391	$24,901	$48,724
Penn	$146,259	$55,584	$40,773	$105,486
Reed	$54,685	$56,340	$33,701	$20,984
Spelman	$37,291	$29,064	$17,303	$19,988

Source: IPEDS. None of the figures include spending on charges for room and board.

[a] Total spending for instruction, research (other than in organizationally separate research centers), academic support, student services, institutional support, and other core expenditures, per full-time-equivalent (FTE) student.

[b] Sticker-price tuition plus mandatory fees. Posted tuitions for City College and Michigan show amounts for both in-state and out-of-state students.

[c] Net revenue per student after deducting institutional grants from posted tuition.

[d] Spending/FTE less net tuition/FTE.

institutional financial-aid grant). Comparing the second and fourth columns, you can see that the average student at Amherst in 2018 was receiving the equivalent of a $61,394 subsidy per year, or about $245,000 over four years.

Competition to offer the largest subsidy naturally leads to the ever-growing size of such subventions over time. In a 2009 article, Stanford economist Caroline Hoxby presented a striking graphic illustration of the growth of per-student subsidies from 1966 to 2006.[8] She grouped colleges and universities into 13 quality categories, based on their admissions selectivity, and then charted, for each selectivity tier, the growth of average educational spending per student and the average subsidy per student (both measured in constant— that is, inflation-adjusted—2007 dollars).

Looking first at educational expenditures per student, in 1966 the highest-selectivity institutions spent about $17,400 per student, whereas the lowest-selectivity group expended around $3,900 (a gap of $13,500). Fifty years later, the highest-selectivity group spent $92,000 per student, and the lowest group, $12,000 (a difference of $80,000). Looking, next, at per-student subsidies, the same picture emerges. In 1966, the difference in the average per-student subsidy between the highest- and lowest-selectivity schools was about $6,000 ($8,000 vs. $2,000). By 2006, that differential had grown to approximately $69,000 ($75,000 vs. $6,000).

Using more-recent data for our profile group, one can readily see how the gap between spending and subsidy by selectivity tier has continued to grow. For example, among our four liberal arts colleges, consider the increase in educational outlays per student per year from 2006 to 2018. At Amherst the increase was 78 percent; at Reed, 45 percent; at Spelman, 38 percent; and at Berea, 34 percent. In 2006, Amherst was spending $22,977 more per student than Spelman. By 2018, that difference had more than doubled, to $51,644.

Spending and Ranking

Not surprisingly, the rankocrats reward and encourage the very behavior that Winston describes and Hoxby chronicles. The formulas used by U.S. News and the WSJ/THE both award approximately 10 percent of their weighting based on how much a school spends per student. Most similar publications do likewise. These assessments depend on data submitted by institutions to the US Department of Education and reported on its IPEDS database. IPEDS charts "core expenses per FTE enrollment," broken down by seven functional categories: instruction, faculty research, public service, academic support, student services, institutional support, and "other."[9] Core expenses do not include noneducational ancillary enterprises, such as cafeterias, dormitories, and separately funded research centers.

Should schools get a boost in their rankings by spending more per student than their peers? Superficially, it seems logical that the answer should be yes. Whether we are talking about refrigerators or college educations, one typically assumes that products costing more to produce are better than cheaper alternatives. But a deeper examination raises legitimate grounds to question that assumption.

First, variations in the amounts spent on each student can occur for many reasons that bear little relationship to the quality of their educational experiences. For universities, the IPEDS expense-per-student figure includes all educational programs offered at that institution, including both undergraduate and graduate programs.[10] In a ranking aimed at prospective undergraduates, rewarding a university for having an expensive medical school or law school can be misleading. This phenomenon may be reflected in Penn's astronomical spending-per-student figure shown on table 10.1.

Even within an undergraduate program, moreover, spending per student can vary widely for reasons other than academic quality. For example, the per-student cost of laboratory science courses vastly exceeds that of, say, most literature courses. This is the primary reason for Caltech's high spending -per-student figure that, in 2000, temporarily catapulted it to the top spot in the U.S. News rankings, as described in chapter 3. Another example is the wide range of extracurricular programs funded by various schools. If a college such as Amherst or Williams chooses to offer an expansive athletic program, its per-student expenses will be higher, for this reason alone, than those at a school, like Reed or Spelman, that chooses not to emphasize sports.

A second problem with grading institutions based on their per-capita spending is that it penalizes schools for operating efficiently. If anything, it encourages wasteful spending. Here I am talking not just about opulent student centers and athletic palaces, but also about the proliferation of administrative departments so characteristic of modern selective institutions. Even if we could show, for example, that City College offers as good an undergraduate education as Notre Dame—for slightly less than half the cost (as shown in table 10.1)—City College would get no credit from the rankers.

Third, rewarding higher educational institutions based on their spending per student discourages wealthy—that is, elite—schools from sharing their educational excellence with more students by expanding enrollments. If you want to maximize expenditures per student, it's important to keep the denominator in that fraction from growing too much. As Jeffrey Selingo explains, over the past 30 years, Ivy League universities have expanded their undergraduate enrollments by only 14 percent, while the population of high-school graduates has increased over three times faster.[11] Imagine what would have happened if the top-tier institutions in Caroline Hoxby's study had used their massive surpluses to double enrollments, rather than doubling spending per student. More students would have benefited from access to their talented faculties, campus facilities, and generous support services. But doing so would have hurt those schools' rankings. By punishing colleges and universities that spread their surpluses across a larger student population, the popular rankings end up accelerating the growing inequality in higher education.

THE FUNDRAISING TREADMILL

Once you are on the subsidy-maximizing treadmill, you are

also necessarily on the income-chasing treadmill. As a dean and then a college president, I often felt that my primary job was figuring out how to generate more and more money to feed the insatiable needs of the spending machine. My staff and I devoted countless hours to cultivating wealthy alumni and parents, nursing relationships with foundations and local businesspeople, building up the staff and budget of the development office, organizing ever-fancier events for alumni, and scheming about ancillary business activities or uses of the campus that might generate a little extra income.

Of course, there is nothing intrinsically wrong with any of this, unless the pressures become so intense that they distort priorities and undercut the institution's true mission. One often-cited example is the enormous investment in varsity football and basketball by universities desperately hoping to join that small coterie of schools whose athletic programs actually make a profit.[12] In the end, most of those institutions are effectively taking money out of the pockets of their students to pay for this folly. Or, to put it another way, they are increasingly in the business of producing entertainment, rather than education. Another example of distortions created by profit seeking is the gradual replacement of arts and humanities courses with vocationally oriented curricula. All across the higher educational landscape, one can see colleges adopting trendy business or technical courses in an effort to attract more full-pay students and channel their graduates into careers that will support higher donations in the future.

A more common—and, I think, more insidious—problem is the pressure to favor wealthy applicants in the admissions process, to the exclusion of poorer ones. A story recounted by Paul Tough in his recent book, *The Years That Matter Most*, provides a poignant illustration.[13] Shortly after arriving at Trinity College (Connecticut) as its admissions dean,

Angel Pérez concluded that the school was admitting too many super-rich kids with high SAT scores but low academic motivation. Indeed, the median family income of students at Trinity—$257,500—was among the highest recorded for any American college.[14] With faculty support, Pérez set out to recruit a larger number of highly motivated, lower-income students and proportionately fewer wealthy goof-offs. He succeeded admirably. But the enrollees that Pérez attracted had lower SAT scores than the more affluent students they replaced. U.S. News rewarded his efforts by dropping Trinity's ranking from 38th to 44th.

The subsidy-maximizing rat race in which competitive institutions are imprisoned creates relentless pressure to admit wealthy students, even those with little noticeable academic ambition. As a law professor for 25 years, I've encountered plenty of them. They graduate from top colleges and universities with B+ or A– averages. They decide to attend law school because, almost literally, they "can't do math and hate the sight of blood." Their writing is flat and formulaic. Their resumés seem machine made. But boy, do they have impressive SAT and LSAT scores!

Stripped to its essentials, the business model that most selective colleges employ is what I call the "lifetime-giving" model. They provide a generous subsidy to their current students on the premise that, as grateful alumni, they will repay this generosity over the course of their lifetimes (and, indeed, through their estates). Of course, not all former students will fully reimburse their alma maters for the subsidy they received. Most will give less, some will donate roughly the full amount, and a few will contribute much more. For the model to be financially sustainable, institutions must harvest from each cohort of former students a cumulative amount at least equal to the school's investment in that group. Moreover, in order to keep fueling the spending rat race, competitive colleges really need each class to produce even more funds than they received.

Schools that employ this business model have powerful—albeit unspoken—incentives to structure their admissions programs to maximize the lifetime income-generating potential of each entering class. These inducements lead them to adopt policies like early decision, legacy and "dean's interest" preferences, merit aid, and other admissions practices that favor the already privileged at the expense of the underprivileged. And, truth be told, often to advantage the academically indifferent at the expense of the intellectually passionate.

The lifetime-giving model also places a very high premium on keeping students happy, so they will graduate on a timely basis and be grateful alumni forever after. I can't help but think that this scheme has contributed to the gradual erosion of required curricula, the disappearance of senior theses (and even long research papers), and the rampant grade inflation prevalent at so many selective institutions.

These phenomena probably would have occurred even in the absence of college rankings. But the widespread practice of assigning prestige points by the amount of money lavished on each student has surely exacerbated them.

PART III

THE GATEKEEPERS

JUDGING COLLEGES BY
WHO GETS IN AND WHO DOESN'T

CHAPTER 11

THE BEST AND THE BRIGHTEST

STUDENT SELECTIVITY AND COLLEGE RANKINGS

An Ivy League admissions officer once said to me, "We admit only the best and brightest." I watched to see if there was even a hint of irony or amusement in his expression. There was none.

My generation would forever associate "the best and the brightest" with David Halberstam's book of the same title.[1] That label referred to members of President John F. Kennedy's inner circle, many of them recruited from the halls of academe. Men like McGeorge and William Bundy, Robert McNamara, Walt Rostow, and Dean Rusk, to name just a few. They had all been academic superstars, with credentials from the likes of the Groton School, Harvard, Yale, and Oxford. And, collectively, they led the United States into the quagmire of the Vietnam War.

To my generation, then, "the best and the brightest" was not always a compliment. As I learned during four decades in academic life, the best students are not always the brightest. And as I also realized, schools full of the brightest students are *not* necessarily the best.

ONLY THE BRIGHTEST

My great-uncle Arthur, who sold greeting cards in Portland, Maine, was fond of proclaiming that his customers were all "fine, upstanding people." But, so far as I could tell, the only qualities of his customers that he really cared about were their willingness to purchase and their ability to pay. So it is with most businesses. But not higher education. To be sure, colleges are concerned about whether an applicant will accept an offer of admission and how much that person's family will be able to pay. But they also care—and care deeply—about various other characteristics of the students they admit, including academic ability, work ethic, integrity, race or ethnicity, and, sometimes, gender identity, athletic ability, musical talent, or religious faith.

At one time, many competitive schools said they were looking only for well-rounded students. In fact, this claim was always hyperbolic and was sometimes used to mask an intent to discriminate against a disfavored group, such as Jews or Blacks.[2] In recent times, the notion of a well-rounded student body has come to replace the well-rounded student. I have even heard some admissions officers talk about their entering class as though it consisted of wholly distinct categories of individuals—using terms such as "academic admits," "athletic admits," "affirmative action admits," and so on.

All that said, it is clear that at most competitive institutions, one quality dominates in the evaluation of candidates: academic ability. These schools will happily admit a new class of applicants with a broad array of athletic skills or musical talents, but not with a wide range of academic abilities. It seems obvious that colleges would want to enroll students with high levels of intellectual capabilities. Most faculty prefer teaching students who can grasp instructional material quickly, ask intelligent questions, and engage in sophisticated discussions. Similarly, administrators want bright individuals who are more likely to graduate and go on to successful careers—not only for the benefit of the students themselves, but also as a way of increasing the likelihood of future alumni support for the institution.

Furthermore, as economist Gordon Winston hypothesizes, many educators at selective colleges believe that they can maximize peer-effect learning by grouping high-ability students together.[3] He even suggests that relying on them to teach each other can enable such institutions to save money on instruction. As an illustration, he cites Harvard College's widespread use of large lecture classes and graduate teaching assistants in social science courses.[4]

Educators often assume that peer-effect learning requires having students with uniform levels of academic ability. That may not be true. Yale's Henry Hansmann speculates that mixing individuals of varying academic abilities might produce better overall educational outcomes.[5] The less able would benefit by learning from the more able, and the latter would profit by helping to teach the former. But virtually no competitive college seems interested in finding out if this is true. By and large, those schools want uniformly smart students.

Which raises obvious questions. How do colleges assess the academic abilities of prospective students before they even arrive on campus? How should they? And, most importantly for our present purposes, are schools that succeed in attracting students who are more academically talented necessarily better—for that reason alone—than institutions that attract less-talented ones?

IDENTIFYING ACADEMIC TALENT IN COLLEGE ADMISSIONS

At Reed, like most selective colleges, making admissions decisions was a painstaking process. We assembled a thick file for every applicant, including high-school transcripts, SAT or ACT scores, letters of recommendations, personal statements, and writing samples. The dossier sometimes included creative work or research papers submitted by the applicant, as well as reports of interviews by admissions staff or alumni volunteers. Once the files were complete, admissions officers would numerically grade each application along multiple dimensions. Those officers would then defend their views in meetings of the entire staff, before making recommendations to the dean of admissions.

Overall, we were looking for a set of qualities that predicted success in Reed's hothouse atmosphere—genuine intellectual curiosity, analytical acuity, a capacity for original thinking, an ability to conceptualize, doggedness in pursuit of understanding, a willingness to take risks and learn from mistakes, and a strong moral compass. We firmly believed that an applicant's high-school record was by far the best predictor of academic success. Of course, this meant giving considerable weight to their GPAs and class ranks. But it also meant assessing the difficulty and range of courses taken, the distribution and year-to-year progression of grades, and the quality of submitted writing samples, teachers' evaluations, and the applicant's own self-assessment.

We knew that GPAs can be misleading, because grading practices often vary widely by high school, course subject matter, and even individual instructor. So we required standardized test scores to help us adjust for those differences. As I discuss below, the SAT and ACT tests have become hugely controversial. Many argue that they are so biased— both by race and by class—that they should either be made optional or scrapped altogether. At Reed, we were well aware of these arguments and agreed that SAT and ACT results should never be determinative. Rather, we viewed them as useful constraints that helped check our instinct about the academic preparedness of, say, applicants who had been home schooled, had been educated at an unfamiliar high school, or had received seemingly aberrant course grades.

We were also acutely aware that race-based and class-based biases can infect all of the indicators used to assess academic promise, from the quality of high-school instruction to the availability of extracurricular activities, internships, college counseling, and assistance in writing admissions essays. The best we could do was to consider every one of these benchmarks—including test scores—with sensitivity to the environmental and demographic realities confronting each applicant.

Largely for the same reasons, we refused to regard maximizing the average test score of the entering class as some sort of institutional fetish. Unfortunately, as I describe below, that has happened too rarely in our sector.

STUDENT SELECTIVITY MEASURES OF INSTITUTIONAL QUALITY

Given the centrality of a student's academic ability in admissions criteria, it should come as no surprise that a common method for evaluating the relative quality of higher educational institutions is to determine how successfully they compete for talented students in the admissions marketplace. This quality is customarily referred to as "student selectivity," or simply "selectivity." Thus, for example, one of the most influential quality-based classifications of American colleges is Barron's selectivity index. In its annual *Profiles of American Colleges*, Barron's assigns roughly 1,650 schools to categories with labels such as "most selective," "highly competitive plus," "highly competitive," and so on.[6]

Barron's selectivity index has been used as a proxy for institutional quality in hundreds of academic studies of higher education, such as Caroline Hoxby's subsidy-per-student research discussed in chapter 10 and the social-mobility investigations of Raj Chetty and his coauthors discussed in chapter 20. Likewise, many college guides use this index or similar measures of admissions success to describe and rate colleges. Selectivity has also been a very important ingredient in college rankings since their inception.

Student selectivity measures, as used to classify colleges by academic quality, fall into two general categories. One focuses on the level of academic talent represented in a school's entering first-year class. The metrics most often employed for this purpose are average scores on standardized admissions tests, such as the SAT and the ACT, and average high-school GPAs or class ranks. The other category of selectivity measures addresses how well a college performs in competition with other institutions to attract and enroll applicants. Criteria employed under this heading include acceptance rate (percentage of applicants admitted), yield rate (percentage of admitted applicants who enroll), and overlap data (based on an institution's win-loss percentages in head-to-head competition with other schools for students admitted in common). Barron's selectivity index combines measures taken from both categories—using average high-school class rank, average high-school GPA, average standardized test score, and acceptance rate.

Because the various selectivity metrics used to rate colleges raise somewhat distinct issues, I discuss them separately in the pages and chapters that follow. In the remainder of this chapter, I concentrate on the issue of whether, and to what extent, it makes sense to judge an institution of higher education by the prior academic performance of its entering students—as measured by either GPAs or class ranks. In the subsequent two chapters, I address the unique and perplexing issues posed by relying on standardized test scores to evaluate both applicants and the schools in which they enroll. Finally, in chapter 14, I consider the three selectivity measures that attempt to assess institutional success in the admissions competition: acceptance rates, yield rates, and overlap data.

RANKING INSTITUTIONS BY ENTERING STUDENTS' PRIOR ACADEMIC PERFORMANCE

At one time, student selectivity rankings of higher educational institutions relied heavily on measures of their entering students' prior academic performance. For example, during the time I was president of Reed, U.S. News was giving a 6 percent weight to the proportion of the college's first-year students who had graduated in the top 10 percent of their high-school classes. Similarly, during the years when I served as a law-school dean, U.S. News assigned a roughly 10 percent weight to the median undergraduate GPA of the students in the law school's entering class. Since then, U.S. News has reduced the weights assigned to these types of indicators, and many other popular rankings have avoided using them altogether—and for good reason, as I discuss below. But these measures are still featured prominently in many college guides, such as the *Fiske Guide* and College Scorecard.

Using Undergraduate GPAs to Rank Law Schools

Law-school rankings nicely illustrate the perils of using the prior GPAs of entering students to rate the schools they attend. When I was dean of the Penn Law School, I found the heavy weight given to undergraduate GPA (UGPA) figures in the U.S. News formula to be particularly troublesome. Early in my tenure, I decided to read about 30 randomly selected application files as a way of putting some flesh on the raw numbers that we reported to the ABA and U.S. News. I could readily see how different applicants' UGPAs depended, at least in part, on their choice of majors, the difficulty of the courses they selected, and the general grading policies of the institutions they attended. But the iron logic of the U.S. News formula made no allowance for such subtleties. The average UGPA for all entering students was the only thing that mattered.

The arbitrariness of using absolute UGPA averages in law-school rankings came home to me with a vengeance when, as Reed College's unofficial pre-law advisor, I tried to explain to various law schools why its graduates' GPAs often seemed low. Reed had a rather distinctive grading policy. Faculty members were expected to return papers and exams to students with copious evaluative comments, but no letter grade. To be sure, they recorded grades and reported them to the registrar for entry into the student's academic record. But instructors didn't inform students about their grades unless asked. And the prevailing anti–grade-grubbing culture was such that the great majority of students did not ask.

If I decided that a student's performance on a paper in my Constitutional Theory course deserved a C, I would write extensive comments explaining what could have been done to make a stronger argument. But the grade I assigned was nowhere to be found in my written comments. The theory behind this practice was that feedback is an essential part of the learning experience. Visibly labeling a student's perfor-mance with a letter grade can distract the instructor from providing an in-depth explanation for that assessment. And it can easily deter the student from paying proper attention to those comments.

As a result, grade levels at Reed have changed very little over the decades. By comparison, at most four-year colleges, GPAs have increased dramatically over time. The "gentleman's C" has virtually disappeared, and grades in the A range (A+, A, and A–) have become so common as to be virtually meaningless. According to research conducted by retired Duke professor Stuart Rojstaczer and published on his GradeInflation.com website,[7] fully 45 percent of all grades awarded by four-year colleges in 2013 fell within the A range, an increase of 280 percent over the comparable figure in 1963! When I joined Amherst's board of trustees in 1998, I was stunned to discover the GPA that had qualified me for a degree *summa cum laude* in 1965 had since become close to the average for the entire school.

Rojstaczer's data also put into sharp relief the variability in GPAs from college to college that bedeviled me as a pre-law advisor at Reed. The poster children for runaway grade inflation are the Ivy League institutions and their elite cousins. At selective private colleges, the proportion of grades in the A range hovers near 50 percent. In 2004, I was quoted in a *New York Times* story about grade inflation at Princeton.[8] At that time, according to Rojstaczer's data, the average GPA at Princeton (3.34) was actually lower than at its Ivy rivals Harvard (3.43), Stanford (3.55), and Brown (3.56). By contrast, the GPA at Reed was 3.11, and at Spelman, 3.20. Since that time, the gap has only widened. According to another website, by 2018 the average GPA at Harvard had risen to 3.63, at Stanford, to 3.68, and at Brown, to 3.73.[9]

If U.S. News had purposefully set out to disadvantage schools like Reed or Spelman in their aspiration to prepare students to study law, they couldn't have come up with a better way than using absolute GPAs to rank law schools. As Rojstaczer and his coauthor put it, at the selective schools, GPAs have become "so saturated at the high end that they have little use as a motivator of students and as an evaluation tool for graduate and professional schools."[10] Or, I would add, as a method of ranking such schools.

Some observers have tried to explain the grade inflation at elite colleges as a product of the increasing academic quality of their students. But scholarly research throws cold water on that rationale. The GPAs at these schools have risen much faster than any plausible measure of their students' academic preparation (such as their average SAT or ACT scores). No, the most widely credited interpretation is sheer consumerism.[11] With the proliferation of student course evaluations, and their increased use for judging faculty members in compensation and promotion reviews, teachers can ill afford to antagonize their students. And higher educational institutions—knowing that they are being judged in part on having high freshman-to-sophomore retention rates and impressive graduation rates—have little incentive to crack down on generous grading practices.

Using High-School GPAs and Class Rank Measures in College Assessments

By contrast to its law-school listings, which are based on entering students' UGPAs, U.S. News uses high-school rank-in-class statistics to assess undergraduate programs. For national universities and liberal arts colleges, the relevant measure is the proportion of matriculating students who finished in the top 10 percent of their high-school classes. This statistic would seem to be a more reliable gauge of prior academic performance than GPAs. High schools, like colleges, vary considerably in their grading policies, making GPA comparisons suspect. Research has shown that grade inflation is rampant in high schools and, as in the collegiate context, especially pronounced in secondary schools catering to the socioeconomically most privileged and academically most advantaged.[12]

Although U.S. News uses class-rank figures rather than

GPAs as a component of their "student excellence" score, many selective institutions report that, in their admissions decision making, they give greater weight to GPAs. This may reflect a belief that GPA numbers somehow capture a student's academic performance more accurately or directly than class standing. But it surely also reflects the unhappy fact that more and more of the most academically ambitious high schools are refusing to report class-rank statistics.[13] Under intense pressure from parents to steer all of their graduates into elite colleges, these high schools only report their inflated GPA data to the institutions to which their students apply. At these high schools, as at Lake Wobegone, all the students are apparently above average.

One could argue, of course, that high-school class-rank numbers, such as those used by U.S. News, are no more reliable than GPAs, as a measure of a college selectivity. Since secondary schools vary in the quality of their educational programs and the academic preparedness of their students, one cannot assume that two individuals from different backgrounds have an equal academic ability merely because they both finished in the top 10 percent of their respective student bodies.

But there is one appealing justification for using high-school class-rank data to compare colleges. It provides an incentive to broaden the range of high schools from which they recruit potential students and thereby provides greater opportunity for applicants who might otherwise be overlooked.

The experience of Texas's state university system lends support to this assertion. In 1997, the Texas legislature adopted a "Top 10 Percent Plan" in response to a federal appeals court decision declaring that the use of racial preferences in admissions was unconstitutional. The plan essentially guaranteed admission to a Texas state university for any applicant who finished in the top 10 percent of any Texas high school's graduating class. (For admission to the University of Texas, Austin, the cutoff was subsequently changed to the top 6 percent.) As scholars have demonstrated, this program has led to a substantial increase in the enrollment of students who come from high schools with heavy concentrations of poor or minority students.[14]

One can only hope that the rankocracy might find ways to reward that sort of behavior among the entire selective tier of American higher education.

CHAPTER 12

SAT

THE ELEPHANT IN THE ADMISSIONS OFFICE AND IN THE RANKINGS

In an attempt to judge entire institutions by the academic credentials of their entering students, college guides and researchers have long relied much more heavily on test scores than on high-school GPAs or rank-in-class measures. The logic of this view apparently runs along the following lines. Colleges all compete to attract the brightest students. The optimal measure of student "brightness" is a uniform nation-wide (now, worldwide) examination that measures qualities predictive of collegiate academic performance. Those schools whose entering classes sport the highest average SAT or ACT scores must, therefore, be the best.

The persuasiveness of this logic depends on the answers to at least two questions. Do the SAT and ACT tests accurately and reliably capture applicants' academic ability? And is a school necessarily excellent if it is full of students who possess whatever it is that these tests measure? The balance of this chapter addresses these queries. In the next chapter, I examine yet another issue that plagues the use of test scores to measure college quality. Does ranking colleges by these scores produce unintended consequences that undermine legitimate educational objectives?

For the sake of simplicity, in the discussion that follows I will talk primarily about the SAT because it has been the lightning rod for most controversies about standardized admissions testing. Like it or not, the SAT is the elephant in the room.

WHAT DOES THE SAT MEASURE: APTITUDE OR ACHIEVEMENT?

As Nicholas Lemann chronicles in *The Big Test*, the SAT examination emerged from an initiative led by Harvard's former president, James Conant, to democratize higher education.[1] Conant's idea was to use intelligence testing to identify a Jeffersonian "natural aristocracy" of talent and ability, replacing the artificial aristocracy of wealth and family that had historically fed most Ivy League universities. Having grown up in a working-class Boston neighborhood, Conant favored using a test that measured aptitude, rather than achievement, to open college doors to kids like himself from less-privileged backgrounds. Hence the label Scholastic Aptitude Test.

Despite Conant's good intentions, however, the SAT has been dogged by controversy throughout its history. One stubborn issue has been the very notion of aptitude. Early testers believed that intelligence was a relatively fixed, biologically determined characteristic—indeed, many still do.[2] This credence helps explain the unfortunate association between intelligence testing and the eugenics movement in the early decades of the twentieth century. Long after that movement was discredited, a lingering association persisted between the notions of aptitude and biological superiority.

Distaste for such measures led Iowan educator E. F. Lindquist to develop a rival exam, which he called the American College Testing Program (now known simply as the ACT). Lindquist's version was achievement oriented—that is, it attempted to measure the extent to which test takers had mastered concepts and knowledge taught in most high schools. The ACT became very popular in the Midwest and began to make inroads even in the SAT's coastal bastions. In response, the College Board (by then, the owner and administrator of the SAT) eventually altered the content of its test to place greater emphasis on achievement and officially scrapped the "Scholastic Aptitude Test" label. Henceforth, it was just "the SAT," which stands for nothing but itself.

DOES THE SAT PREDICT ACADEMIC SUCCESS?

In addition to the controversy about biological determinism, disputes have also swirled about the reliability and validity of tests like the SAT. In psychometric parlance, reliability is a measure of reproducibility—that is, the extent to which a test produces the same results, no matter how often it is administered. The College Board insists that the SAT is very reliable in this sense, and most researchers agree.[3] The big issue in this regard, however, is the extent to which test results can be altered by coaching. A huge test-preparation industry, populated by the likes of Kaplan and the Princeton Review, rests on a bet that coaching does indeed raise scores. Or at least that test takers can be convinced that it does.

This development has been the subject of numerous scholarly studies. The research pretty consistently shows that coaching can produce, on average, gains of about 6 to 9 points on the SAT verbal test and about 14 to 18 points on the math test.[4] On a score scale running from 200 to 800 for each portion of the test, that may not seem like much. But it just might be sufficient to flip an application from the "almost but not quite good enough" pile to the "barely good enough" pile in a college admissions office—that is, from reject to wait list, or even from wait list to admit.

Validity, the other psychometric standard, focuses on a test's significance—that is, the accuracy with which it measures an important underlying quality. The principal means of determining the SAT's validity is the extent to which an applicant's score can predict that person's academic performance in college, especially as determined by first-year grade-point average (FYGPA). Studies of the SAT's validity have produced varied results. Most evaluators seem to conclude that the best overall statistical predictor of FYGPA is a combination of high-school GPA and SAT (or ACT) scores. Between the two, most investigators have found that high-school GPA alone is a somewhat more accurate predictor than an SAT or ACT score alone.[5] But there is other research demonstrating that standardized test scores correlate somewhat more strongly with college performance, especially when there is a wide range of such scores represented within the student body of a particular institution.[6]

My conclusion from these studies is that, on average, SAT results are, in fact, valid predictors of college GPAs—especially for students whose scores are significantly below or above those of most of their classmates. For this reason, it makes good sense to use SAT scores as a check on admissions decisions that are based heavily on other fallible indicators of academic preparedness, such as high-school GPAs and class ranks, as well as various qualitative—and, therefore, inevitably subjective—criteria.

CLASS AND RACIAL BIAS IN THE SAT

Whatever one concludes about the validity of the SAT, however, the basis for the fiercest criticism is the undeniable correlation of SAT performance with test takers' family incomes, parental education levels, and racial/ethnic groups.[7] Striking visual confirmation of this point appeared in a graphic accompanying a 2019 *Wall Street Journal* article.[8] It featured color-coded bell curves showing the distribution of

SAT scores by these three criteria. As one progressed down the tiers of family-income categories, for example, the bell curves marched steadily to the left (i.e., toward lower distributions). Students from families with incomes above $200,000 had an average SAT score of 1230, a number that dropped steadily by income levels, reaching a low of 970 for students whose parents made less than $20,000. A similar pattern occurred as one progressed down the tiers of parental-education levels, or as as one compared average SAT results by racial and ethnic groups. Asian Americans posted the highest average (1223), followed by Whites (1123), Hispanics (990), and African Americans (946).

Attempts to Mitigate the Tests' Biases

The demographically divergent pattern of such scores has been a headache for the testing organizations, triggering recurrent efforts to eliminate, or at least reduce, those differences. For example, these organizations have tried to remove identifiable traces of racial or cultural bias, such as the infamous question once used on the SAT, asking students to define the term "regatta." They have also attempted to counteract the advantage possessed by students able to afford expensive coaching lessons by offering free advice on how to prepare for the tests and providing sample practice questions. But despite dogged efforts, the demographic biases have persisted.

Another tactic tried by the testing organizations has been to correct for those biases through various adjustments to the scores themselves. During the 1990s, a statistician at the Educational Testing Service (which was then administering the SAT) dreamed up a "measure of academic talent" that would adjust each SAT score to account for different test takers' demographic characteristics—such as family income, parental education, and race.[9] The idea met with a sufficiently hostile reception that it never saw the light of day. In 1999, after states such as California and Washington had outlawed the consideration of race in admission to their public universities, the College Board developed a program called Strivers, which would have compared a person's actual SAT score with a predicted SAT score based on that individual's background factors.[10] Another chilly reception, another idea shelved.

Adversity Scores

Undaunted, the College Board tried once again in 2019, floating the idea that it would calculate an "adversity score" for each SAT test taker. Unlike the earlier proposals discussed above, this computation would be based, not on the personal characteristics of the individual test taker, but, instead, on the socioeconomic attributes of the population living in that person's neighborhood and attending the same high school. The College Board also developed an "Environmental Context Dashboard" for every high school in the country, showing the school's overall score, as well as the various component measures on which it was based.

The adversity calculation was not intended to adjust or revise the student's actual SAT results. Rather, it was designed to accompany the test taker's SAT score in college applications. The College Board successfully beta-tested its plan with Yale and Florida State. It then expanded the experiment to 50 other institutions, over 90 percent of which reported that the system helped them make more-objective evaluations of individual applications. Florida State even credited it with helping to increase the enrollment of non-White students.

But not everyone applauded. The experiment's critics saw the adversity score as a kind of scarlet letter, branding both individual applicants and their high schools. An interactive graphic published online by the *Wall Street Journal* drove this home by comparing the adversity scores with average SAT results from over 10,000 high schools. According to its author, viewers could quickly determine which high schools were "overperformers" and "underperformers."[11] By August 2019, the College Board backed down and dropped the idea.[12] I have often wondered, albeit mischievously, whether the experiment would have proved more acceptable had it been flipped on its head, to produce a "privilege score."

Although it ceased computing and reporting an overall adversity statistic, the College Board has continued to publish the underlying data on which it had been based. Now renamed "Landscape," this service is designed to give typically under-staffed admissions offices at least one relatively uniform and objective basis for comparing the thousands of high schools—and the neighborhoods—from which their applicants come.[13] I give the College Board credit for trying to help level the playing field, at least a little. But it is unfortunate, for rank-ing purposes at least, that the College Board has been unable to find an acceptable way to adjust SAT scores to reflect test takers' varied socioeconomic and environmental advantages and disadvantages.

As long as schools are graded on the basis of the raw SAT averages of their entering classes, they will have an incen-tive to favor privileged applicants and a disincentive to admit promising lower-income students, first-generation students, or students of color who happen to have lower results. This condition probably contributes to the failures of elite higher educational institutions to do more to promote racial equity and social mobility, as discussed in chapters 15 and 20.

DO HIGH SAT SCORES MEAN "BETTER" COLLEGES?

If SAT and ACT scores are useful, although flawed, ways to

judge *individual* academic ability, are they also a useful means for evaluating *institutional* academic quality? Most people reflexively assume that the answer is yes and, therefore, that the best schools must enroll the highest-scoring students. Sure enough, there is a pretty strong correlation between a school's position in popular best-college listings and the average SAT scores of its entering classes.

Table 12.1 displays SAT-score ranges for the fall 2019 entering classes at our eight profile schools. Among the universities, the ordering by that variable—Penn at the top, then Notre Dame, Michigan, and City College—generally tracked their positions in most of the popular comprehensive rankings. At the top of the prestige pyramid, Penn's 1450-1560 score range corresponded to the 96th–99th percentiles of all SAT test takers that year.[14] Among the liberal arts colleges, as one would expect, Amherst's numbers were higher than those attributable to Berea and Spelman. Amherst's range matched the 87th–99th percentiles, whereas Spelman's corresponded with only the 55th–78th percentiles.

Reed was an interesting exception to the general correlation between SAT data and rankings. Its range, as shown on table 12.1, was the same as Amherst's, even though Reed trailed Amherst by a wide margin in all the popular listings. This suggests that a few schools with particularly strong intellectual reputations may be able to attract students with top SAT scores, even though they lag behind in other factors included in the formulas. Still, the general pattern holds. Elevated SAT scores and top-tier rankings go together. But should they? Does the enrollment of higher-scoring students necessarily demonstrate that an institution has a superior academic quality? One argument relies on a kind of wisdom-of-crowds theory. Since applicants with impressive test scores presumably have a wide choice of schools to attend, the fact that they

TABLE 12.1.

Entering-class SAT scores (for fall 2019)

College	25th Percentile	75th Percentile
Amherst	1310	1520
Berea	1090	1298
City College	1040	1250
Michigan	1340	1530
Notre Dame	1400	1550
Penn	1450	1560
Reed	1310	1520
Spelman	1080	1230

Source: IPEDS.

Note: Scores are for the combined evidence-based reading and writing and math portions of the SAT test. Percentiles reflect the score distribution in each school's fall 2019 entering class.

select, say, Penn rather than Michigan must mean that Penn is better than Michigan. I assess the logic and illogic of this argument in chapter 14.

The other—and to me, more substantive—claim is that smarter students are associated with higher levels of teaching and learning. This, in fact, is the argument that U.S. News employs to explain its reliance on "student excellence" measures: "Students who achieved strong grades and test scores during high school have the highest probability of succeeding at challenging college-level coursework; enabling instructors to design classes that have great rigor."[15] By implication, the magazine's editors are saying that a college is "best" if it offers "challenging" and "rigorous" courses, and that it will do so only if its students excel on the SAT. A related theory, echoing Gordon Winston's peer-effects argument discussed in the previous chapter, is that students learn more from smarter fellow students than they would from less-smart peers.

Scholarly research on these theories has produced

decidedly mixed results. A recent review of the literature by Stanford's Graduate School of Education concludes that student selectivity—that is, the average test scores and GPAs of a college's entering student body—is "not a reliable predictor of . . . learning."[16] Matthew Mayhew and his coauthors summarize scholarly research published between 2003 and 2014 by saying that "little evidence suggests that selectivity is related to measures of students' self-reported gains in learning, let alone verbal, quantitative, or subject matter competence measured by standardized tests."[17] This finding, they report, "has been consistent over the past 40 to 50 years." These same authors did, however, find a positive but "small" association between student selectivity and "general cognitive development" (usually described as "critical thinking") and the use of "good educational practices" (i.e., instructional techniques identified by numerous scholars as conducive to effective learning, discussed in more detail in chapter 17).[18]

Yet other studies question the latter conclusion. In one recent article, researchers conducted a "quantitative observational study" of classroom teaching in 587 courses taught at nine colleges, ranging in selectivity from low to high. Using a widely accepted rubric for good instructional practices, they concluded that the low-selectivity schools scored higher on teaching quality than the high-selectivity ones.[19] Another publication, focusing on a sample of liberal arts colleges, found no correlation between student selectivity and the intensity with which students were exposed to sound educational techniques.[20]

Like all of the literature on learning, much depends on the particular variables used to measure the quality of teaching and student learning, the selection of control variables, the particular schools or educational segment being studied, and so on. Reviewing this body of research, it seems to me that one can only conclude that the link between selectivity, on the one hand, and the quality of teaching and learning, on the other, remains to be demonstrated. Or, perhaps, it simply cannot be demonstrated.

So, can we conclude that high average SAT scores tell us which colleges are best? No, we cannot.

One consequence, however, emerges very clearly. There is a close correlation between test scores and most-popular-college rankings. For that reason, educators have believed for decades that one of the surest pathways to improving their standing in the pecking order is to increase their average SAT scores. But, as we shall see in chapter 13, their efforts to feed the SAT-score "elephant in the room" have often produced serious distortions and unanticipated consequences.

CHAPTER 13

CHASING HIGH SAT SCORES

THE GAMES COLLEGES PLAY

At Reed, as at all selective colleges, we cared about the average SAT score of our entering classes and felt a sense of accomplishment when that number increased. And, like all of our peers, we employed various practices designed to attract high-scoring applicants. We bought lists of test takers with top marks from the College Board. We personally recruited at academically demanding high schools. In our literature, we ceaselessly touted our rigorous academic standards. And we considered an applicant's test score to be an important factor in making admissions decisions. But, because we did not cooperate with U.S. News or its competitors, we were not enslaved by the goal of continually boosting our average SAT number. We always felt free to reject applicants with high scores who showed little evidence of intellectual passion. And we always felt free to admit those with low scores who did.

I well understood from my prior experience as a law-school dean, however, that for a rankings-obsessed school, maximizing the average test-score figures for its matriculants can easily become an end in itself, distorting admissions practices and often undermining educational goals.

MAXIMIZING LSAT SCORES
IN LAW-SCHOOL ADMISSIONS

The imperative to inflate an institution's test-score averages is especially potent in law-school admissions, where a very large factor in the U.S. News formula depends on LSAT figures. During my days as the dean of Penn Law, I confess to having been a willing participant in trying to maximize LSAT scores as a way of raising our ranking. Because U.S. News, at that time, based its assessments on an average of the school's 25th and 75th percentile LSAT scores, we watched those numbers like a hawk. My admissions dean would sometimes charge into my office, gushing with excitement about an unusually talented applicant—perhaps a person of color, or an older student who had overcome enormous life challenges. I would listen sympathetically and invariably say: "Sure. Go ahead and say yes, as long as your prized candidate doesn't drag down our 25th percentile number." Shame on me.

So when I became the de facto pre-law advisor at Reed, I knew exactly how the game was played. I recall a day early in my presidency when a student whom I knew very well came to request my help in getting admitted to a top-tier law school. I had spent the academic year supervising his senior thesis project on a constitutional law topic. The finished product was superb, equivalent in quality to most student-authored writings published by leading law reviews. I was on good terms with the dean of the law school he aspired to attend and offered to put in a good word. No sooner had I concluded my spiel than my dean friend fired back, "What's his LSAT score?" My answer elicited precisely the response I had expected: "Well, that's below our 25th percentile. I'll have to put him on the wait list."

I told my advisee: "They'll probably hold out until the last minute to see if admitting you will hurt their numbers, and then you just might get admitted. So, put down a deposit at your second-choice school and keep your fingers crossed." Sure enough, on the last day of August, he called me: "I just found out I've been accepted! But I've missed new-student orientation." "Never mind," I said. "Pack your bags and go! You won't be sorry you did." He went. And he never did regret it. He was a star student, even though, according to the implicit value system decreed by U.S. News, he didn't belong there.

MERIT AID: "BUYING" HIGH-SCORING APPLICANTS

At the undergraduate level, the mad scramble to enroll students with high SAT scores to boost one's rankings has led to all kinds of game playing and distortions of educational values. A particularly troubling example is the phenomenon of using financial-aid grants to "buy" top-scoring applicants, through the mechanism of merit aid. At Reed, as at Amherst and Penn among our profile schools, we awarded financial-aid grants solely on the basis of documented financial need. We did not give merit aid—a euphemism for what I used to call "throwing money at rich kids with high SAT scores." For us, it was a matter of principle. For every dollar you give to a smart rich student, that's one fewer dollar you have to attract a smart poor one. But, like most principles, it cost us dearly.

Year after year, I would hear about yet another of our competitors who had started using merit aid in an attempt to steal some of our best applicants. My financial-aid director once came to see me, lamenting the fact that a prime admissions prospect had just called to see if we would match a $10,000 grant offer from a competitor whose president I knew—and liked—very well. "Oh no," I said. "Have *they* started using merit aid?" Our financial aid office didn't budge, and, sure enough, we lost the applicant.

A month later, I ran into the president of that school at a professional meeting. "How could you do this?" I asked, half in jest. "You used to be a big believer in need-only aid. Where are your principles?" "Principles?" he answered, smiling. "This is about my pocketbook. Think of it this way: you guys have to give a $50,000 grant to get one low-income student with a 1400 SAT score. I can now give five $10,000 grants to get five higher-income students with 1400 SAT scores." He didn't have to say what I knew he was thinking: "Those five students do more to boost our average SAT score than your one student." Yes, I thought, if I were a slave to rankings, and if I were dead set on maximizing my average SAT score, that's how I would think, too.

The Growth of Merit Aid

Merit aid has ballooned since the 1990s. While there are multiple explanations, the growing dominance of college rankings is surely one important reason. A 2011 report by the US Department of Education documented the explosion. Among full-time students at four-year institutions, the proportion receiving this form of financial assistance grew from 8 percent in 1995 to 44 percent in 2007.[1] By that point, more students were receiving merit aid than need-based assistance. But it gets worse. The average size of the merit-based grant (in inflation-adjusted dollars) has also grown. That same year, private nonprofit colleges were offering an average merit award of $8,400, an amount that was $700 higher than the average need-based grant. At public institutions, the average merit-aid figure was also larger ($4,200 vs. $2,700). As one might expect, compared with need-based support, merit funds went primarily to students from higher-income families, who were less likely to be Black or Hispanic and more likely to have high SAT scores.

The heaviest dispensers of merit aid are private non-profit schools, especially those that are moderately selective and charge high tuitions. The *Wall Street Journal* recently reported that George Washington University has been giving non-need-based grants to nearly half of its students.[2] But the public sector is catching up. As states have increasingly switched from the old low-tuition/low-aid model to the private sector's high-tuition/high-aid pattern, the public sector has turned to merit aid with a vengeance.

A watershed event was the 1993 creation of Georgia's HOPE scholarship program, designed to encourage that state's best and brightest high-school graduates to stay home, rather than flee to what they might think were greener academic pastures elsewhere. A recent New America study asserts that Georgia's entire financial-aid budget is now focused on merit, rather than need-based aid.[3] And most of its neighbors in the southeastern United States have followed its lead. Over the past two decades, public universities have tripled the amount they spend on merit grants. Much of this growth reflects the arms race for out-of-state students who pay much higher fees than their in-state counterparts, even after taking into account whatever tuition discounts they may receive.

Arguments for and against Merit Aid

Advocates argue that merit-aid programs give students— particularly those from lower-income families—an added incentive to perform well in high school, apply to four-year colleges, and persist to graduation. A large body of scholarly research has attempted to assess the validity of these assertions, with decidedly mixed results. Illustrating one side of the debate is a series of papers by Susan Dynarski, focused on the Georgia HOPE program and its Arkansas counterpart.[4] Exemplifying the contrasting view is an investigation of a Massachusetts merit-aid program by Sarah Cohodes and Joshua Goodman that shows how such programs can backfire by inducing academically underprepared applicants to attend schools where they are less well supported and less likely to graduate.[5] As summarized in a more recent article by Charles Clotfelter and his coauthors, most other studies have yielded conclusions landing somewhere between these two extremes.[6]

Whatever one concludes about the incentive effects of merit aid, however, its most glaring drawback is its tendency to exacerbate income inequality. This was the primary reason that we refused to dispense scarce tuition-assistance dollars to wealthy students while I was at Reed. As Michael McPherson and Morton Schapiro argued decades ago, this type of financial support effectively takes money out of the pockets of poor students and gives it to richer ones.[7] The College Board's report, "Trends in Student Aid 2019," puts this in rather dramatic focus.[8] Among full-time students attending four-year private colleges during the 2015–2016 academic year, the average unmet financial need was $18,980, while the average figure for grants in excess of need was $13,760. Even in the wealthiest parental-income group (those with earnings over $200,000 per year), the average grant in excess of need was $15,370.

In the public sector, the numbers were almost as bad: $14,400 in average unmet need, $6,170 in average over-met need. One can see the effects by looking at the financial-aid statistics for schools ranked below the top tier in the U.S. News pecking order. One repeatedly sees schools that award merit-aid grants, typically averaging over $10,000 per recipient per year, while only meeting the full documented need of less than half of their lower-income students. Merit aid, in other words, is a reverse–Robin Hood program, fueled by the intense competition for highly credentialed applicants. And I think it's fair to say that it's also driven by prestige-based rankings that give heavy weight to a school's average test scores and other indicators of institutional privilege.

RAISING SAT AVERAGES
BY NOT REPORTING LOW SCORES

Seeking to maximize reported average test scores in order to improve one's rankings creates strong temptations to fudge the data. As we saw in chapter 6, the history of U.S. News rankings has been plagued by the misreporting of SAT scores. In addition to simply lying, postsecondary institutions have frequently resorted to the gambit of what might be called selective reporting of scores—that is, including only categories of admitted students who customarily perform well on standardized tests.

Selective reporting came to the attention of the media decades ago. According to a 1995 story in the *Wall Street Journal*, Northeastern University had chosen not to submit the test scores for both its international and its "remedial" students, collectively representing fully 20 percent of the school's enrollees.[9] Boston University refused to report SAT verbal scores for matriculants from foreign nations. New York University and Manhattanville College were excluding the scores of their economically disadvantaged students.

The problem of selective reporting apparently continues to this day. In the methodology statement accompanying its recent rankings, U.S. News has acknowledged that some schools fail to report the SAT scores of their "athletes, international students, minority students, legacies, or students admitted by special arrangement."[10] Think about that. Some colleges are apparently claiming that SAT scores are valid and useful only for their ordinary, White, domestic, non-athletic students, so those are the only numbers they will report.

I've already mentioned two other gaming tactics. Many

schools shunt applicants with low SAT scores or low GPAs to a January term start so that their scores are not included in the report of fall-semester enrollees. And some universities steer those with less impressive admissions credentials to an organizational unit of the institution—wholly separate from its primary undergraduate college—for which they report no data.

DISPENSING WITH SAT REQUIREMENTS: FROM TEST OPTIONAL TO TEST BLIND

Test Optional: How to Boost Your SAT Averages

During the time when I was president of Reed, I noticed that a growing number of moderately selective liberal arts colleges were adopting a practice called "test optional," in the parlance of college admissions professionals. In effect, these schools told potential applicants that they were free to submit an SAT or ACT score if they wished, while reassuring them that failing to do so would not hurt their chances of admission. The school would simply consider all of the other factors—high-school academic record, letters of recommendation, applications essay, and the like—and make its decision.

I became convinced that the growth in test-optional policies could be attributed in large part to rankings pressures. By implicitly encouraging applicants with low SAT scores not to submit them, institutions would be able to report only the higher figures for those who did. For example, what if the students in the lower half of a college's SAT distribution had an average score of 1220, and the ones in the upper half had an average score of 1380? If the school could convince all the students with the lower scores not to include them in their applications, its reportable average would rise from around 1300 to 1380. And its ranking would presumably go up along with it.

This is not just hypothetical. A study of the experience at Bates College showed that the average SAT score of non-submitters was about 160 points below the average for submitters.[11] Bates went test optional well before 1983, but dozens of other schools followed suit after test score–based rankings became a dominant force in the higher-education marketplace. If adopting such a policy was motivated at least in part by a desire to move up a few rungs on the ladder, then one would expect that most of its practitioners would be somewhere in the middle of the pack, not at the top. And, sure enough, that's precisely what was happening in the early 2000s.

The test-optional advocates appeared to be saying that SAT scores were valid predictors of academic ability only if an applicant were a good test taker. In other words, such marks proved to be useful if they were high, but not if they were low. That argument, it seemed to me, was the equivalent of saying, "We will look at a high-school GPA only if it's above 3.5, but ignore it, or not ask for it, if it's below 3.5."

In 2006, I published an op-ed piece in the *New York Times*, arguing that the growth of test-optional admissions was largely rankings driven.[12] Not surprisingly, I received a lot of angry pushback from my peers at schools that had recently adopted the practice. They quite appropriately cited all the criticisms of standardized tests. And they argued passionately that those were the reasons for going test optional, not a cynical effort to manipulate their position in the competitive standings. Yes, I replied, the SAT and the ACT are certainly imperfect. But compared with what?

All of the methods conventionally used to evaluate applicants' college readiness are flawed—whether they involve high-school GPAs, quality of high school attended, extracurricular activities, college essays, or enrichment activities such as internships or foreign travel. Most of them favor students from wealthy families and children of well-educated parents, while they often disadvantage low-income, first-generation, and minority students.[13] For all of these factors, including test scores, the proper corrective is not to throw them out the window altogether, but to give them only the weight they deserve, taking into account the range of opportunities and disadvantages faced by that particular applicant. That is precisely what we did at Reed, and what most holistic admissions programs attempt to accomplish.

The debate over the wisdom and the efficacy of test-optional admissions continues to rage unabated and certainly cannot be resolved in these pages.[14] For my part, I remain persuaded by the arguments against the policy. As I make clear in subsequent chapters, I heartily endorse the test-optional defenders' professed goal of increasing the racial and socioeconomic diversity of our college-going population. But giving applicants a choice in whether to submit test scores is not a proven way of achieving that aim. While there are anecdotal reports that this practice has led to an increase in the diversity of some higher-education institutions' applicant pools and enrollments,[15] careful statistical investigations suggest caution in leaping to that conclusion.

A good example is a 2014 study based on the experience of 180 selective liberal arts colleges from 1992 to 2010.[16] Throughout that entire period, the test-optional schools persistently lagged behind those requiring tests in terms of their percentages of students of color and Pell grant recipients. On average, going test optional did not close either gap. Adopting that posture did, however, produce an increase in the total number of applications and an upswing in the reported average SAT/ACT score for the college—precisely the effects that would tend to help it move up in the rankings. By using the test-optional gambit to make themselves appear more competitive, these institutions were able to attract more highly credentialed—that is to say, academically and economically privileged—applicants. The result was that it became harder, not easier, for many low-income students and students of color to compete for admission.

Rather than encouraging academically less-prepared individuals to *avoid* taking standardized tests, many believe that a better strategy would be to *require* all public high-school students to take the SAT or the ACT. Yes, there is always the prospect that high schools will teach to the test, but the very experience of preparing for and taking a college-entrance exam provides a stimulus for students who might not otherwise imagine higher education in their futures. In fact, the evidence supports this supposition. Studies have shown that, in states where it is mandatory for secondary-school students to take the SAT or the ACT, low-income students and students of color are more likely to enroll in a four-year college.[17]

Going Test Blind: How to Hurt Your Ranking

If, contrary to my view, an institution feels that standardized tests are so flawed that students should have the choice not to report them at all, then the appropriate course of action seems obvious: drop consideration of test scores altogether. The college should go test blind.

The big problem with doing so, however, is that it hurts a school's ranking. The experiences of colleges like Sarah Lawrence and Hampshire offer a cautionary tale. When Sarah Lawrence went test blind in 2005 and thus failed to submit any test-score figures, U.S. News simply made them up.[18] It revealed that it had arbitrarily assigned a number that was 15 percent below what Sarah Lawrence's peer schools were reporting. Three years later, U.S. News decided to drop test-blind institutions from its rankings altogether. Goodbye Sarah

Lawrence! The same fate befell Hampshire College when it concluded, after an internal validity study, that the SAT and the ACT added nothing useful to its admissions criteria, given its highly idiosyncratic curriculum.[19] Imagine that. A news magazine, in effect, decrees the illegitimacy of a considered decision made by professional educators about the best way to serve their scholastic mission!

And guess what? In the case of Sarah Lawrence, at least, U.S. News won. In 2012, the college caved in and adopted a test-optional policy, so it could be restored to U.S. News's good graces.

The End of Standardized Tests?

Whether rankings-fueled or not, the test-optional movement has continued to spread, both promoted and documented by an advocacy group called the National Center for Fair and Open Testing (or Fair Test, for short). As the movement has grown, the positions of test-optional schools have gradually inched upward from the middle of the pack toward the top. This is no surprise. As more lower-tier institutions have used this technique to raise their ranking scores, they have begun to nip at the heels of their upstream rivals. The decision by the University of Chicago to go test optional in 2018 received a lot of attention, because it suggested that this practice had finally reached the top selectivity echelon.[20] Still, as recently as 2019, most of the other highly selective schools continued to require that applicants submit SAT or ACT scores.

And then along came the COVID-19 pandemic. Testing companies repeatedly encountered difficulties in administering their exams remotely and securely, leading to widespread applicant frustration. In response, dozens of colleges, including most of the elites, decided to suspend requiring test scores for at least one or two years.[21] Many of them said they would use this interval as an experiment to see if they could live without standardized tests in the long run. But the most ominous news for the testing industry was the announcement by the chancellor of the University of California system in May 2020, stating that its campuses would abandon the use of the SAT or the ACT by 2023.[22] To be sure, the chancellor also said that the California system would attempt to create an alternative standardized test to be used in future admissions decisions. But commentators have expressed understandable skepticism that California will be able to do what the established testing organizations have tried for decades to accomplish, without success—develop a statistically reliable and valid test of academic ability that is free of socioeconomic or demographic bias.[23]

These developments prompted U.S. News to announce a month later that it would figure out a way to rank test-blind colleges.[24] And sure enough, for its 2021 edition, U.S. News returned over 60 formerly unranked test-blind schools to its good graces. But those institutions paid a heavy price, because—for hierarchical purposes—the magazine assigned them "the lowest test score by a ranked school in their category."[25] Hampshire College, once proudly unranked from 2008 to 2020, now finds itself dumped into the bottom quartile of national liberal arts schools.

I continue to believe that well-designed admissions tests can serve an important purpose for colleges and universities that insist on attaining high academic standards. As selective schools become ever more national and international in their reach, they need a uniform, standardized measure of academic ability to discipline what are otherwise largely subjective judgments about the quality of an applicant's high-school performance and personal attributes. Numerous studies have demonstrated the reliability and predictive validity of the SAT and the ACT. But their use must always be tempered by an awareness of their bias in favor of applicants with economic and social privilege. They must never be used in a formulaic or deterministic way to decide whom to admit and whom to reject.

For similar reasons, standardized test scores should never have been used as the basis for formulaically ranking undergraduate programs. The decision by U.S. News, and later adopted by its competitors, to sort and evaluate colleges by SAT scores unleashed a wave of evasive behavior. Too many colleges shifted their scholarship dollars away from those students with greatest financial need toward those with highest test scores. Many institutions distorted the true picture of their student body's academic abilities by selectively reporting SAT scores. And dozens increased the subjectivity—and, potentially, unconscious biases—of their admissions process by going "test optional" to inflate their reported scores.

I recognize that the days of using standardized tests in undergraduate admissions may well be numbered. The California system's search for a replacement exam may founder on the same shoals of racial and socioeconomic bias that threaten to shipwreck the SAT. Elite schools, having adjusted to making admissions decisions without SAT and ACT scores during the pandemic, may simply drop them permanently. If most higher-education institutions abandon the use of standardized tests, many people will applaud, but a number of others will not. I will be among those who regret the loss of a useful measure of academic preparation. But I will be grateful for the silver lining: the era of ranking colleges by their students' SAT scores will, blissfully, end.

CHAPTER 14

INTERCOLLEGIATE ADMISSIONS COMPETITION

WINNERS AND LOSERS

In the competitive world of higher education, the admissions process sometimes feels like yet another intercollegiate varsity sport. Everyone, it seems, is trying to outscore their opponents by attracting more of "the best and the brightest" students described in the previous chapters.

During admissions season, even at noncompetitive (and non-varsity athletic) Reed College, one of my trustees would routinely ask me, "How are we doing?" In much the same way, a trustee at another school might interrogate the basketball coach. In the world of intercollegiate admissions, someone always wants to know, "Are we winning or losing?"

WINS AND LOSSES: OVERLAP REPORTS

When I was dean of the Penn Law School, every year I would receive an overlap report from the Law School Admission Council (the folks who administer the LSAT). This report would show how well Penn Law fared during the latest admissions cycle in competing with its rivals. I could readily see, for example, how many of the applicants admitted by both Penn and Columbia chose to attend each of those schools. It was a sobering report. All year long I might have been able to kid myself that we were more competitive than Columbia, but there it was in black and white. No, we weren't. They were winning.

As a trustee at Amherst, I got to see similar overlap reports from the College Board, showing how Amherst fared in head-to-head competition with the likes of Williams and Brown and Dartmouth. The overlap reports at Penn Law and Amherst were strikingly similar in one respect. Each institution was genuinely competitive with only a few other schools. And the list of its true rivals was remarkably stable from year to year. Furthermore, there was often a stunningly high correlation between the overlap reports' winning percentages and the rankings. At Penn Law, we routinely got clobbered by most law schools that U.S. News said were better than us, and we routinely trounced the ones it said were worse. I sometimes wondered if its editors had a secret pipeline into LSAC's confidential database. But, of course, the causal chain ran in the opposite direction. Applicants based their matriculation decisions (captured in the overlap reports) on the rankings.

At Reed, these reports revealed a different pattern, which was somewhat more diffuse and showed greater variability from year to year. We did not have huge overlaps with anyone—nothing like Amherst's with Williams, or Penn Law's with Columbia Law. Mostly we had a modest number of overlaps with a wide variety of other institutions, including some research universities, such as Chicago or Berkeley, and many liberal arts colleges, such as Oberlin or Wesleyan. The number of admissions offers we made in common with each of those schools, and even our winning percentages in those rivalries, seemed to drift up and down from year to year. Still, it was a scorecard, and we paid close attention.

I have sometimes wondered whether overlap data such

as those could be used to construct college rankings. After all, if the goal is to capture relative prestige, as reflected in market position, why not look at how consumers in that marketplace actually vote with their feet? Well, it turns out that some people have.

Ranking Colleges by Elo Points

If you want to construct a hierarchical list of colleges based on the results of multiple pairwise competitions for admitted students (Amherst vs. Williams, Amherst vs. Brown, etc.), you need a method of aggregating that information into an overall score for each contender. One plausible technique is the system used to rank masters in the world of competitive chess. In January 2021, this method decreed that Magnus Carlsen was the best chess player in the world.[1] Fabiano Caruana was number two. And a little further down the chess ladder, Matthew Sadler came in at number 41, edging out Bassem Amin at number 42. How do we know these things? Because the World Chess Federation (FIDE) has a system for ranking chess players (not just grand masters, but even relative newcomers, like my precocious grandson).

FIDE uses a system invented by a Hungarian physics professor named Arpad Elo. It assigns "Elo points" to players, based on how they perform in head-to-head competitions. It's not necessary—in fact, it's impossible—for every master to play against every other master, as if in a single, gigantic March Madness tournament. So long as there are sufficient chess matches among a wide enough sample of players, the system makes it possible to assign relative positions to everyone, based on their total number of Elo points. Very similar methods are used in many competitive undertakings, including college sports, professional tennis, ping-pong, video games, and Scrabble. I even have a US Squash ranking, thanks to this system.

TABLE 14.1.

A revealed-preference ranking of selected colleges (2004 data)

College	Ranking	Elo points
Amherst	9	2,363
Michigan	42	1,978
Notre Dame	13	2,279
Penn	12	2,325
Reed	68	1,837

Source: Avery et al. (2013).

Given the prevalence of this technique, it's no surprise that some enterprising researchers have used it to compare colleges. In a 2013 journal article, Christopher Avery and his coauthors computed Elo-point scores for 105 colleges and universities, based on their won-lost records in head-to-head competitions for students.[2] They called it a "revealed-preference" ranking, derived from a theory developed by economists to measure the relative preferences of consumers among multiple product choices. The researchers' data came from a survey of students with high GPAs, selected by college counselors at 510 high schools. All told, 3,240 students responded. Based on their replies, Avery and his colleagues assembled an ordinal listing, with Harvard at the top, followed by Yale, Stanford, Caltech, and MIT. More or less what one would expect. Table 14.1 shows the ranking and Elo-point scores of five of our profile schools. (No results were reported for Berea, City College, and Spelman.)

The Parchment Student-Choice Rankings

The revealed-preference study by Avery and his coauthors was a one-time piece of research. But it evidently inspired a company named Parchment to do an annual student-choice ranking using a similar methodology.[3] Headquartered in Scottsdale, Arizona, Parchment provides a "digital-credentials service" for the storage, transmission, and reporting of academic credentials, such as high-school or college transcripts. In addition, Parchment surveys a large number of college-going students each year and asks them to name the schools to which they applied, by which they were admitted, and at which they enrolled. It then computes something like Elo points for each institution, based on that school's wins and losses in its competition for students.

As described in its methodological statement, the algorithm used by Parchment seems to be very elegant and sophisticated. But the actual results generated by that algorithm are strikingly peculiar. In its 2020 listing, the top five schools were MIT, the Air Force Academy, Pomona, the Naval Academy, and Swarthmore. Amherst came in 7th, Michigan 11th. This ordering might sound plausible. But wait. That same year, Parchment assigned Yale to the 62nd spot and Harvard to the 74th. Penn came in 33rd, trailing behind Baker College in Cadillac, Michigan (29th) and the University of Texas at Tyler (32nd). Notre Dame, which was 44th, finished behind Goldey-Beacom College in Wilmington, Delaware, at 43rd. Even more puzzling are the wild swings in the Parchment orderings from year to year. Swarthmore College lurched from 55th in 2019 to 5th in 2020; Texas-Tyler soared from 141st to 33rd; Columbia dropped from 7th to 38th; and Notre Dame plummeted from 2nd to 44th.

What is going on here? One can only guess. Perhaps many students are fibbing in their responses to the Parchment survey. That's certainly conceivable, but it's not obvious why such a pattern should change dramatically from one year to the next. Parchment claims that it has student reports for over 2.4 million matriculation decisions in its database. The respondents can't all be lying. A more likely contributor to the oddness of Parchment's results might be variations in the numbers of responses from college to college. For example, the 2020 score awarded to Goldey-Beacom College (with an undergraduate enrollment of approximately 730) rested on a mere 85 data points, compared with Notre Dame's 2,336 data points, or Michigan's 20,369. Another possibility is that student responses from different colleges fluctuate wildly year by year so that some schools' scores reflect more-recent data than those for other institutions.

But the most obvious problem with these rankings is their attempt to jam together into one linear list schools from wildly divergent competitive niches. What does Baker College have in common with the University of Pennsylvania? How many degrees of separation are there between Goldey-Beacom and Notre Dame? When two institutions are both located within a well-established overlap group, consisting of schools with similar missions—think Amherst and Williams, or Penn and Columbia—one can perhaps use this method with confidence. But when colleges and universities are located in widely disparate overlap groups, the value of student-choice computations diminishes rather quickly. Schools with distinctive missions simply cannot be reliably compared by this method. The fact that Parchment's 2020 top-five list includes two military academies illustrates my point. I assume that most students who apply to the Air Force Academy are attracted precisely because they want to serve in the military and have a career in aeronautics. They might also apply to MIT or Stanford, but if they are admitted to the Academy, that's where they will go.

For the same reason, when I was at Reed, I felt it made no sense to use win-loss ratios to determine whether we were in some sense "better" than, say, Berkeley. Yes, in a typical year we shared something like 30 or 40 overlaps. And, yes, both schools appealed to iconoclastic, intellectual applicants. But the two institutions differed enormously in size, complexity, tuition and fees, social climate, and a thousand other dimensions. The reasons why students chose to attend Reed or Berkeley were simply too numerous to capture in any single metric.

So, aside from Parchment and occasional academic research papers, nobody uses student choice or Elo points to rate colleges. And no one should. Instead, as we shall see, the rankers have fallen back on even cruder and much more manipulable metrics to measure wins and losses in the intercollegiate admissions game—acceptance rates and yield rates.

ACCEPTANCE AND YIELD RATES
AS SCORECARDS FOR THE ADMISSIONS GAME

At Reed we often talked about our "admissions funnel." Fed into the top were the tens of thousands of high-school students with whom we had some sort of contact through mailings, email blasts, unsolicited inquiries, high-school visits, and the like. That number was then distilled into the few thousands (late in my tenure, around 3,500) of individuals who sent in a completed application for admission. The next section in the funnel included roughly 1,400 applicants to whom we tendered offers of admission. Then there were the 350 or so admitted applicants who sent in their tuition deposits. And, finally, emerging from the bottom of the funnel, were the roughly 340 who showed up at freshman orientation, with parents in tow.

The numbers concealed what was almost always an agonizing process of choice by both applicants and college admissions staff, filled with all of the anxiety and hand wringing documented in published accounts of the college admissions frenzy.[4] But in the end, all of that drama was distilled into two cold, hard, numerical measures of competitive success: acceptance rate (percentage of applicants whom we admitted) and yield rate (percentage of admitted applicants who enrolled). The unstated goal was to keep reducing our acceptance rate and increase our yield rate.

Although popular best-college rankings have gradually de-emphasized these measures, they still loom large in the evaluation of institutions by bond-rating agencies, accrediting bodies, and college guides. The theory behind assessing schools by their acceptance and yield rates is obvious. Since colleges, unlike for-profit businesses, artificially limit their output, they signal quality by exclusivity. Rather than maximizing the number of satisfied customers, their objective seems to be to maximize the number of disappointed applicants. Every year, stories in the media breathlessly report further declines in the acceptance rate of brand-name colleges. Where we were once impressed if a school admitted fewer than a quarter of its applicants, now you make headlines with acceptance rates below 10 percent. In the 2020 IPEDS data, Stanford reported a 4 percent acceptance rate, edging out Princeton, at 5 percent. And the surge in applications to elite institutions following the COVID-19 outbreak merely exacerbated that pattern. Harvard reported admitting only 3.4 percent of its applicants for the 2021 entering class.[5]

Curiously, yield rates tend to receive less attention from the media than acceptance rates. Perhaps this is based on a view that, say, a 10 percent acceptance rate is intrinsically more dramatic than a 60 percent yield rate. Or perhaps it reflects an assumption that the two measures are essentially duplicative as quality indicators. Indeed, as the data on our eight profile schools in table 14.2 show, they do tend to exhibit an inverse correlation. As one would expect, the institution with the lowest acceptance rate (Penn, at 8 percent) had the highest yield rate (70 percent). Conversely, the colleges with

TABLE 14.2.

Acceptance and yield rates (for students who entered in fall 2019)

College	Acceptance rate (%)	Yield rate (%)
Amherst	11	39
Berea	30	69
City College	46	15
Michigan	23	46
Notre Dame	16	58
Penn	8	70
Reed	35	17
Spelman	43	13

Source: IPEDS.

the highest acceptance rates (City College and Spelman) had the lowest yield rates.

Berea College provides an intriguing exception to the inverse correlation of acceptance and yield rates observed in table 14.2. Given its somewhat idiosyncratic mission, Berea is a classic self-selection school. It appeals to a very small segment of the college-going population—young people of modest means, residing mostly in Appalachia, who are attracted to its work-college philosophy and its zero-tuition policy. Thus, while only relatively few individuals apply (contributing to the school's high acceptance rate), the vast majority of those who are admitted choose to enroll (producing a very high yield rate). This illustrates a general problem with using admissions statistics to compare institutions pursuing a highly distinctive mission with those having a more generic character.

Gaming the Metrics

Using metrics like acceptance and yield rates to evaluate postsecondary institutions invites all kinds of gaming behavior.

Probably the most common way to drive down acceptance rates is to inflate the number of applicants by marketing aggressively, eliminating application fees, and the like. This has spawned criticism that colleges and universities deliberately set applicants up for disappointment by presenting a false picture of admissibility—engaging, in other words, in a "recruit to reject" strategy.[6] Another gambit employed by many of them is the so-called two-part application. The first part consists of a simple expression of interest in applying, followed later by the submission of an actual completed application form (the second part). By reporting the first part as an "application"—even if never followed by a second part—a school can artificially boost its number of "applications" and ratchet down its acceptance rates.

Yet another common way to manipulate these measures is by admitting only those applicants whom you are quite sure will accept your offer. A particularly cynical version of this tactic, allegedly employed by many schools and publicly documented in a few cases,[7] is not to admit your most desirable applicants—those who, because of their stellar credentials, are least likely to accept your offer. These are the students who presumably applied to your college only as a safety school. Since the chances are good that they will, in fact, receive an offer from a preferred—and typically higher-ranked—school and thus turn yours down, why not put them on the wait list, instead of admitting them? As Paul Marthers, my admissions dean at Reed, once told a reporter, "If you want a great acceptance rate and a great yield, just put everyone on the waiting list."[8]

Using Early Admissions to Boost the Score

A far more pervasive method of reducing the acceptance rate—and increasing the yield rate—is to use early admissions as a way of inducing applicants to signal their intention to attend.

Early-admissions programs come in multiple flavors. The two generic versions are early decision, in which the applicant promises to accept an offer if made, and early action, in which the college provides a decision in December, leaving an admitted applicant free to consider other offers later in the cycle. If you know ahead of time who is most likely to accept, you can significantly reduce the number of applicants you need to admit in order to fill your entering class.

Although early-admissions programs predate the rankings era, they expanded dramatically once the rankocrats began employing acceptance and yield rates in their formulas. During the period when I served as Penn's law-school dean, I noticed that the university made especially aggressive use of early decision. Each year I would read stories in the student newspaper about the growing proportion of undergraduate class seats filled with early-decision candidates. The share got up to over 40 percent one year, significantly higher than the corresponding figures at other Ivy League schools. But those institutions soon followed in Penn's footsteps. Ivy League universities now routinely fill over 40 percent of the places in their entering classes through early-admissions programs. Indeed, in recent cycles, Penn has filled more than 50 percent of its first-year class via early decision.[9] No wonder its yield rate, as shown on table 14.2, was 70 percent.

This might not be a problem if early admissions were indistinguishable from regular admissions. But they are not. In fact, such programs have come in for withering criticism over the years. For one thing, detractors say the early-admissions process forces high-school seniors to choose their college destinations prematurely, on the basis of too little information, causing them (once admitted) to treat the rest of their high-school senior year as a kind of academic afterthought.

More tellingly, early decision clearly favors upper-income

applicants, for at least two reasons. First, it takes what one article labeled "cultural capital"—namely, access to sophisticated precollege advisors—to calculate the costs and benefits of applying early versus later.[10] In a book titled *The Early Admission Game*, Christopher Avery and his coauthors sought to capture the mysteries of this system by likening it to a fictional gambling game they called "Martian blackjack."[11] Second, and even more importantly, committing to a single college in December robs the admitted applicant of an opportunity to compare tuition discount offers from multiple schools during the spring cycle. Financially needy students are thus deterred from using this option.[12]

Because early-decision applicants tend to be wealthier than regular-cycle ones, they are particularly valuable to schools that characterize their admissions process as need blind. By using that self-description, these institutions claim that they evaluate all applicants solely on the basis of their academic merits, never on the basis of their ability to pay. Yet, as Matthew Kim has pointed out, early admissions give such schools a reliable way to identify wealthy applicants in advance, without having to ask them about their family's finances.[13] By thus locking in roughly half of your entering class by January, not only can you reduce your acceptance rate and increase your yield rate, but you can also control your financial-aid budget while preserving your prized need-blind status. In fact, the perceived institutional payoff from such admissions programs is great enough that colleges often apply more-generous admissions criteria to early-decision applicants than to spring-cycle ones. Writing in 2004, Avery and his coauthors estimated that the advantage in applying for early decision was equivalent to an extra 100 points on one's combined SAT score.[14]

Responding to criticisms such as these, Harvard, in 2006, announced that it was abandoning early admissions altogether. Princeton quickly followed suit. Many observers imagined that other elites would join this parade of virtue. But they did not. The advantages of early decision, especially to schools a little bit further down in the prestige pecking order, was too great. Indeed, five years later, Harvard and Princeton backpedaled, adopting non-binding early-action programs.[15] Although that form of early admissions commendably gives needy applicants a chance to compare financial-aid awards from other schools, it still tends to push them to make premature decisions and rewards access to the cultural capital necessary to evaluate competing options.

Granting Special Admissions Preferences

Early-admissions programs overlap considerably with another way to lower acceptance rates and boost yield rates—namely, giving an advantage to certain categories of applicants whom the admissions office knows are most likely to accept offers. Recruited athletes nicely fit this description, because college coaches have typically prescreened the applicants, not only for athletic ability, but also for eagerness to accept an admissions offer. By this process, schools like Amherst and Williams, which fill roughly a quarter of their freshman class with recruited athletes, gain a large acceptance-rate and yield-rate advantage over colleges like Reed and Spelman, which have no varsity teams. Some observers defend athletic recruiting as a way of attracting and enrolling students of color or those from low-income families. That is undoubtedly true at some universities and in some sports. But at the highly selective institutions, many recruited athletes—especially in sports like squash, golf, lacrosse, or rowing—tend to be children of privilege, not of disadvantage.[16]

Another example of this strategy is the common practice of elite schools to favor legacy applicants (children, and sometimes grandchildren, of alumni), as well as the offspring of faculty and staff, and those of former or even prospective donors. As we know from the data generated in the 2019 Harvard affirmative-action lawsuit, applicants in those categories had a dramatically greater chance of being admitted than other, similarly talented aspirants.[17] There are, to be sure, many plausibly legitimate reasons for favoring applicants in these categories, but the prospect of earning a numerical boost from this practice cannot be dismissed as a motivator.

Reducing the Size of the Entering Class

Another obvious means of reducing a college's acceptance rate is to decrease the size of the entering class, thereby lowering the number of students it needs to admit. Of course this option is too costly in foregone tuition revenue for most schools to consider, except under unusual circumstances. But there are ways to compensate. As I described in the previous chapter, some undergraduate programs have shunted their lower-credentialed applicants to a spring-semester matriculation option. Since most measures of selectivity are based on fall-semester first-time enrollees, this gambit enables an institution not only to inflate its SAT numbers, but also to reduce its apparent acceptance rate. Indeed, this tactic can yield yet an additional statistical payoff. The graduation rates reported to IPEDS and used in most ranking formulas are based on tracking those who enroll in the fall semester. As studies have repeatedly shown, students with lower academic credentials are less likely to graduate than those with higher levels of preparation. If a school can shunt its academically weaker students into a spring semester start, their performance will not be reflected in the school's reported completion rates.

A somewhat similar method to pay for decreasing the size of the freshman class is to increase the number of students admitted as transfer students in their sophomore or junior years. A version of this tactic made its appearance in law schools shortly after U.S. News started judging them according to their acceptance rate for first-year students. Before 1990, transferring was almost unknown among top-tier law schools. In a typical year, one might lose a handful of students after their second semester, most of whom left for personal reasons, such as following a spouse to another city. (The late Ruth Bader Ginsburg, a former Supreme Court justice, is a celebrated example, having transferred from Harvard to Columbia when her husband took a job with a New York City law firm.)

With the advent of law-school rankings, however, transfer numbers increased markedly. I began to see a noticeable outflow of our Penn Law students leaving in their second year to attend schools positioned just above us. As I looked at the statistics for these institutions, I could see exactly what was going on. They were reducing the size of their first-year law classes and paying for the lost tuition by beefing up their transfer admissions. And increasing their average LSAT scores and acceptance rates in the process.

WHAT DO ADMISSIONS NUMBERS TELL US ABOUT ACADEMIC QUALITY?

As we have seen repeatedly throughout this book, the metrics used in college rankings—in this case, student-choice calculations and acceptance and yield rates—have a tendency to distort institutional behavior. But the deeper question is whether such measures capture something essential about relative institutional quality. At bottom, the intuition behind ranking schools by their admissions numbers is the wisdom of crowds. By this argument, the "crowd" of college-goers tell us which schools they consider better by their actual application and matriculation decisions.

Comparing two schools of roughly equal size, one might conclude that if more people apply to, say, Penn than to Notre Dame, they must believe Penn is better. Therefore, so the reasoning goes, Penn *is* better. Comparing schools of unequal size, one could infer that if Michigan attracts more applications, relative to its size, than Reed—reflected in its lower acceptance rate—Michigan must be better. Likewise, according to this argument, the crowd of admitted applicants signals which school is superior by its matriculation decisions. If Berea has a higher yield rate than City College, it must be better. Or if Amherst has a higher Elo-point score than Penn, computed from head-to-head competitions between multiple schools, then Amherst has more to offer.

The flaws in these arguments should be obvious. First of all, there is no single crowd whose collective judgment tells us anything useful about the relative merits of all these different institutions. As I have argued repeatedly, there are, instead, millions of college-bound applicants seeking to pursue their personal ambitions and dreams. The crowd that applies to Penn is not the same as the one that seeks out Notre Dame or Amherst. And it is certainly very different from the crowd that applies to Michigan or Reed or Berea or City College.

Second, using the wisdom of crowds to determine where a school belongs on the hierarchy suffers from a fatal circularity. The unstated point of commercial rankings is to influence where the college-going public will apply and enroll. To the extent that the number crunchers are successful in this ambition, they will influence the very statistics—acceptance rate, yield rate, student-choice rating—that they then use to establish the next set of comparative orderings. No wonder college rankings so often turn out to be self-fulfilling prophecies!

CHAPTER 15

AFFIRMATIVE INACTION

RACE, ETHNICITY, AND RANKINGS

When I arrived at the Penn Law School in 1989, the percentage of Black students was negligible. The faculty admissions committee genuinely hoped to increase this number. But it had imposed minimum thresholds for applicants' LSAT scores and undergraduate GPAs, thus making that job difficult. I pressed the committee to relax the standards. They did, to a degree, and the next year we were able to double the proportion of Black students in the entering class—from a miniscule 2 percent to a meager 4 percent. The student newspaper announced the results in a story under the headline "Diver-City." Congratulatory? Ironic? I wasn't sure.

When I got to Reed, the proportion of Black students was, once again, 2 percent. With sustained effort we managed, in a good year, to get it up to 3 or 4 percent. No clever headlines in the student newspaper this time. I heard similar stories from deans and presidents so often that I began to wonder whether there was some sort of iron law in operation. The explanation, I heard repeatedly, was the racial performance gap—the alarming nationwide disparity between African American and White students in conventional measures of academic aptitude and achievement. More than 140 years after Lincoln emancipated the slaves, 50 years after the US Supreme Court outlawed Jim Crow segregation, and 40 years after race-based affirmative action began, the gap stubbornly persisted.

After a while, we in academia broadened our targeted racial and ethnic categories to include Hispanics, Native Americans, and Asian Americans. Lumping them all together made the numbers look better. The Asian figures improved impressively, though we all knew that category included many academic high-achievers, while at the same time concealing widely varying national and ethnic identities, some of which still faced performance gaps of their own. The Hispanic cohort—today often called Latinx—showed steady gains, mostly reflecting progress being made by second- and third-generation Hispanic families. Even the Black category showed some advances. But on closer examination, much of the growth in Black enrollment could be attributed to children of recent immigrants from African and Caribbean nations, many of whose parents were well-educated professionals.[1] The numbers of Black students who were descendants of American slaves barely budged.

Selective higher education was not making much of a dent in redressing America's shameful racial history.

WHY RACIAL AND ETHNIC DIVERSITY MATTERS

Is it the job of higher education to help atone for America's racial sins? Most educators would surely answer yes, and I would emphatically agree. If so, one would suppose that a best-college ranking should attempt to measure how well institutions are meeting that challenge. As we shall see, however, the rankocracy has been reluctant to incorporate racial and ethnic diversity into their formulas. There are, perhaps, good reasons for this. To understand those rationales and decide whether they are good or not, we need to review a little history.

How Diverse Is Selective Higher Education?

Many of our profile colleges, as described more fully in the appendix, illustrate the early linkage between higher education and racial justice. It is most obviously present in the origins and continuing commitment of the historically Black colleges and universities (HBCUs), most of them, like Spelman, founded after the Civil War to educate freed slaves and their children. That commitment is also reflected in Berea's abolitionist roots and its early, racially integrated student populations. Consider also Michigan's origins in a school devoted in part to educating Native American children. Or City College's founding and continuing mission to educate children of New York City's burgeoning immigrant population.

What about today? Is that spirit still alive? Yes, emphatically so. Are we making progress? From a nationwide perspective, the answer is partly yes, but mostly no. On the positive side, the overall numbers and proportions of Black and Hispanic students going to college have increased steadily, though slowly. In 2017, the US Department of Education's National Center for Education Statistics (NCES) reported that the percentage of Black young adults (aged 18–24) who were enrolled in a postsecondary institution grew from 31 percent in 2000 to 35 percent in 2015.[2] More impressively, the college-going percentage of Hispanic youth grew from 22 percent to 37 percent.

But on the negative side, too few of these students of color are enrolled in selective institutions. According to a Georgetown study, among the increased number of minority students attending college during the period from 1995 to 2009, almost three-quarters went to non-selective, open-admissions schools.[3] In those years, the percentage of Black college students attending the most selective institutions barely budged (from 8 to 9 percent). Likewise, the percentage of Hispanic students at those schools only inched up from 11 to 12 percent.

Writing in 2015, the Brookings Institution's Jonathan Rothwell showed that racial and ethnic disparities had not significantly changed in over 25 years.[4] Indeed, while the overall attendance differential had remained roughly the same, both the Black-White and the Hispanic-White degree gaps had widened. Compared with their White and Asian counterparts, Black and Hispanic students mostly attended colleges with "significantly worse outcomes"—such as lower graduation rates, smaller post-graduate earnings, and higher student-loan default rates. Among those who had started at a four-year college in 2012, only 48 percent of Blacks and 57 percent of Hispanics had earned a degree within six years, compared with 72 percent of Whites and 77 percent of Asians.[5]

These patterns continue to hold true across segments of higher education. At the selective public universities, for example, most schools admit a percentage of Black students that is well below the corresponding figure among young adults in their states. A recent study assigned letter grades to 101 of the most selective public institutions, based on how well they performed in this regard.[6] The University of Michigan, with a Black student population of 4.3 percent, in a state with a 16.4 percent Black college-age population, received an F. It was not alone; virtually every public university in a state with a large minority population flunked.

The Remedial Justification for Affirmative Action

Both the popular and scholarly literature contain dozens of arguments explaining why institutions of higher education, particularly selective schools, should educate larger numbers of non-White students, especially Blacks and Hispanics. As the tortured legal history of affirmative action demonstrates, those rationales generally fall into two clusters: remedial action and educational benefits.

The original justification for affirmative action was avowedly remedial. Because postsecondary schools serve as essential pathways to positions of economic success and societal leadership, they should make a deliberate effort to assist members of groups held back by centuries of oppression. President Lyndon Johnson summed up the argument nicely in his 1965 commencement address at Howard University: "You do not take a person who, for years, has been hobbled by chains and liberate him, bring him up to the starting line of a race and then say, 'you are free to compete with all the others,' and still justly believe that you have been completely fair."[7] Although Johnson used the singular noun—"a person"—he clearly meant to refer to a population. An important point about this reasoning is that it justifies providing a remedy for an entire disadvantaged group, not simply isolated individuals.

During the years that followed, many selective American colleges and universities eagerly embraced Johnson's statement as a kind of moral imperative. They not only expanded their recruitment of African American applicants, but they also often set hard or soft quotas for their admission. In virtually all instances, they used a more generous benchmark for Black applicants in conventional quantitative measures of academic preparation. On average, for example, highly selective institutions admitted Black students whose average SAT scores were a full standard deviation below those of Whites. That, of course, was before the era of college rankings. Now, admitting lots of students with lower SAT scores could cost a school dearly.

The Legal Backlash

As the composition of the US Supreme Court shifted to the right in the Nixon era, support for racial preferences dwindled. The court's 1978 decision in *Regents of the University of California v.*

Bakke effectively drove a stake in the remedial justification for affirmative action. Race-based preferences, said the court, may not be employed for the purpose of remedying past discrimination against an entire racial group.[8] But, said Justice Lewis Powell, speaking only for himself in a decisive concurring opinion, race may still be used as one among multiple admissions criteria in the service of achieving educational diversity. So long as race is not determinative or used in a set-aside or quota system, it might be considered a plus factor—along with other characteristics, such as geography, social class, and the like—to help produce a class whose multidimensional composition promotes student learning.

In recent decades, an increasingly conservative Supreme Court has tightened the diversity rationale. More and more justices have questioned whether educational diversity can be considered a "compelling state interest" that is worthy of constitutional protection. And a clear majority of the court has insisted that any use of racial or ethnic categories—no matter how assertedly benign—must be "narrowly tailored" to achieve that goal.[9] Narrow tailoring implies looking for nonracial proxies to achieve the desired degree of diversity, as well as ensuring that the admissions process is truly "holistic"—that is, based on a consideration of the whole person in all of that individual's many dimensions and attributes.

To compound the growing skepticism about the propriety of racial preferences under federal law, several states, including Arizona, California, Michigan, Nebraska, and Washington, have enacted prohibitions on the explicit use of race as a criterion for the admission of students to their public universities. The year after California's version (Proposition 209) took effect, Berkeley saw a 61 percent drop in the numbers of Blacks, Hispanics, and Native Americans in its entering class. UCLA saw a 36 percent decrease.

The Educational Benefits of Racial and Ethnic Diversity

The *Bakke* decision set off a mad scramble among educators to document the educational benefits of having a racially diverse student population. Academic researchers have conducted dozens of studies attempting to ascertain whether increases in racial/ethnic heterogeneity are associated with favorable educational outcomes. These investigations have used the federal government's racial/ethnic classifications, which require each college to disclose the percentages of its students who self-identify in one of the following categories: "Hispanic or Latino, American Indian or Alaska Native, Asian, Black or African American, Native Hawaiian or Other Pacific Islander, and White."[10]

Studies of the educational payoff from student diversity vary widely in their approaches. One method is to look at the impact of what investigators sometimes call "interactive diversity." This body of research tries to determine whether sound educational outcomes correlate with the amount and intensity of social interactions among students across racial and ethnic lines. One popular technique for measuring interactive diversity (the Gini-Simpson index) has been imported from the field of ecology. This metric estimates the probability that any two randomly chosen members of a general population will belong to two different subgroups within that population.[11] The implicit justification for using this measure to test for educational diversity is the assumption that more learning-related beneficial interactions will occur in a statistically more heterogeneous student population.

The literature on the educational effect of cross-racial interactions is far too vast and varied to summarize here. Matthew Mayhew and his colleagues have attempted that feat, for research up through 2014.[12] My impression of their summary is that interactive diversity clearly promotes a higher level of social understanding and tolerance. A different question is whether this type of diversity produces learning gains, in the form of improved cognitive skills or knowledge acquisition. Here, the reported results seem to be mixed and inconclusive.

Another set of studies looks at the effects of what has been called "curricular diversity"—that is, the number and range of courses about non-European, non-White groups that a college offers, or even requires. As Mayhew and his coauthors summarize it, the literature suggests that this type of instruction can produce learning benefits, especially if students take multiple courses and their classwork is reinforced by favorable social interactions.[13] Since curricular diversity could (at least conceivably) be achieved in an ethnically homogeneous college, it does not, by itself, provide a justification for enrolling a large number of minority students.

In most of this research, it appears that White students tend to realize the greatest educational payoff from attending ethnically heterogeneous colleges. This troubles many observers, who complain that Blacks and Hispanics are, in effect, being "used" for the education of Whites. But even if Whites are the primary beneficiaries of diversity, one can also reasonably argue that they are the ones who most need a racial awakening to the privileges they have inherited and routinely take for granted.

Back to Remediation

Notwithstanding the *Bakke* decision and its successors, and despite Proposition 209 and its progeny, the remedial justification for affirmative action has not gone away. Almost 60 years after Lyndon B. Johnson's speech at Howard, his exhortation still resounds in the swelling chorus of calls to dismantle a culture built on White supremacy. The remedial argument focuses not so much on the supposed educational virtues of heterogeneity as on the moral imperative of righting a terrible wrong done to specific racial and ethnic groups—in particular,

African Americans and Native Americans, but probably also Chinese, Japanese, Hispanics, and other groups systematically oppressed throughout our national history. By this account, selective institutions of higher education, serving, as they do, as gatekeepers for leadership positions in our society, should pursue two related goals. First, enroll a larger number of students from those groups. Second, ensure that they persist, graduate, and go on to fill those leadership positions.

Many observers worry that there is a conflict between these two goals. Given the stubbornly persistent racial performance gaps in society in general, and in elementary and secondary education in particular, selective postsecondary schools have great difficulty admitting more students of color unless they alter their customary quantitative standards of academic preparation and aptitude. To the extent that these standards are, in fact, predictive of academic success, critics claim that relaxing them may condemn some students of color to a kind of academic purgatory, leading to disappointment and even withdrawal from a school.

This, in essence, is the basis for the "mismatch" critique of affirmative action. Perhaps the most prominent spokesman for this argument is Richard Sander, a law professor at UCLA. In a 2004 law review article, he asserted that, by employing affirmative action—indeed, by being pushed to do so by their accreditors—law schools were effectively condemning most Black students to attend institutions in which they were ill equipped to succeed.[14] In a 2012 coauthored book, Sander later expanded his reasoning to apply to undergraduate education.[15]

Sander's writings have provoked a storm of criticism, addressed to both his statistical methodology and the inferences he drew from his data. As William Kidder noted in summarizing this literature, the Sander thesis flies in the face of a large body of scholarship demonstrating quite convincingly that minority students do, in fact, achieve good outcomes from attending selective schools.[16] The pathbreaking study in this genre is *The Shape of the River*, by former Princeton and Harvard presidents William Bowen and Derek Bok. Using multiple measures, they convincingly documented the post-graduate success of Black students who had attended a sample set of elite institutions.[17] More-recent studies, focusing specifically on both graduation rates and post-graduate earnings, reinforce those conclusions.[18]

This is not to say that it's easy for selective colleges, or law schools, to achieve significant increases in their proportions of Black, Native, and Hispanic enrollees, while still ensuring that they will succeed academically. So long as such institutions maintain their insistence on matriculating only the best and brightest students, as traditionally defined—that is, high SAT scores and high GPAs from academically challenging high schools—they will be locked in a zero-sum competition for a disproportionately small pool of minority applicants. And, to the extent that they give explicit preferences to applicants of color, the threat of lawsuits will continue to hang over their heads, as the 2019 litigation involving Harvard's undergraduate admissions process illustrates.

Still, despite the difficulties, some selective colleges simply do a better job of recruiting and educating minority students than others. Amherst is a good example. You can see it in the numbers. In fall 2019, according to IPEDS, almost a quarter of its student body was Black (10 percent) or Hispanic (13 percent). The six-year graduation rate for both its Black and Hispanic students (97 percent) was slightly higher than its overall graduation figure (95 percent). Even more impressively, it achieved these results while also having a relatively high percentage of low-income students and refusing to employ merit aid to "buy" high-income minority students.

Most of the other highly selective institutions among our

profile group reported much lower percentages of Black and Hispanic students in 2019 (Michigan, 11 percent; Notre Dame, 15 percent; Penn, 18 percent; Reed, 11 percent), though their minority-student graduation rates generally tracked their overall graduation rates. Of course, the surest way to achieve a high proportion of students of color is to be a school whose defining mission is to serve minority students, such as Spelman, or whose mission is to serve educationally disadvantaged students, like Berea or City College.

RACE, ETHNICITY, AND RANKING

In a different world, the college rankings industry might have been a powerful instrument for encouraging the most selective tier of higher education to promote the cause of racial and ethnic diversity. But in *this* world, it has not played that role. Indeed, the rankocrats have been notably hesitant to incorporate diversity metrics into their formulas. The WSJ/THE listings give a small amount of weight (3 percent each) to measures of student and faculty diversity, based on the Gini-Simpson biodiversity index. Niche includes an unexplained "diversity index" as a very small ingredient among the literally hundreds of factors in its formula. Meanwhile, Forbes and Money make no explicit reference to racial factors in their methodologies. Nor does U.S. News.

Although race does not figure in its overall best-colleges listings, U.S. News does not ignore the subject entirely. On its website, it presents a separate list of schools ranked according to a "diversity index." This category presumably uses a formula akin to the Gini-Simpson index, designed to estimate the probability that a student will "encounter" another student from a different ethnic group.[19] The schools with relatively high diversity-index scores compose an eclectic mix of private elites and lower-ranked colleges, as well as lots of public universities, all of which have a relatively wide distribution of students from the seven IPEDS racial/ethnic categories. Based on fall 2018 student data, U.S. News concluded that the most heterogeneous national university was the University of Hawai'i at Hilo. City College came in 7th. Among liberal arts colleges, Amherst held the same position. Sadly, but perhaps tellingly, the liberal arts school with the highest diversity-index score that year, Pine Manor College in Massachusetts, was under such financial stress that it could no longer continue as an independent entity. It was acquired by Boston College in 2020.[20]

So, give U.S. News some credit. But its diversity index—like the similar factor used by the WSJ/THE—addresses only *interactive* (not remedial) diversity. Furthermore, U.S News has buried its diversity ranking, like its other specialized, single-variable listings, deep in its website, overshadowed by the best-college beauty contest, with its eye-catching headlines.

Why, I wonder, does U.S. News—and, for that matter, do most of its cousins—shy away from giving race and ethnicity more prominence? One reason might be disagreement about the purposes and value of demographic heterogeneity in higher education. It is certainly true that racial diversity is legally fraught and politically controversial. Debate continues to rage about whether affirmative action should serve remedial or educational purposes. Many educators predict that the current Supreme Court will drive the final nail in its constitutional coffin. Others think that voters in various states are lining up to ban it. A recent poll indicates that even large majorities of Blacks and Hispanics oppose using race as an explicit factor in college admissions decisions.[21]

All true. But it seems to me that the real reason for the rankocracy's hesitancy to feature race and ethnicity in their formulas is that, in our society, prestige is still largely synonymous with Whiteness, and the leading rankings are all about prestige. Giving a heavier weight to racial and ethnic diversity could upend the order of things. As I explain more fully in the concluding chapter, I am opposed to any form of one-size-fits-all standard of college quality. We should truly let a thousand flowers bloom. But, as long as the rankers insist on trumpeting a single, all-encompassing grading system, surely they should reward schools that devote more of their wealth, prestige, and academic talent to serving the cause of racial justice.

On several occasions, I have cited *How College Affects Students*, the multivolume, multiauthor summary of research on the impacts of higher education. In the vast literature on this broad topic, one of the more depressing passages appears in the most recent volume of this series. Summarizing several decades of academic research, the authors conclude:

> The weight of the evidence suggests that with regard to cognitive development, college is hard-wired for White student success compared with African American students. African American students begin college with significantly lower scores on measures of aptitude and intellectual and cognitive development. . . . Evidence shows that this initial gap widens during the course of study. . . . When compared to White students, African American students have been and continue to be disadvantaged in college.[22]

In the face of such findings, the virtual silence of the rankocracy on the importance of remedial racial diversity and its corollary of racial success is deafening. But it's worse than silence. This is not just inattention. It's affirmative *inaction*.

By overwhelmingly basing their comparative assessments

on institutional selectivity, wealth, and reputation, these publications reward colleges and universities for admitting privileged, mostly White and Asian students, who are already programmed for success by the prevailing measures of academic achievement. And their best-college rankings exact a heavy price from schools, such as Spelman and City College, that want to make a sincere contribution toward atoning for the nation's history of racial oppression.

PART IV

HIGHER GOALS FOR HIGHER EDUCATION

OUTCOMES, VALUE ADDED, AND
THE PUBLIC GOOD

CHAPTER 16

INSIDE THE BLACK BOX

CAN LEARNING GAINS BE MEASURED?

One spring semester during my tenure as Reed's president, I co-taught a course on American Constitutional History and Theory with a colleague from the Political Science Department. Every Monday evening, the two of us and 22 students would spend three hours discussing Hume and Locke, the Federalists and the Anti-Federalists, de Tocqueville and Mill, and, of course, the US Supreme Court.

Heading off to class, sometimes in the middle of a business meeting, I would occasionally feel a twinge of guilt that teaching was a distraction from my "day job" (and evening and weekend job, for that matter) as president. But the moment I settled into my chair at the conference table, I knew that this was why I had come to Reed.

Having taught law students for over 25 years, I thought I had mastered all the tricks of eliciting classroom performances from reluctant participants. In my Reed seminar, I needed no tricks. One of us would pose a question, and the conversation would take off. There were no requests from students to "pass"—the term often used by law students who are either unprepared or unwilling to participate in class discussion. And there were no questions about what would be on the exam. We could talk freely about Plato or Aristotle, confident that everyone had studied their writings in the required freshman humanities course. We could expect students to plow through lengthy reading assignments and complete six written exercises, all without complaint. And we could count on our office hours being filled with inquisitive students.

As I reflected on my one and only teaching experience at Reed, I thought to myself, Wouldn't it be nice if educational institutions were actually graded on how well they educate? But they are not. Most rankings don't even try to take student learning into account. And those that do so end up making a pretty sorry mess of it.

DIRECT MEASURES OF LEARNING

What would it take to produce a direct measure of student learning that could enable magazines and newspapers to make "objective" comparisons? The most plausible method would be to create a test of academic-skills development or subject mastery (or both) that could be administered to students as both incoming freshman and exiting seniors. In this way, one could theoretically rank colleges and universities by calculating the average improvement for all test takers in each school and then comparing the results.

There are, in fact, some existing tests that could conceivably be used as the basis for such an undertaking. Three of the most widely recognized ones are the Collegiate Assessment of Academic Proficiency (CAAP), the Educational Testing Services' Proficiency Profile, and the Collegiate Learning Assessment (CLA).[1] CAAP, which purports to assess general cognitive learning, contains modules on reading comprehension, mathematics, writing skills, scientific reasoning, and critical thinking. The Proficiency Profile measures achievement in reading, writing, and mathematics. The CLA uses "performance tasks" to judge critical thinking, analytical reasoning, and written communications skills.

While all of these tests have their supporters and users, they have not penetrated the higher-education establishment very deeply. For example, only about 250 institutions have administered the CLA exam since its inauguration in 2002. A few of those schools, such as Kansas State University and St. Olaf College, have—to their everlasting credit—been willing to publicize their students' results on the CLA website, for all the world to see.[2] The vast majority of schools that do use such tests, however, keep the results a closely guarded secret, because they either don't trust the findings or don't like what they say.

Occasionally, someone penetrates this veil of secrecy. In 2017, for example, the *Wall Street Journal* obtained data on improvements in average student CLA scores from about 100 public universities, using state freedom-of-information laws to pry loose the results.[3] The gains the *Journal* found were generally pretty modest, consistent with the findings of researchers Richard Arum and Josipa Roksa in their widely read 2011 indictment of American higher education, *Academically Adrift*.[4]

One reason for skepticism about measuring collegiate learning in this fashion is that these are low-stakes tests. That is, at most schools, students take these exams voluntarily, with no rewards or punishments for performing well or badly. Unlike, say, LSATs or MCATs, performance on the CLA does not affect admissibility to graduate school. Nor does it factor into an individual's college GPA or rank in class. Nonetheless, the evidence seems to suggest that most students do take them seriously. For example, when participants are asked to indicate, on a five-point scale, how much effort they invested in taking the CLA, most of them report a relatively high level. If students knew the results were going to be used to rank their schools, they would probably exert themselves even more intensely.

Another objection is that these instruments essentially assess the same abilities that standardized pre-admissions tests already claim to have measured. Given the controversy over the fairness and even usefulness of the SAT and the ACT, as discussed in chapter 12, one can understand why few higher educational institutions want to adopt yet another, similar test. A related criticism is that general cognitive skills, of the sort assessed by tools like the CLA, are already baked into students by the time they go to college. What postsecondary education is supposed to instill, critics claim, is something else—a more advanced order of ability that simply cannot be measured on a 90-minute exam. This probably helps explain why very few highly selective schools have administered these tests, or at least why they have not done so more than once, perhaps after satisfying their curiosity about them. And if the selective institutions aren't interested in using such tests for internal diagnostic purposes, there is little reason to believe they could be persuaded to administer them as the basis for a published college ranking.

GRADUATE ADMISSIONS TESTS

Some commentators have suggested that one could compare colleges by the average scores of their students on graduate- and professional-school admissions tests, such as the GRE, GMAT, LSAT, or MCAT. In fact, at least some of the organizations that administer those tests already compute such averages. During my service as dean at Penn, the Law School Admission Council informed us of the average LSAT score for test takers from each undergraduate institution whose seniors or graduates had applied to Penn Law that year.

There are, however, obvious objections to using graduate admissions tests as indicators of collegiate learning. To be sure, they do measure an important set of academic skills at a particular moment in time. But they provide no basis for determining whether, and to what extent, those skills were enhanced by the test taker's college experience. Furthermore, each of these examinations has been designed to gauge only the distinctive cognitive abilities and knowledge content needed for success in a particular field. To the extent that they do assess general cognitive processing abilities, such as reading comprehension, analytical reasoning, and the like, their use will once again raise the familiar issues of validity and fairness associated with undergraduate admissions tests.

COURSE GRADES

Aside from tests of general cognitive-skills development, one might consider quantifying learning simply by looking at students' grades in their college courses. In theory, the more a student has learned, the higher the grade that student receives. Average GPA—or, better yet, average GPA increases from the first to the fourth year of study—might tell us something about the relative effectiveness of different colleges at stimulating learning. But objections leap to mind. The widely documented phenomenon of grade inflation, discussed in chapter 11, leads many observers to doubt that grades are really measuring learning, as opposed to appeasing consumerist students and their helicopter parents. Likewise, grading patterns vary widely by discipline, with courses in STEM areas (science, technology, engineering, and mathematics) customarily producing scores that are lower than those in arts and humanities courses. And, as I experienced firsthand at Reed, GPAs can vary widely from one institution to the next, for reasons wholly unrelated to relative learning achievement.

SELF-REPORTED LEARNING GAINS

Another plausible way to measure educational attainment is

simply to ask students how much they have learned during their years in college. This is one of the goals of two survey instruments widely used in higher education: the National Survey of Student Engagement (NSSE) and the College Student Experiences Questionnaire (CSEQ).[5] Both ask students, at various points in their undergraduate years, to estimate, on a numerical scale, the extent to which their educational experience has enhanced various academic skills or knowledge. In principle, for each college, one could compute the average gains in these scores between, say, the sophomore and senior years and compare different schools by their results.

U.S. News has exhibited no interest in using measures such as these in its rankings. But some other publications, such as the WSJ/THE, Forbes, and Niche, have made a stab at including student engagement (including learning) in their formulas. Each of these organizations bases its engagement measure on the results of a survey administered to a large sample of college students. I give them credit for trying to assess learning in this fashion. It is far from clear, however, that such analyses produce reliable results. Aside from the usual methodological problems with surveys, scholarly research tends to show that students are "highly inaccurate" in reporting the degree to which their own knowledge or skill levels have improved over time.[6] When they select a rating on a question that asks how much they have learned, or how well, what they usually do is rate their satisfaction with the instruction they have received (a topic that I address in the next chapter), but not learning per se.

STUDENT EFFORT INVESTED IN LEARNING

As we all know instinctively, even the most brilliant instructors will not produce good learning results if their students are unmotivated or distracted away from academic pursuits.

The research literature clearly and repeatedly supports this intuition. The more time and effort students devote to their studies, the more they learn, at least as measured by grades and self-reported gains.[7] A number of survey instruments, such as the NSSE, attempt to assess the quantity of student effort, typically measured by self-reported hours of study time per week.

Overall, the results of these surveys indicate a dispiriting decline in the amount of work invested by America's college students. Reviewing the results of a half-century's worth of student surveys, Philip Babcock and Mindy Marks report a steady decrease in the average reported time students spend on academic pursuits—dropping from 40 hours per week in 1960 to 27 hours in 2011.[8] In *Academically Adrift*, Arum and Roksa point to the combination of declining student effort and grade inflation as evidence of a "disengagement compact" between academically lazy students and research-focused faculty at American colleges and universities.[9]

However valid Arum and Roksa's accusation might be, surely the amount of academic effort expended by students varies among different institutions. For example, research confirms that, in schools known for their party atmosphere, the average student devotes less effort to their studies than the average student in schools known for their academic intensity. That being the case, one could conceivably use student surveys to distill a metric that measures the average number of hours invested in academic activities by the students at each institution, and then rank them accordingly. The results would probably be eye opening. But I am not aware of any such survey data. Already embarrassed by how little effort their students expend, most colleges are probably in no hurry to cooperate with such a data-gathering effort. And, of course, if students knew that their school was going to be ranked on

the basis of their self-reported estimates of study time, well . . .
how would you expect them to answer the survey?

All of the metrics discussed above have some value in
certain settings, especially if interpreted through the lens of
professional educational judgment. But none of them provide a solid, objective, easily administered basis for ranking
schools by their contributions to student learning *outcomes*.
Nonetheless, before we throw up our hands in frustration,
it's worth asking whether we could evaluate educational programs by *inputs* into learning—namely, by looking at *what*
students are being taught and *how well* they are being taught.
Those are the topics to which I now turn.

CHAPTER 17

PROXIES FOR LEARNING OUTCOMES

INSTRUCTIONAL CONTENT AND QUALITY

During my service as Reed's president, I was fortunate that members of my board of trustees generally agreed with my views regarding college rankings. But there were always a few skeptics. When the topic arose at a board meeting, someone might say to me: "Okay, I understand why you think the rankings are garbage. But, compared with what? If we don't use them as a basis for judging ourselves, how can we ever know whether we are doing a good job educating our students?"

Fair question.

In response, I would sometimes cite the college's practice of requiring students to pass a junior-year qualifying exam, as a measure of the extent to which they had mastered the methods and literature of their major fields. Or I might invoke the senior thesis as an indicator of the research and writing skills acquired over four years of study. To me, those were about the best evidence of actual learning outcomes that I could think of.

More often, however, I would answer such a question by talking about inputs into the learning process. I would mention the intricate structure of the curriculum, including the required freshman humanities course and extensive distributional requirements. I would wax eloquently about the "conference method" of instruction. I would recite the elaborate process we used to evaluate faculty members' teaching abilities, not only for tenure and promotion reviews, but also for biennial salary determinations. I would remind the trustees that we did not use part-time instructors. And, never missing an opportunity to rattle my little tin (fundraising) cup, I would remind them of how hard we worked to pay competitive faculty salaries, equip science laboratories, operate a research nuclear reactor, build sets and create costumes for theater productions, satisfy demands for the latest piece of information technology, and so on. Somehow, talking about inputs into the educational process was always easier than talking about outcomes.

For the same reasons, those who make it their business to assess the quality of colleges' and universities' educational programs—guidebook publishers, researchers, accreditors, and rankers—also typically fall back on input-based proxies for learning. In this chapter, I canvas three types: the content of the curriculum (what students are being taught), the caliber of instruction (how well they are being taught), and the resources devoted to instruction.

RANKING COLLEGES BY WHAT THEY TEACH
Breadth of Curricular Offerings

The WSJ/THE ranking is the only popular one that attempts to measure an institution's academic quality by the breadth of its undergraduate curriculum. Its methodology assigns a small amount of weight (3 percent) to the sheer number of courses offered at an institution. This measure seems to reflect what one might call a department-store model of higher education. In effect, it says that the best school is the one that offers students the biggest selection of courses. This is similar to saying that Home Depot is better than the corner hardware store, or Walmart is superior to a neighborhood boutique.

Students' academic preferences are indeed highly diverse. But it is far from clear that the best way to maximize the satisfaction of those preferences is for a single school to cater to all of them, as opposed to having a diverse set of institutions, each of which appeals to a narrower set of predilections. I know of no research that suggests that the sheer breadth of a curriculum correlates with better learning outcomes. Small, teaching-intensive colleges like Reed or Amherst or Berea cannot possibly rival huge universities like Michigan or Penn for the number of course offerings. But does that fact alone make Michigan better than Reed, or Penn better than Amherst? I don't think so.

Curricular Structure

An alternative, content-based proxy for learning might focus on the structure of the curriculum. It might ask, What courses are required? Are they arranged in a logical progression? Do cognitive tasks cumulate and reach some sort of apex in the final year? There was once a widely held view that offering a high-quality academic program at the baccalaureate level required a curriculum featuring disciplinary breadth and intellectual progression. By this precept, all students should be exposed, in at least an introductory way, to the methodologies and classic literatures of the major academic disciplines. And the offerings in each field should be arranged in such a way that knowledge, technique, and mastery build progressively from course to course, year to year, leading, in the senior year, to a major integrative capstone exercise, such as a research thesis. This is a view with which I heartily concur, informed as it is by my own experiences—as a student during the era of Amherst's (now-defunct) "New Curriculum" and, more recently, as the president of Reed, with its tightly structured program of study.

However, none of the mainstream college rankings attempt to measure curricular excellence in anything like this fashion. The closest approximation of which I am aware is a course-content grading system devised by the American Council of Trustees and Alumni (ACTA). The organization describes itself as a staunch defender of academic freedom and excellence. To the folks at ACTA, an academically "excellent" curriculum includes at least one required course in each of seven disciplines: composition, mathematics, foreign language, science, economics, literature, and American government or history. Since 2009, ACTA has issued an annual publication called "What Will They Learn?" It assigns letter grades to institutions based on how many of those seven subjects they require.[1] Of the 1,132 schools graded in ACTA's 2019–2020 edition, only 23 received an A, and another 352 were awarded a B. St. John's College, the "great books" school with campuses in Annapolis and Santa Fe, garnered an A. Harvard got a D. Amherst—with its open curriculum—flunked.

Wholly apart from the ideologically conservative leanings of ACTA, any ranking system that awards a failing grade to most schools is unlikely to gain much traction. And the problem goes well beyond the disappearance of required courses in, say, American history or mathematics. The very notion of requiring disciplinary breadth, course prerequisites, and intellectual progression seems to be disappearing.[2] At this point, any attempt to reverse that trend, much less to grade institutions by the quality of their curricula, would probably founder on the furious debate over the "canon." Perhaps this will change. But for now, a curricular-based ranking of colleges is doomed to be a fringe undertaking, perhaps favored by a handful of ideologues or antiquarians, but unlikely to gain widespread acceptance.

RANKING SCHOOLS BY HOW WELL THEY TEACH

A more common method of evaluating a college's educational programming is to assess the caliber of instruction that it offers. This approach rests on the universally held assumption that good teaching produces good learning outcomes. But, as any professional educator will attest, evaluating teaching turns out to be a mare's nest. Do we look at the pedagogical techniques that are used? Ratings of teaching quality by other educators or by students? Resources invested in teaching? All of the above?

Prevalence of Sound Pedagogical Practices

Research on the neuroscience and sociology of learning has produced a solid consensus on the practices that tend to produce optimal learning outcomes.[3] Give students intellectually and cognitively challenging assignments. Require them to solve problems and produce research findings. Promote interactive exchanges between the instructor and students and among class members. Provide frequent constructive feedback on learners' performances. Encourage students to engage in collaborative projects and activities. Insist that instructors be accessible and available, well-prepared for class, and well-organized in their presentations.

Various educational organizations and advocates have attempted to distill these practices into prescriptive frameworks—such as the "Valid Assessment of Learning in Undergraduate Education" rubric created by the Association of American Colleges and Universities, the Lumina Foundation's "Degree Qualifications Profile," or Arthur Chickering and Zelda Gamson's "Seven Principles for Good Practice in Undergraduate Education."[4] Each of these provides not only checklists of desirable pedagogical practices, but also methods for evaluating the extent to which—and even the level at which—individual instructors employ them.

Could they also be used to rank entire academic programs? In principle, yes. As I mentioned in the concluding section of chapter 12, several researchers have employed such frameworks in an attempt to determine whether the caliber of an institution's teaching correlates with its degree of student selectivity.[5] But, as these investigations have demonstrated, using this method to assess the instructional quality of an entire educational program would be prohibitively expensive. It would require dozens of well-trained evaluators, observing multiple classes for each course. Moreover, to minimize the variability among raters, it would probably be necessary to have several different observers assess each class. Anyone who has conducted reviews of a tenure candidate's teaching skills will tell you that observation of classes—especially small classes—is inherently obtrusive and usually alters the behavior of both the instructor and the students. The idea of using this method to produce annual rankings of entire schools is simply impracticable.

Peer Assessment of Institutions Based on Instructional Quality

Some people think the best way to evaluate the quality of instruction offered by various schools is to consult the opinions of experts. A leading example is the Times Higher Education's annual "Academic Reputation Survey," the results of which contribute 10 percent to the WSJ/THE rankings of colleges. THE invites educators from around the world to nominate up to 15 institutions they regard as "producing the best teaching" in their subject area.[6] U.S. News employs a variation on this theme. The survey form that it uses to conduct its overall peer assessment, discussed in chapter 8, includes a question asking respondents to nominate up to 15 schools "with a strength in undergraduate teaching." Although the replies do not factor into its comprehensive best-college rankings, the magazine publishes a separate list of the entities that received the most nominations.

As one might expect, there is a reasonably strong correlation between the institutions at the top of the U.S. News "best-teaching" list and those heading its overall "best-colleges" ranking. Still, there are some surprising exceptions. For example, the 2021 best-teaching list showed Williams and Agnes Scott tied for number two among liberal arts colleges, even though the overall ranking of Williams (1st) and its peer-reputation score (4.6 on a five-point scale) were both far above those of Agnes Scott (61st and 3.4, respectively). This suggests that many respondents were indeed making an effort to isolate their opinion of a school's teaching excellence from their view of its overall quality.

Still, one has to wonder whether the recipients of surveys such as those administered by THE or U.S. News can possibly know enough about the institution-wide teaching quality at peer schools to provide reliable responses. THE says that it invites "proven scholars" to make such assessments. So far as we can tell, these are people known by the caliber, quantity, and influence of their published scholarship. Perhaps the respondents know a great deal about the quality of *research* produced by faculty at peer institutions—at least in their academic field—and THE also asks them about that. But what do they know about the excellence of *teaching* at these colleges and universities? Perhaps they assume that levels of scholarship and teaching are positively correlated, but I know of no studies that confirm such a view. Indeed, many educators believe that the opposite is true.

In contrast to THE's survey, the U.S. News questionnaire goes to college presidents, faculty deans, and admissions deans. Are they more likely than THE's proven scholars to have informed opinions about teaching quality across the entire range of institutions in their Carnegie classification? Probably not. For reasons I canvas in chapter 8, these respondents are likely to have highly incomplete, and possibly biased, views of both the caliber of teaching and the overall excellence of their peers. Indeed, since instruction is less visible to outsiders than faculty scholarship or institutional accomplishments, I suspect that one's knowledge of another school's teaching quality is especially suspect. For these reasons, I can understand why U.S. News has chosen not to incorporate peer assessments of teaching into its overall ranking, but, rather, has published the results as a specialized listing for its readers to take or leave as they see fit.

Student Assessment of Overall Instructional Quality

While academic administrators and scholars have only a rather shaky foundation for making pronouncements about the overall quality of teaching at other schools, one might suppose the students are better positioned to do so. There have been several studies of student learning in which one of the independent variables is just such a rating. This research does seem to confirm that positive student perceptions of teaching excellence correlate with better student learning outcomes.[7]

Several publications ask students to assess the overall instructional quality of their institution. For example, the "US Student Survey," administered by THE, feeds data into an "engagement with learning" criterion that contributes 7 percent to the WSJ/THE rankings. Niche has its own student survey, whose data receive similar weight in their overall assessments. Forbes imports the Niche survey results as a factor in its own listings.

The Princeton Review may be the "student survey king." Every few years, it asks samples of college students to evaluate their experiences along multiple dimensions and then reports its findings in books like its 2021 edition, *The Best 386 Colleges, 2021.*[8] Among the 62 categories in which the Princeton Review publishes top 20 lists, there are a few that are serious attempts at gauging teaching quality, such as its "best classroom experience" and "most accessible professors" categories.

Student Assessment of Individual Instructors
An alternative to asking students for an overall institutional evaluation would be to aggregate their appraisals of individual instructors and courses, using some sort of common survey instrument administered by an independent organization. Enter RateMyProfessors.com.[9] Wildly popular with college students, it claims to have obtained over 19 million ratings of roughly 1.7 million professors in the United States, Canada, and the United Kingdom. This website publishes ratings of both individually named professors and entire institutions.

How seriously should we take its survey results? The methodological problems are obvious.[10] First, there is the omnipresent selection-bias problem. Who chooses to respond to these surveys? Mainly students who are happy with their teachers and their school, or primarily those who are unhappy? Second, there is the sample-size issue. A small college like Berea or Reed might have only 25 to 30 students replying to one of these surveys. Is that enough?

Even more troublesome is the issue of divergence among the various groups of students whose opinions are being sampled. The reliability of ratings depends on the extent to which a common group of individuals have experienced the products or services being compared. Does it make sense to choose between two Chinese restaurants, based on their relative consumer-rating scores? Probably, on the assumption that enough of the people giving their opinions have eaten at each of those restaurants. Does it make equal sense to use this method to choose between, say, Chinese and Ethiopian restaurants? Perhaps not. It depends on whether there is much overlap between the set of Chinese-cuisine lovers and Ethiopian-food aficionados, and, if not, whether their standards differ in some systematic way.

Applying this logic, it presumably makes sense to trust student views of instructors in choosing among courses in the history department at Penn. But perhaps it is less practical to rely on those assessments in choosing between a computer science course and a literature course at Penn. And, by extension, it seems absurd to choose to attend Penn rather than, say, Reed, based on the average course evaluations by enrollees at the two institutions. Not only is there virtually no overlap in the set of students whose views are reflected in those ratings, but there also is no reliable basis for assuming those two cohorts have the same preferences.

RANKING SCHOOLS BY THE RESOURCES THEY DEVOTE TO INSTRUCTION

Given the difficulty of reliably measuring the *quality* of instruction, most systems for evaluating colleges typically fall back on comparing the *resources* invested in instruction. U.S. News makes heavy use of such criteria. Its 2021 formula gave a 10 percent weight to expenditures per student, which included instructional costs. Its other proxies for teaching excellence included a "class size index" (worth 8 percent) that rewarded schools for having small classes; average faculty compensation (7 percent); the proportion of full-time faculty with "terminal degrees" (mostly PhDs) in their field (3 percent); the proportion of faculty who were full time (1 percent); and student/faculty ratio (1 percent). Other ranking systems use some of these same metrics, as well as various measures of faculty research productivity and professional recognition.

All of the instructional resource measures used by U.S. News and similar organizations have a plausibly positive connection with the quality of learning that occurs at a college or university. But there are also reasons to be skeptical about the strength of that connection.

Factors That Reward Research but Not Necessarily Teaching

As I pointed out in chapter 10, the per-student expenditure figures used in college rankings encompass a number of non-instructional activities, including faculty research. Schools reporting the highest levels of spending per student may well be allocating much more money to supporting faculty research than their lower-ranked peers, rather than investing more heavily in student instruction. Likewise, it turns out that metrics such as faculty compensation, the proportion of faculty with terminal degrees, and student/faculty ratio often share the same drawbacks. Why is that?

Consider faculty compensation. Is an institution with high faculty salaries necessarily "better" than one that pays lower amounts? Having dedicated 10 years trying to attract and retain star faculty at the Penn Law School, I know full well that faculty at research-intensive schools are compensated primarily on the basis of their published scholarship, not their teaching. I also know from sitting on campus-wide promotion review committees at Boston University and Penn that virtually no one gets tenure at a research university based solely (or even primarily) on teaching excellence. Research output— both in quantity and in quality—is the currency of the realm in those institutions. Increasingly, that is also becoming true at the most selective liberal arts colleges. The proportion of faculty with terminal degrees is another factor more strongly connected to research than to teaching ability. As countless academics lament, graduate school mainly trains you in how to become a productive scholar, not how to become an effective instructor.

Another potentially deceptive measure in the U.S. News formula—and one that is prominently featured in virtually every college guide—is student/faculty ratio. Many people assume that a low ratio is a reliable indicator of high-quality instruction. So, an institution that has an 8:1 ratio—that is, one faculty member for every eight students—must surely be offering its students greater course-selection opportunities and more instructional attention than a school that has a 12:1 ratio. But this is not necessarily the case. Indeed, it is quite often *not* the case.

What matters for instructional purposes is not the raw headcount of faculty members, but what they are doing with their time. For purposes of computing student/faculty ratios, the IPEDS database's glossary defines "faculty" to include staff members whose tasks consist of "conducting instruction, research or public service as a primary activity."[11] Faculty in research-intensive schools tend to have lower annual teaching loads (typically three courses per year) than those for faculty in teaching-focused schools (often five or even six courses per year), so the former can devote much more of their time to research. They also are inclined to have generous research-leave policies, for the same reason. As a result, the students in the school with the 12:1 student/faculty ratio may well have a choice of more courses and smaller classes than those in the one with an 8:1 ratio.

All this is not to say that research is unimportant. Indeed, many college rankings—especially the global university listings discussed in chapter 2—avowedly recognize research productivity as the leading measure of comparative institutional prestige. But, for the most part, these are assessments addressed to governmental funding agencies, prospective faculty, and potential graduate students. Ratings of the sort that I focus on here, by contrast, are targeted primarily at prospective undergraduates, who presumably care much more about what, and how well, faculty teach than what they publish. Indeed, U.S. News says that its five faculty-resources metrics have been chosen to "assess a school's commitment to instruction."[12] Unfortunately, however, four of those five factors are often more likely to take into account a school's commitment to faculty research than to instruction. Which brings me to the fifth factor, class size.

Class-Size Measures

Among all of the resource-related proxies for instructional quality used by U.S. News and its competitors, the class-size index measure strikes me as the most useful. Of course, any numerical standard can be attacked as arbitrary and will inevitably invite gaming. As we know from the Northeastern University example discussed in chapter 5, basing class-size metrics on fall-semester classes could encourage rankings-obsessed administrators to backload the large classes to the spring semester. Further, there is no magic in the number 20, the cutoff used by U.S. News (and reported by IPEDS) to define the optimal ceiling on class enrollments. Still, my experience, both as a student and as an instructor, tells me that small classes do, in fact, lead to more-active, engaged, and successful learning. And the weight of scholarly research on the subject tends to validate this belief.[13] Given that finding, it seems somewhat odd that U.S. News gives its class-size index only about a quarter of the overall 30 percentage points of weight allocated to instructional-quality proxies in its formula. But at least it's something.

DO PROSPECTIVE STUDENTS
CARE ABOUT TEACHING AND LEARNING?

Long-time higher education researcher Robert Zemsky offers a bleak answer to that question. "It is clear," he writes, "that learning does not matter in the marketplace. Instead the marketplace favors selectivity, brand names, national visibility, winning sports teams, and, in the case of the nation's medallion universities, major research portfolios."[14]

As a lifelong educator, I consider Zemsky's assessment to be too dire. In my experience, the marketplace—at least the prospective-applicant portion of that marketplace—does care about learning. The available research supports the view that a desire to learn receives heavy weight in most applicants' educational aspirations. The 2019 CIRP freshman survey asked entering students at (mostly selective) four-year institutions to identify those possible reasons for attending college that they considered "very important." The two choices receiving the largest number of affirmative answers were "to learn about things that interest me" (83 percent) and "to gain a general education and appreciation of ideas" (75 percent).[15] Nearly three-quarters of the respondents said that they aspired to attend graduate or professional schools; among that group, the importance of learning was even higher. Likewise, it's clear that, once they become undergraduates, most students select courses and majors based primarily on what they want to study and whom they want to study with. My experiences at Penn, Amherst, and Reed support that conclusion, and I'm sure the same is equally true at Berea, City College, Notre Dame, Michigan, and Spelman.

Perhaps the reason that "the marketplace" appears to

care primarily about the criteria on Zemsky's list is because those factors are more readily quantifiable than the quality of teaching and learning. Therefore, those elements are more amenable to being fed into ordinal rankings. But this hardly indicates that teaching and learning are unimportant to participants in the educational marketplace. It just means that choosing a college by its educational excellence requires application of the very skills and attitudes that effective education instills—a careful gathering of evidence, diligent analysis, and thoughtful judgment.

CHAPTER 18

CROSSING THE FINISH LINE

RANKING SCHOOLS BY GRADUATION RATES

When I retired as Reed's president, I realized that I had presided over 21 commencement ceremonies during my life in academe. They were among my most treasured memories. There was something about the medieval pageantry, the mixture of solemnity and exultation, that touched my soul to its core.

Upon first arriving at Penn, I was unimpressed with the choice of venues for the law school's commencement ceremony. So I decided to spring for the cost of renting Philadelphia's iconic Academy of Music. Designed to mimic Milan's Teatro alla Scala, the Academy had long served as the home of the Philadelphia Orchestra. Standing on its venerable stage, surrounded by dozens of berobed faculty members, and staring out at 1,500 graduates, adoring parents, and friends, I could almost imagine myself, baton in hand, ready to conduct Brahms's *Academic Festival Overture.*

But to my mind there was nothing that could compare to a Reed College commencement. Held under a huge tent surrounded by towering sequoia and Douglas fir trees, the ceremony perfectly embodied Reed's distinctive character. The focus was completely on the graduating students, every one of them treated identically—no prizes given to just a handful of selected seniors, no overpaid celebrity commencement speaker, no honorary degrees awarded to perfect strangers, no alumni honors bestowed on major donors. Just a brief set of remarks by the president and an alumnus or alumna selected by the graduating seniors, a musical interlude performed by a student chorus, and then row after row of proud, exhausted, sometimes slightly bemused graduates marching across the stage.

Commencement featured one of Reed's numerous charming traditions. In exchange for the obligatory handshake and well-earned diploma, many graduates handed the president whimsical gifts—stuffed teddy bears, wizard hats, plastic trumpets, comic books, you name it. One year, after I had made a fateful decision to bulldoze several acres of community gardens to build new dormitories, I received dozens of potted plants. All in good humor. I think.

What moved me most deeply about Reed's commencement exercises was the feeling of accomplishment that I shared with the graduates. I had known so many of them, having shaken every single entering student's hand at freshman orientation, and then followed them through four years of struggle and triumph. I had hugged them all, sloppy with sweat and champagne, as they cavorted through the administration building at the conclusion of the senior thesis parade. I knew, as perhaps only the president of a small liberal arts college can, how hard it was to make it all the way from the starting gate to the finish line.

EARNING A DEGREE
Why Graduation Matters

The prevailing view is that graduation rates are an essential measure of our nation's program of higher education. A host of influential players, ranging from President Obama to the Lumina and Gates Foundations, have identified college completion as an urgent national priority.[1] Macroeconomic studies have shown that increasing the college completion rate would increase America's gross domestic product, raise average income levels, and reduce unemployment.[2] A majority of states have adopted performance-based funding initiatives in which the size of appropriations made to their public universities depends, at least in part, on improving their graduation rates.[3] This emphasis on college completion is understandable, since only about 60 percent of those who start at four-year colleges finish within six years.[4]

Why is it so important for students to complete their program and earn a degree? Part of the reason is that learning is cumulative. As numerous studies show, the longer you stay in college, the more you learn and the longer you retain what you have learned.[5] But the primary reason is the "sheepskin effect." Like it or not, getting a degree is a necessary precondition for admission to most graduate and professional schools. And it is also viewed by many employers as an important signal of a person's job readiness. So, to the extent that we value postsecondary education as a gateway into lucrative and prestigious careers, a subject I discuss in the next chapter, a baccalaureate degree is a virtually indispensable ticket. And a college's graduation rate has therefore become an essential measure of institutional performance.

Why Students Don't Finish

When I attended Amherst College, I marched straight through its academic program in four years, never imagining that there was any other way. On the scheduled date for our graduation ceremony, there I was, sitting in the dazzling sunshine of a late spring day with all of the students whom I remembered from freshman orientation. Later, when I taught at Boston University and Penn, I observed that most students had the same expectation about their college experience—everyone gets a degree, and almost nobody transfers, takes time off, or flunks out.

When I arrived at Reed College, however, I discovered a different reality. A mere 50 percent of the students graduated in four years, and around 65 percent in six years. During my tenure as president, I once awarded a diploma to a "student" who had started more than 50 years earlier. He had dropped out in his senior year but somehow managed to earn a doctorate elsewhere and enjoyed a long and productive career as a college professor. In retirement, he returned to Reed to finish his senior thesis! And right after graduation, he joined his onetime classmates to celebrate their fiftieth reunion.

Some of the faculty viewed Reed's low graduation rate with pride. "It shows that we maintain high academic standards," said one old-timer. "We don't just give As and Bs; we still give Cs, Ds, and even Fs. The workload is heavy. We assign students graduate-level reading. You've got to pass a junior qualifying exam and write a senior thesis. If you can't hack it, you should go somewhere else."

Talk like that reminded me of a moment during my student orientation at the Harvard Law School some 37 years earlier. Erwin Griswold, a gruff, intimidating presence nearing the end of his 21-year reign as dean, was addressing 500 incoming students, arrayed before him in a huge amphitheater classroom. Griswold devoted much of his speech to lamenting the relaxation of academic standards at his beloved law school. "Not that long ago," he remarked, "I greeted the entering class by saying: 'Look to your left. Look to your right. By this time next year, one of the three of you will be gone.'"

Beyond Reed's uncompromising academic standards, there were other reasons for its low graduation rate. Reed famously attracted rebels, freethinkers, iconoclasts—students, in other words, who marched to the beat of their own inner drum and not to the metronome of the traditional academic schedule. The most famous person ever to have attended Reed was a young man from Los Altos, California, named Steve Jobs. He enrolled as a student for exactly one semester and then dropped out, deciding that Reed's classical curriculum wasn't meaningful enough to justify the high tuition.

After hanging around for another semester playing with computers in the basement of the administration building and auditing courses in calligraphy and folk dance, Jobs spent a couple of years living in Indian ashrams and Oregon communes. Then he teamed up with his old buddy Steve Wozniak and formed a company called Apple that audaciously marketed "personal" computers to ordinary people. And he never looked back. Even 30 years later, there were plenty of students like that at Reed. I'd hardly get to know them, and then they would disappear, off to work on a fishing boat in Alaska or try their hand at writing software in their basements. Or maybe transfer to Berkeley to save tuition money and study Japanese.

But these factors barely scratch the surface of reasons why many students don't graduate at most American colleges. By far the biggest reason is financial. Lined up behind that are family trauma, emotional struggles, health challenges, and plain old discouragement. Students run out of money. They have to take jobs to get by. They have to go home to take care of a sick parent. They suffer from untreated depression. They plunge into the abyss of drug addiction. They become pregnant or get their girlfriend pregnant.

Beneath the cultivated composure of campus settings, these are the stubborn realities that routinely confront too many of America's undergraduates. Higher education cannot be expected to solve all of the underlying social dysfunctions that feed these problems. But schools can nonetheless take steps to ameliorate the impact on their students' academic performance and progress. In a recent book entitled *The Dropout Scandal*, Berkeley professor David Kirp suggests several "proven" strategies to boost completion rates.[6] Use data analytics to track students who are most susceptible to stumbling off the path. Consciously steer them into experiences that promote a sense of community and belonging. Redesign those pesky "gateway" courses in math and science so struggling students can earn promotion to upper-level instruction.

To be sure, there are no panaceas, no easy fixes. All of these things cost money, a commodity usually in short supply at institutions with the lowest completion rates. And using data analytics to track students raises uncomfortable images of a police state.[7] Still, given the importance of obtaining a degree and the high cost of failing to do so, that old sink-or-swim attitude exemplified by Erwin Griswold's orientation address is simply no longer acceptable.

So, yes, perhaps Kirp is right in calling the current dropout rate a "scandal" and suggesting that a few institutional leaders' heads should roll for failing to tackle it. But, at a minimum, the problem of low completion rates should be clearly exposed. Before taking a leap that they might regret, college applicants need to be made aware of the barriers they may face. So it comes as no surprise that for many years, one of the most salient metrics for describing, comparing, and ranking postsecondary schools has been their graduation rates.

GRADUATION RATES AND RANKINGS

There are many ways to calculate graduation rates. One variable is the category of students whose progress is being recorded. The most commonly used measures track the success of full-time, first-time students (as opposed to transfer students) who matriculated in the fall semester. But one can sometimes find

TABLE 18.1.

Six-year graduation rates (for students who entered in fall 2013)

College	Graduation rate (%)
Amherst	95
Berea	68
City College	56
Michigan	93
Notre Dame	96
Penn	96
Reed	76
Spelman	75

Source: IPEDS.

other measures based on the completion rates of transfer students, part-timers, and spring matriculants. A second variable in computing completion rates is the timeframe employed to assess students' progress. The measurement periods most often used for baccalaureate colleges are eight years and six years. The US Department of Education's College Scorecard, for example, uses an eight-year period. This choice is designed to make ample allowance for the multiple reasons why many students—especially those at less-selective schools—struggle to complete their college education in the standard four years. Most commercial college guides and rankings publications, by contrast, prefer to use a six-year measure, and a few even use four or five years.

As an illustration of the variation in completion rates among reasonably selective institutions, table 18.1 presents data on the six-year graduation rates for the 2013 entering cohort at our eight profile schools—that is, the percentage of those 2013 matriculants who had received a degree by 2019.

U.S. News relies very heavily on completion measures in

constructing its best-colleges rankings. With somewhat laughable precision, its 2021 formula assigned exactly 17.6 percentage points to a four-year rolling average of a school's actual six-year graduation rate for all students, an extra 8 percent to a "graduation-rate performance" metric, discussed below, and an additional 5 percent to graduation levels for lower-income students receiving Pell grants. Most other publications also relied heavily on similar statistics in their recent issues. Forbes gave a 12.5 percent weight to "on-time" graduation (using both the four-year and six-year periods). The WSJ/THE assigned an 11 percent weight to these factors (rather sensibly using the six-year rate for full-time students and the eight-year one for part-timers). Washington Monthly employed a 17 percent weighting for various graduation-rate measures (using the eight-year period).

PROBLEMS WITH USING GRADUATION RATES
While graduation rates are undeniably important measures of college outcomes, they need to be employed with sensitivity to their limitations. Giving heavy weight to these numbers in a college-ranking formula can change institutional behaviors in unexpected ways. For example, some observers believe that a fixation on college completion has contributed to a relaxation of academic standards and an escalation of grade inflation.[8] Others fear that the perceived imperative to raise graduation rates may discourage institutions from taking the risk of admitting more lower-income or minority students and then having to invest the resources necessary to ensure their success.[9]

Tracking Students Who Transfer
A particular drawback with graduation-rate measures that bedeviled me at Reed was their tendency to penalize schools

TABLE 18.2.

Outcomes eight years after enrolling (for students who entered in fall 2011)

College	Graduated (%)	Transferred Out (%)	Withdrew (%)
Amherst	95	4	1
Berea	66	24	10
City College	49	30	20
Michigan	92	5	3
Notre Dame	96	4	0
Penn	96	2	2
Reed	81	15	4
Spelman	77	17	6

Source: IPEDS.

Note: Figures do not necessarily add to 100%, because some students were still enrolled or their status was unknown.

whose students transfer to another college to complete their education. Table 18.2 presents data on the percentage of students who switched to another institution within eight years of starting at one of our eight profile schools. (I use an eight-year outcome measure in table 18.2, unlike the six-year data in table 18.1, because many colleges do not report transfer-out statistics in their six-year figures.)

As table 18.2 illustrates, students rarely transfer out of the most elite schools. By contrast, those who start at colleges or universities that are farther down the pecking order, or schools with distinctive missions, are more likely to transfer and finish elsewhere. Perhaps we should fault such institutions for failing to support, or satisfy, their students well enough to retain them all the way to completion. But there are many perfectly understandable reasons why individuals who start at, say, Berea or City College may want—or need—to complete their education elsewhere. In many cases these colleges should be given credit for giving their students a solid academic foundation and a sense of direction.

When I was Reed's president, I felt that our low graduation rate presented a somewhat unfair impression. From anecdotal evidence, I was convinced that most of our non-graduates had not, like Steve Jobs, withdrawn altogether but had instead transferred to another school from which they eventually received a degree. But we had no systematic way to find out. Fortunately, that problem has now been solved by the National Student Clearinghouse (NSC), a nonprofit organization created by the higher-education community to collect and report information about student enrollments and degree completions.

NSC is now able to track students who transfer from one institution to another. Its national data show that, among those who matriculated in fall 2012 at a *public* four-year university, 60 percent had earned a baccalaureate degree from that same institution within six years. Another 10 percent had received a degree from a different school.[10] At *private* nonprofit colleges, the numbers were 68 percent and 11 percent, respectively. Although NSC now tracks students who transfer, those who publish comprehensive best-college listings still customarily use graduation rates that omit transfer data.

The Self-Selection Issue

Perhaps the biggest problem with using raw graduation rates to rank colleges is selection bias. As table 18.1 illustrates, the schools with the highest graduation figures attract students with the greatest levels of academic ability, achievement, and wealth—precisely the category of enrollees who are most likely to satisfy academic requirements and persist in completing their degrees, no matter where they go to college. Would City College have the same graduation rate as Penn if it had similar students? Possibly (indeed probably, if it also had an amount of wealth comparable to Penn's).

Gaps between graduation rates for low-income students (conventionally identified as those receiving Pell grants) and all other students present some evidence for the self-selection hypothesis. According to NCES data, for the 2011 cohort entering four-year schools, the nationwide six-year graduation rate for Pell recipients was only 48 percent, compared with 70 percent for students not receiving federal subsidies.[11] The racial disparities were equally disheartening—the completion rate for Asian students (74 percent) was almost double that for African Americans (40 percent). It is for this reason that some of the most passionate critiques of graduation-rate metrics come from presidents of historically Black colleges. For example, Walter Kimbrough of Dillard University has argued that the fixation on graduation numbers disadvantages colleges whose very mission is to offer opportunity to our society's most academically disadvantaged.[12] So long as we judge schools by their raw graduation rates, we risk falling into that old trap of rewarding brand value and prestige, rather than actual institutional performance.

GRADUATION-RATE PERFORMANCE MEASURES

For over a decade, U.S. News has tried to compensate for the self-selection problem by including in its formula a measure of graduation-rate "performance." Washington Monthly uses a similar criterion. These metrics attempt to determine the value added of attending a particular college or university. They do so by computing the difference between its *actual* graduation rate and the figure that would be *predicted*, given various attributes of its student population (such as academic aptitude and socioeconomic and racial composition) and characteristics of the institution itself (such as its financial resources).

According to the data underlying the U.S. News 2021 edition, the two schools in our profile group that had the highest absolute six-year graduation rates were Notre Dame and Penn, both at 96 percent (table 18.1). Pretty impressive! But their predicted graduation rates were also 96 percent. So they got a zero on performance. No rankings enhancement there. Contrast them with Berea College, whose actual graduation rate was only 65 percent, but whose predicted rate was a mere 45 percent. As a result, it presumably received a big boost in the rankings.

Not surprisingly, among our eight profile schools, the ones with the best performance figures were Berea, Spelman, and City College. To be sure, one can quibble with this system. U.S. News refuses to make public the formula it uses to compute that factor, so we have no real way to verify its calculations or critique its assumptions. Indeed, at least one researcher has questioned whether these figures have any validity at all.[13]

In my view, however, a more troubling feature of the U.S. News approach is the fact that it still gives more than twice as much weight to absolute graduation rate as it does to graduation-rate performance. Thus it persists in favoring prestige-rewarding inputs over performance-based outputs. But I give U.S. News credit for making a good-faith effort to correct for selection bias and, thus, to reward institutions like Berea and Spelman that really make a difference in the lives of the students they enroll.

As Princeton's former president, William Bowen, and his coauthors argued in their important book, *Crossing the Finish Line*, earning a degree is an essential goal for most would-be college students.[14] At least it is for the vast numbers of those lacking the gifts—or good fortune—of such famous college dropouts as Steve Jobs, Bill Gates, and Mark Zuckerberg. Therefore, getting students across that finish line should be an essential goal for any self-respecting academic administrator.

At Reed, I voted with my feet on this issue. After a year trying to rationalize the school's historically low graduation rates, I rolled up my sleeves and began doggedly pursuing a plan to increase the completion rate. Not because it would boost our numbers in some arbitrary formula, but because it was, frankly, the right thing to do.

To deepen the sense of student community, we built more dorms. To relieve the pressures of academic overload, we strengthened student services and enriched extracurricular opportunities. To promote teamwork and spur creativity, we expanded the performing arts departments and built them a stunning new home. As a result, the graduation rate crept up to around 80 percent. Reed students were still famously independent, and its curriculum remained a challenging obstacle course. But at least more of its students got to cross the threshold into the next phase of their life's journey. As they should have.

And the assessment of my performance as president included how much Reed's graduation rate had improved on my watch. As it should have.

CHAPTER 19

MAKING
A LIVING

THE WINDING ROAD FROM COLLEGE TO CAREER

At the Penn Law School, the career-counseling program was a pretty straightforward matchmaking operation. Every fall, representatives from law firms and corporations would show up on campus by the hundreds to interview both second-year students for summer jobs and third-year students for post-graduation employment. For weeks, neatly scrubbed students in sober business attire would run from class to interviews (or just skip class for interviews). Employers would then invite some of the students to callbacks at their home offices, eventually offering positions to those who impressed them the most. It was more challenging to help students find jobs in the public and nonprofit sectors, because openings tended to be few and far between, and employers rarely recruited in person. Still, for the most part, we had it down to a science.

By contrast, running a career-counseling program at Reed was anything but a science. Very few employers came to campus to conduct interviews, because Reed's enrollment was small and its students were rather famously countercultural. The investment banks and consulting firms that recruited at Penn took a pass on Reed. Another challenge was that Reed's seniors were so fixated on completing their thesis projects that few of them seemed to have much bandwidth for thinking about the future—other than, perhaps, graduate school.

Nonetheless, we labored away at providing programs to steer students onto productive career paths. We invited alumni to give talks about their chosen professions. We created internship opportunities. We urged graduates and parents to post job openings available at their workplaces. An enterprising professor from the Russian department even organized mock interview luncheons, which, to the surprise of many, were wildly popular. "Don't order pasta with tomato sauce at an interview lunch," she might have said. "And remember, the small fork is for salad."

At Reed, we talked endlessly about "education for education's sake." But we knew that even our precious—and pricy—education had to lead somewhere, and a very important aspect of that "somewhere" was a job.

Not surprisingly, many who rank colleges also believe that higher education should lead to a remunerative career and, therefore, that institutions should be evaluated by their graduates' employment success. In searching for metrics by which to conduct such an evaluation, the two most obvious candidates are the percentage of a school's recent graduates who are gainfully employed or their average earnings.

POST-GRADUATE EMPLOYMENT RATE

To my knowledge, none of the best-colleges publications use raw employment-rate statistics to assess undergraduate programs. Aside from the difficulty of obtaining information from far-flung graduates, the variability in types of jobs obtained by baccalaureate-degree recipients—ranging from, say, dishwashers to data analysts—would probably make such information meaningless. As we shall see later, assessments of undergraduate schools tend to rely instead on post-graduate earnings measures.

By contrast, law-school rankings have depended heavily on employment-rate data. Late in my tenure as dean of Penn Law, U.S. News began asking law schools to report the percentage of their graduates who were employed, both immediately following graduation and nine months later. That seemed perfectly sensible. Legal education is, after all, designed to prepare students for entry into a particular profession. The quality of law schools should, therefore, be reflected, at least in part, in the ability of their graduates to parlay their JD degrees into jobs in that profession.

But, as with everything involving law-school rankings, once U.S. News tossed another ingredient into its recipe, the gaming began.

Law schools had, of course, been collecting post-graduate employment figures long before U.S. News came along. But once they became an important factor in national rankings, the pressure mounted to track down every graduate. And the visibility of that data increased exponentially. At Penn, I was always pleased that our employment numbers were solidly above 90 percent. But looking at the figures reported to U.S. News by our competitors, some of them seemed impossibly high, approaching 100 percent. After making a few inquiries, we discovered that several of our peers were counting just about any job that their graduates managed to scrape up—such as waiting on tables at restaurants, stocking supermarket shelves, or bartending. Even worse, to my mind, we discovered that some schools were manufacturing short-term jobs for their unemployed graduates—working as research assistants or file clerks in the admissions office. These so-called jobs often lasted only a couple of weeks, just long enough to enable the school to count these graduates as employed on the U.S. News survey.[1]

The manipulation of employment-rate numbers got particularly egregious when the 2008 financial meltdown led to a collapse in the job market for lawyers. At that time, the National Association for Law Placement was calculating that only about 60 percent of recent law-school graduates were able to find jobs in the legal profession. Yet most law schools continued to report placement numbers above 90 percent. Groups of angry unemployed graduates, burdened by hefty student loans, brought class-action lawsuits against 15 law schools, alleging misrepresentation of their employment numbers. Two US senators demanded that the Department of Education's Inspector General launch an investigation.

In 2011, the American Bar Association finally took action. It issued a new accreditation standard, requiring law schools to report substantially more-detailed information about the positions their graduates had accepted. This standard classified jobs by their intended duration, full-time or part-time status, and type (e.g., those that require passing a bar exam, or those for which a JD degree would be an "advantage").[2] A couple of years later, the ABA again revised its regulation, requiring law schools to list separately any positions for which the law school or its university was the employer.[3]

All this information is now publicly available on the ABA's website, and U.S. News has incorporated it into its formula. The magazine assigns varying weights to the different categories of jobs, rewarding schools that steer their graduates into real, full-time, long-lasting legal positions. In its profiles on individual law schools, U.S. News essentially replicates the ABA reports. In theory, the fact that these numbers come from the law schools' national accrediting agency offers an assurance of their reliability. But even the ABA, through its periodic reaccreditation reviews, is not able to verify the absolute accuracy of the data reported by the law schools. I know from experience that tracking down some graduates nine months after their departure and confirming their employment status can be difficult. Given the sorry history of gaming the rankings in the world of legal education, one has reason for skepticism.

POST-GRADUATE CAREER EARNINGS

Most publications that evaluate undergraduate programs use average post-graduate earnings as the primary measure of a school's success in preparing its students for the world of work. The reason for this is obvious. The ability to parlay a baccalaureate degree into a remunerative career matters greatly to young people, influencing both their decision about whether to go to college and their choice of which school to attend.[4]

The two leading sources of post-graduate earnings data are College Scorecard and PayScale.com. Both are used in popular comprehensive rankings, such as those published by the WSJ/THE, Forbes, Money, and Washington Monthly. PayScale also publishes its own listings, based on average midcareer earnings and return-on-investment calculations. Curiously—given its obvious fixation on prestige and wealth—U.S. News has not used earnings data in its formula.

College Scorecard Earnings Data: Uses and Limitations

On its statistical dashboard for each undergraduate institution, College Scorecard prominently reports median early-career earnings data, based on the salaries received by individuals 10 years after they first enrolled at that institution. This information comes from federal tax records, so is as accurate as earnings data can be. But there are several problems.

First, the population covered includes only students who have received either a federal grant or federally guaranteed loan. Only about 60 percent of all American college students fall into those categories. Thus the earnings figures reported for any particular institution may not be representative of that school's entire student body. For some, like Berea College, where roughly 95 percent of the students receive federal Pell grants, this is not a problem. But at most of the selective elites, only a relatively small percentage of their students have either Pell grants or federally subsidized loans (or both). In 2019, for instance, only 13 percent of Penn's undergraduates were receiving Pell grants. And 13 percent were taking out federal loans, a group that presumably overlapped considerably with Pell recipients.

A second problem stems from the fact that College Scorecard reports earnings data for students who initially enrolled at a particular college, regardless of whether they graduated from that school, transferred to another institution, or dropped out altogether. As we saw in table 18.2, graduation, transfer, and withdrawal rates can vary widely, even among relatively selective colleges. Thus, for example, comparing Scorecard's earnings data for City College and Penn would be difficult, since only 49 percent of the students who started at City finished there, as compared with 96 percent of those who matriculated at Penn.

A related problem with Scorecard's earnings reports is that they do not distinguish between individuals who went on to graduate or professional school and those who did not. When, for example, one observes a difference in average earnings between degree holders who started at City College and those who began at Penn, how much of that disparity is directly attributable to these two schools, and how much to the post-baccalaureate programs that some of their graduates attended?

A final problem has to do with timing. Early-career earnings (at roughly age 28) are not very good predictors of longer-term outcomes. Even among those who graduated with a bachelor's degree, some who earned it in four years will have been employed for six years, while those who completed it in eight years will only have been working for two. Some will have already received degrees from a graduate or professional school, while others may still be enrolled in such institutions.

PayScale Earnings Data: Uses and Limitations

PayScale solves some of these problems.[5] It attributes earnings data to a particular college or university only for those individuals who actually graduated from that school. In addition, it reports salaries for all former students, not just those who received federal grants or loans. PayScale's data also cover a longer time period. Although it does include early-career information, it also prominently reports (and uses for its primary ranking) midcareer data (roughly 10 to 20 years following graduation). Research shows that salaries at approximately age 35 tend to be much more reliable predictors of lifetime earnings. There is, of course, a price to be paid for this degree of accuracy. If you evaluate a college by its graduates' actual midcareer earnings, you are essentially judging the college, not as it is today, but as it was 10 to 15 years earlier. Believe it or not, some institutions of higher education do change faster than that!

Table 19.1 presents recent PayScale earnings data for our eight profile schools. As the table indicates, the organization separately reports data for two categories of graduates. The first (the column labeled "Undergraduate degree only") includes only those whose higher-education careers ended with a baccalaureate degree from that school. The second ("All alumni") includes both the "Undergraduate degree only" individuals and other graduates who went on to obtain a postgraduate degree of some sort. Which of these two measures is preferable? It's hard to say. The former isolates the vocational value of an undergraduate school's educational program from the confounding effect of some other (graduate-level)

TABLE 19.1.

Average midcareer earnings for the colleges' graduates (2020–2021 data)

College	Undergraduate degree only[a]	All alumni[b]
Amherst	$127,100	$139,800
Berea	$70,900	$72,700
City College	$96,400	$102,400
Michigan	$112,300	$121,500
Notre Dame	$136,900	$142,300
Penn	$142,900	$152,900
Reed	$109,700	$114,900
Spelman	$82,600	$93,600

Source: PayScale (2020).
[a] Alumni of the college whose highest degree is a baccalaureate degree.
[b] All alumni of the college, including those who subsequently earned a graduate or professional degree.

institution's program. But the latter reflects the extent to which that undergraduate school prepares its students for graduate-level education. So both measures appear to have value.

For all its apparent advantages over College Scorecard, PayScale has plenty of detractors. The biggest criticism stems from the fact that all of its data come from survey responses by individuals who use PayScale's website for salary comparisons and job searches. To what extent are the responders representative of the entire population of college graduates? How large are the samples for individual schools? Money magazine, which heavily weights PayScale's data in its annual college rankings, asserts that these figures are "reliable," citing PayScale's claim that over 3 million people have filled out the survey over a 10-year period. This sounds impressive. But that number translates into an average of only 300,000 survey responses per year. When spread out over the 4,000 colleges in PayScale's database, the average college would be represented in only about 75 graduates' salary reports per year. Probably for this reason, it's no surprise that the earnings figures and relative standing of schools on PayScale's website tend to shift quite noticeably from year to year.

Additional Problems with Ranking Colleges by Post-graduate Earnings

Aside from concerns about the accuracy and representativeness of the data, there are several problems with judging colleges by their former students' earnings. One is the lamentable, but pervasive, reality of employment discrimination. The alumnae of Spelman are likely to be doubly disadvantaged. One wonders what Spelman's midcareer earnings figures, as shown on table 19.1, would look like in a world in which Black women were employed and compensated at the same rates as White men.

A second problem is the rather dramatic variation in earnings by field of study. Both PayScale and College Scorecard report this data not only by college or university, but also by college major within an institution. Looking at recent Scorecard figures, one can see that at Penn, the reported median early-career salaries ranged from $29,300 for English majors to $135,200 for computer and information science majors. This variability also means that, in judging overall earnings numbers for an entire institution, one must be alert to the mix of academic programs it offers. Perhaps not surprisingly, schools that specialize in preparing graduates for careers in engineering, technical, and health care careers heavily populate the top of PayScale's ranking, along with the usual elites. For this reason, some publishers, such as Money and Washington

Monthly, commendably use a formula to adjust the various schools' overall earnings figures by the distribution of academic fields in which their graduates majored.

A third problem with using career earnings to compare institutions is the differential cost of attending them. For example, table 19.1 tells us that the average salary for Penn's graduates was much higher than that for City College's alumni. But students also had to pay more to attend Penn. According to US Department of Education data for academic year 2019 (see table 20.1), the *total* cost of attending Penn for four years was approximately $298,000, compared with roughly $120,000 for City College. Likewise, Penn's *average net* cost of attendance (after taking into account scholarship grants) was also much higher than the comparable figure for City College ($99,100 vs. $13,600). Did it still make sense to choose Penn over City College?

RETURN ON INVESTMENT

To answer questions such as the one I just raised, many researchers and rankers compare institutions of higher education by their students' average return on investment (ROI). The "return" in this computation is the students' lifetime earnings; the "investment" is their cost of college attendance. The calculation is complicated and inescapably arbitrary. One needs to estimate a career-long stream of future income and a near-term stream of expenses, and then apply the proper discount rate to express both streams as present values. Ideally, one must also include risk estimates that reflect the expected distribution of outcomes—for example, the range of income trajectories, the differential odds of graduating, and the disparate periods of time from matriculation to earned degree.

Despite these difficulties, calculations of the returns on attending different colleges abound. PayScale, for example, computes an ROI figure based on average salaries 20 years after graduation.[6] Its formula looks at those who received only a baccalaureate degree. For this group, it compares average net earnings (after factoring in the average cost of attendance) with hypothetical earnings had these individuals not attended college at all. Once again, as was the case with its midcareer earnings lists, the upper tier of its ROI lists includes many schools that specialize in preparation for technical, engineering, and health care jobs, as well as the usual roster of elite schools. But now the US military academies rise to the top: high gross return, zero cost of attendance! Similarly, Michigan's standing improved from its 144th position in earnings to 81st in ROI. Good payoff, lower cost. By contrast, Penn's position declined, from 14th in earnings to 30th in return. High payoff, but also high cost.

The folks at Georgetown's Center on Education and the Workforce performed an even more complicated calculation, ranking schools by their estimated returns on investment over multiple 10-year intervals following graduation. Judged by the average return over a 40-year career, the top schools were, once again, those that specialize in engineering and health care.[7] Maybe my father was right. I should have attended MIT 40 (plus) years ago!

One might think the lesson is clear. If you want to maximize your ROI, go to an engineering school, or a maritime academy, or perhaps a pharmacy school—or, if you can get in, an elite university. But don't go to a "niche" liberal arts school! Of course, the payoff depends on so many variables, such as family financial circumstances and career preferences, that the personal return on investment for a student at any of these schools can vary enormously. Consider family income, for example. As we will see in chapter 20, for low-income students, the net cost of attendance at schools like Amherst or Penn is very comparable to the net costs of going to City College, thanks to generous financial-aid grants. Or consider field of study. The student who enrolls at Penn and majors in English may have a much lower income and ROI than the one who chooses Reed and majors in computer science.

WHY DO GRADUATES OF ELITE COLLEGES MAKE MORE MONEY?

Leaving aside the relatively high earnings associated with some schools specializing in technical and health care fields, it is generally true that the more selective a college or university, the higher its graduates' earnings.[8] One can see this relationship in table 19.1. Why is that? Scholars have advanced three theories, sometimes referred to in the literature as "selection bias," "human capital," and "signaling." Consider again the differential in average earnings between graduates of Penn and City College, as shown on table 19.1. The selection-bias theory explains this result as a product of the different sorts of students who are attracted to Penn and City College. Penn, according to this explanation, draws many more enrollees from academically, economically, socially, and demographically privileged backgrounds than City College—precisely the sorts of individuals who would have successful careers no matter where they went to college. Thus Penn gets credit for their career successes, not because of anything the university has added to its students' set of precollegiate qualities, but simply because they selected Penn.

The human-capital and signaling theories, by contrast, are value-added explanations. They ascribe the observed salary differentials to something that the institution has actually bestowed on its students—some attribute that makes them more valuable in the marketplace. But these two theories focus on different types of contributions. The human-capital argument would explain Penn's higher graduate-earnings figure by saying that Penn—through both its formal curriculum and its informal culture—provides its students with more of the skills, knowledge, attitudes, and contacts that lead to career success.

The signaling theory focuses instead on the brand value conferred by a particular college's degree—essentially, what I call "pedigree" in chapter 7. According to this explanation, employers in high-paying sectors are more likely to hire someone with a Penn credential than a City College degree, simply because of Penn's perceived superior brand value. And graduate and professional schools are more likely to admit an applicant from Penn than one from City College, again for just that reason.

For the purpose of evaluating and comparing Penn with City College, should it matter which of these theories is correct? Some people would say no. All that counts, they would argue, is that Penn graduates make more money, so anyone who can get into Penn should go there (unless, of course, they could get into Harvard or Stanford). This is the implicit message of PayScale's earnings-based rankings. Others would say that it *does* matter which explanation is correct. How can we find out? And how can schools be rewarded for what they add to a graduate's earning capacity?

Self-Selection or Institutional Value Added?

There is a robust body of research literature that attempts to tease out the effects of self-selection, human-capital, and signaling theories. It is dense, complex, and—no surprise—not slam-dunk definitive. Consider the investigations that try to separate self-selection from value-added explanations. Exemplifying one side of the scholarly debate is a pair of well-respected articles by Princeton researchers Stacy Dale and Alan Krueger. They conclude that, after you control for the individual qualities of students—such as their precollege academic preparation, family incomes, and demographic profiles—the institutional differences among schools do not explain much, if any, of the observed disparities in post-graduate earnings results.[9] Illustrating the opposite view are two papers, one by Harvard economist Raj Chetty and his coauthors, and the other by Stanford economist Caroline Hoxby, that find a strong, positive association between institutional characteristics and average earnings.[10] Indeed, Chetty and his colleagues estimate that about 80 percent of the observed salary differentials are attributable to the characteristics of the undergraduate school attended, and only about 20 percent to attributes of their matriculants. Several other studies also side with the Chetty-Hoxby position.[11]

Given the sophistication of the methodology used by this latter group of authors and the comprehensiveness of their data, I believe their conclusion is more likely to be the correct one. If so, elite colleges and universities really do add value beyond the simple fact that they attract ambitious, high-achieving students. So, by this theory, if applicants want to improve their prospects to earn a substantial income, then it really does matter which school they choose to attend.

It is, of course, unlikely that any commercial enterprise would expend the resources necessary to use similar techniques to compute annual college rankings. But a somewhat simplified version is possible, as illustrated by a Brookings Institution study published in 2015. Brookings computed a value-added measure, based on the extent to which the average midcareer salaries of an institution's graduates were above or below a level predicted by a formula based on various characteristics of the school's student body and institutional wealth.[12] That calculation yielded a very intriguing list—with Caltech on top, followed by Colgate University, MIT, the Rose-Hulman

Institute of Technology, and Carleton College. The WSJ/THE and Money magazine use variations on this method to compute their earnings component (worth about 5 percent in the overall formula).

Human Capital or Signaling?

Assuming that colleges do, in fact, add value to their students' career prospects, there remains the question of whether they produce this effect by enhancing their students' job-readiness skills or simply by bestowing a valued pedigree. Research by Brad Hershbein strongly suggests that signaling brand value is a very large part of the explanation.[13] His theory is that when employers initially hire someone, they have very imperfect information about that person's capabilities, so they rely on rather crude signals, like the candidate's undergraduate GPA and the prestige of the school attended. Over time, he asserts, employers can make much more accurate assessments of one's productivity, so the strength of those signals fades.

Hershbein looked at early-career earnings of recently hired baccalaureate-degree graduates and found that their salary levels were much more strongly correlated with the relative prestige of the institution from which they graduated than with the GPA they earned. In fact, the predictive value of GPAs fell as institutional prestige rose. To those of us familiar with the rampant grade inflation at elite schools, this comes as no surprise. If I were hiring someone, I, too, would probably be much more impressed by a degree from Amherst or Penn than a 3.6 GPA. Once again, we see the dominant power of institutional prestige, and we understand why the leading rankings feel the need to capture and celebrate that attribute.

As I discuss in chapter 21, making a good living is not the only purpose for getting a college education. But most applicants and students certainly want to be successful in whatever careers they pursue. And most institutions seek to prepare them to achieve that goal. So it is fair that schools should be held accountable for how well they succeed in that endeavor. Earnings, of course, are only one indicator of career success. But in our materialistic culture, they are the dominant measure and, for the purposes of constructing ordinal rankings, probably the best one available. Furthermore, the crucial issue of college affordability, discussed in the next chapter, requires us to ask whether the cost of attendance will produce sufficient financial rewards to repay that investment.

That said, anyone who wants to evaluate colleges by their graduates' earnings should be extremely sensitive to the limitations of using that measure. As we have seen, the available sources of salary data are highly imperfect. College Scorecard's information may be comprehensive and accurate, but only for a subset of students—those who received federal aid and who started, but did not necessarily finish, at a particular school within 10 prior years. PayScale's data look only at a college's graduates but are subject to the problem of small, possibly biased, and possibly stale survey responses. Both sets of statistics reveal very wide variations in earnings by fields of study within and types of specialization across schools. None of the available data seek to reflect the enormous variation in institutional missions that most commercial rankings systematically suppress.

Most importantly, in judging colleges and universities by the career trajectories of their graduates, we must always keep in mind the essential role played by human agency. Students are not automatons who are programmed by higher-education technicians to perform certain productive tasks. They are complex packages of temperament, character, need, drive, skill, and talent, only some aspects of which are amenable to modification by their collegiate experiences. The statistical correlations that purport to link the college that students attend with their midcareer earnings conceal a vast variation in the human qualities—to say nothing of the random events—that contribute to those outcomes.

CHAPTER 20

SOCIAL
IMMOBILITY

COLLEGE RANKINGS AND THE AMERICAN DREAM

The most electrifying moment in my four years as a student at Amherst occurred on a crisp October day in 1963. President John F. Kennedy had come to help dedicate the college's new library, named for its occasional lecturer and beloved poet, Robert Frost. In that Boston-accented cadence we had come to know so well, Kennedy intoned:

> What good is a private college or university unless it's serving a great national purpose? The library being constructed today—this College itself, all of this, of course, was not done merely to give this school's graduates an advantage, an economic advantage, in the life struggle. It does do that.
>
> But in return for that, in return for the great opportunity which society gives the graduates of this and related schools, it seems to me incumbent upon this and other schools' graduates to recognize their responsibility to the public interest. Privilege is here, and with privilege goes responsibility.[1]

Kennedy's speech that day, an eloquent ode to the "cleansing" power of poetry, would be his last major address. Less than a month later, an assassin's bullet would take his life, and with it the dreams of my generation.

INCOME INEQUALITY AND HIGHER EDUCATION

Among the "responsibilities" of a privileged college, as Kennedy stated, was confronting the growing income inequality in the United States. "Although Amherst has been in the forefront of extending aid to needy and talented students," he said, "private colleges, taken as a whole, draw 50 percent of their students from the wealthiest 10 percent of our nation. And even state universities and other public institutions derive 25 percent of their students from this group."[2]

Higher Education's Responsibility to Promote the American Dream

As a descendant of Irish immigrants who had clawed their way to the top of the economic and social ladder in Yankee Boston, Kennedy knew something about the American dream: every generation should be able to achieve a higher standard of living than their parents. For almost a century prior to Kennedy's presidency, that vision was fulfilled for many in this country, thanks to the growth of well-paid jobs in manufacturing and the skilled trades. But by the 1960s, the tide was turning. The blue-collar industries that had fueled much of America's prosperity were already in decline, producing a steady exodus of high-wage, mostly unionized jobs—first to nonunion shops in southern states, and then to sweatshops in Third World countries. With it came the long, slow death of the dream for too many of Kennedy's countrymen. Among Americans born in the mid-1940s, roughly 90 percent ended up making more money than their parents. But for those born in the mid-1960s, that number would drop to 60 percent, and for those in the mid-1980s, to 50 percent.[3]

As the US economy shifted from occupations requiring

only a high-school certificate to those demanding advanced education, the burden for fulfilling the American dream came to rest more heavily on the shoulders of our nation's colleges and universities. For over a century, that obligation had been borne primarily by state-funded public universities, many of them non-selective or even open-enrollment institutions. But that was not good enough, Kennedy was saying to us in 1963. Even the most-selective institutions of higher education needed to carry their share of responsibility.

Progress and Impasse

Has higher education responded to JFK's exhortation? Yes and no. In recent years, the number of American children who attend an undergraduate institution has steadily increased, and, with it, the amount and percentage of students from lower-income families. One way to see this evolution is to compare the family income levels of those who enroll in postsecondary schools with the income levels of the general population. In 1986, the average college student came from a family that was richer than 70 percent of all American families. By 2014, that number had fallen to 50 percent.[4] In other words, over those 28 years, America's college-going population became less comparatively wealthy and more middle-class. Another way is to calculate the proportion of traditional college-age students coming from low-income families. That number grew from 12 percent in 1996 to 20 percent in 2016.[5] That's progress.

But maybe not. When one looks at where all those lower-income students go to college, it is still overwhelmingly in the lowest-selectivity tier of American higher education. As illustrated by table 9.2, elite institutions are still very much the preserve of the rich. Research by Raj Chetty and his coauthors, discussed in more detail below, provides stark confirmation of this fact.[6] At the 12 Ivy-plus universities in their sample, only about 4 percent of the students came from families in the bottom quintile (i.e., the lowest 20 percent) of the national income distribution. In fact, only about 19 percent came from the *bottom three quintiles* of that distribution, while approximately an equal proportion came from families in the *top 1 percent*. These percentages remained essentially unchanged from 2000 to 2011. At 99 "other elite" schools in their sample, shares of low- and moderate-income students actually declined slightly during that period. I don't think this is what JFK would have called progress.

In the face of this sobering—many would say depressing—reality, many observers and commentators have quite properly begun to ask selective colleges what they are doing to address the problem of economic inequality in our nation. In the balance of this chapter, I discuss the measures most commonly used to answer that question: a college's affordability to lower-income students; their share as a percentage of the student body; their odds of graduating; the amount of debt they typically incur to pay for their education; and the odds that they will be able to move up the economic ladder after graduating.

AFFORDABILITY:
THE PRICE THAT LOWER-INCOME STUDENTS PAY
Full Cost and Net Cost

What is the true cost of attendance at a given college or university, and what has the school done to make that outlay more affordable for students from economically challenged families?[7] The US Department of Education has attempted to answer those questions. It starts by calculating the full cost of attendance at each institution. This figure is the sum of its sticker-price tuition and mandatory fees, as well as its self-reported estimates for what students pay per year for room and board, books and supplies, and other living expenses. In theory, this amount

TABLE 20.1.

Total cost and average net cost of attendance, by selected family income groups (academic year 2018–2019)

College	Total cost[a]	All students	Family income $0–$30,000	Family income $30,001–$48,000
			Average net cost[b]	
Amherst	$73,966	$16,339	$6,079	$4,423
Berea	$49,854	$5,156	$5,296	$5,296
City College	$29,967	$3,397	$704	$2,947
Michigan	$30,298	$17,357	$3,166	$5,887
Notre Dame	$71,801	$30,536	$12,498	$15,609
Penn	$74,408	$24,771	$3,181	$4,833
Reed	$73,207	$32,069	$13,630	$13,123
Spelman	$52,929	$43,042	$40,517	$42,714

Source: IPEDS.

[a] Total cost of attendance for students living on campus.

[b] Total cost less the average amount of grants or scholarships per student from any source. Net cost figures include only students receiving some form of grant or scholarship. Figures for City College and Michigan are for in-state students only.

represents what a full-pay student would have to shell out to attend that school for one year. Of course, even for full-pay students, the actual cost will vary, depending on whether they live on or off campus, what kind of meal plan they select, whether they enroll in courses with especially expensive textbooks and supplies, and so on. But it's a start.

In fact, at most institutions, the majority of students don't pay anything like the full cost of attendance, because they receive various forms of grants and scholarships. Here is where affordability calculations get especially convoluted. The DOE tries to capture that complexity by calculating the average net cost of attendance for various categories of students. For example, its IPEDS database reports net-cost figures for those who receive any sort of grant or scholarship (both need-based and merit-based) from any source (governmental or institutional). It also separately computes net-cost figures for various family-income categories. As an illustration, table 20.1 presents academic year 2019 data on our eight profile schools, showing the total cost of attendance, average net cost for all students receiving financial aid, and average net cost for subsets of those students coming from lower-income families.

As you can readily see, the average student receiving financial aid at all of these schools paid a great deal less than the nominal full cost. And, generally, those with the lowest incomes paid even less, as one would hope and expect. The lowest net-cost figures belong to the institutions with the greatest wealth, like Amherst and Penn, and those with the lowest tuitions, like Berea, City College, and Michigan. But remember that the City College and Michigan figures are for in-state students only. An out-of-state student at Michigan, facing a nominal $49,350 tuition price, surely paid much more than the $15,262 charge confronting an in-state student (see table 10.1).

Ranking Colleges by Net Cost of Attendance

Several publications have incorporated IPEDS data on the net cost of attendance into their formulas. Prominently, Money magazine, which seeks to highlight schools that offer good value, bases fully one-third of its overall ranking on affordability measures.[8] Of that component, roughly half comes from the net price of attendance for all grant-receiving students, with a separate calculation for the net price paid by those from low-income families. Similarly, Washington Monthly gives some weight to the average net price paid by students with family incomes below $75,000.

Money magazine and Washington Monthly deserve credit for directly addressing the affordability issue, especially insofar as they focus on net costs for less wealthy students. Measuring affordability by the net cost for *all* grant and scholarship recipients, however, is more problematic, because it does not distinguish between poorer students who are receiving need-based assistance and more-prosperous students who are receiving merit aid. As I discussed in chapter 13, many colleges and universities have been throwing money at wealthy students in an effort to maximize reportable student SAT scores—often diverting funds from needier students. A ranking based on the total dollar amount of grants awarded—both need based and merit based—does nothing to discourage this tactic.

A further caveat is that the IPEDS net-cost figures, by themselves, don't tell you what proportion of a school's total enrollment receives tuition assistance. Should we give more credit to a school that gives 5 percent of its students a free ride (and charges everyone else the full cost), or a school that provides a half-price discount to 50 percent of its students? In fact, in our sample, the proportion of students who receive aid ranges widely, from Berea's 100 percent and Spelman's 82 percent down to Penn's and Reed's 52 percent. For these reasons, affordability rankings typically, and appropriately, combine data on an institution's net cost and its proportion of lower-income students, a topic that I now address.

RANKING BY PROPORTION
OF LOWER-INCOME STUDENTS
Pell Share as a Measure of Socioeconomic Diversity

A common way to calculate the proportion of a school's student population that is financially needy is to look at how many of those students receive, or are at least eligible for, federal Pell grants. This statistic, usually called "Pell share," is readily available from the IPEDS database and prominently

TABLE 20.2.

Pell shares and average Pell grant (academic year 2019–2020)

College	Pell share (%)[a]	Average Pell grant
Amherst	24	$4,777
Berea	82	$5,303
City College	56	$5,082
Michigan	17	$4,903
Notre Dame	9	$4,709
Penn	13	$4,823
Reed	13	$4,778
Spelman	47	$5,359

Source: IPEDS.

[a] Students receiving Pell grants as a percentage of total undergraduate enrollment.

reported on College Scorecard. The Pell program provides direct tuition support to students who meet certain family-income standards. For 2020-2021, the maximum Pell grant was $6,345, awarded to a student whose parents were sufficiently poor that their expected family contribution (EFC) to the cost of their child's college attendance was zero. The smallest Pell grant was $895, going to a recipient whose EFC was around $5,400. There is no absolute income limit for Pell eligibility, since EFC is a function not only of family income, but also family size and expenses (including other children's educational costs).

Since its creation in 1978, the Pell program has had its ups and downs, or, rather, its downs and ups. In inflation-adjusted dollars, the monetary amount of Pell grants declined steadily from 1978 to 1993 and then increased from 1993 to 2021.[9] By 2021, the maximum Pell grant had recovered to its 1978 level. The problem is, however, that the cost of attending college has grown more than twice as fast as the general cost of living. For that reason, Pell grants today contribute a much smaller percentage of the costs that recipients actually face. For public four-year institutions, the maximum Pell grant today covers only about 28 percent of the charges for in-state students, while for private nonprofits, the proportion is a mere 12 percent.

Still, what matters for our purposes here is the utility of Pell share as a measure of an institution's concern about social mobility. Table 20.2 displays the Pell shares at our eight profile schools in academic year 2020. As one would expect, given its mission to serve poor children from Appalachia, Berea had by far the largest Pell share, with City College and Spelman also reporting impressive numbers. By contrast, the most highly selective institutions, such as Notre Dame and Penn, had the lowest shares. It's also revealing that Berea, City College, and Spelman reported the highest average grant per student, signifying the relatively greater poverty levels of their Pell populations.

Amherst's figure of 24 percent, the highest among the elite schools in our sample, is no accident. After I returned to Amherst as a trustee in 1998, the college, under the leadership of its new president, Tony Marx, committed itself to increasing the socioeconomic diversity of its student body. The college dramatically expanded its search for talented students from low-income families and enhanced the attractiveness of its financial-aid packages to lowest-income students by substituting outright grants for loan obligations. As a consequence, Amherst was able to increase its Pell share from about 12 percent to over 20 percent, an achievement that earned Marx national acclaim, as well as admiration and, frankly, envy among many of his peers.

Pell Share Skepticism

Nonetheless, the use of Pell data to measure a school's commitment to socioeconomic diversity has come in for some criticism. In a 2017 Brookings report, Jason Delisle argued that roughly a third of Pell recipients were not truly poor, but "middle income," in the sense that they fell near the median earnings level for American families.[10] He also claimed that for various reasons, roughly 30 percent of truly low-income students didn't receive—or even apply for—Pell grants. As a consequence, he said, a school's Pell percentage is not a good indicator of the true extent to which it is serving the poor. And variations in the range of Pell recipients' income levels make interschool comparisons suspect.

The research findings of Raj Chetty and his colleagues add some fuel to the Pell skepticism fire. As they pointed out, while Ivy-Plus universities increased their Pell shares from an average 12.1 percent to 16.8 percent between 2000 and 2011, that entire upswing could be attributed to congressional expansion of the income-based eligibility criteria. Another, somewhat more damning criticism is that many schools, under pressure to raise their Pell numbers, have gamed the system by admitting lots of middle-class students with family incomes just below the Pell cutoff and very few students with incomes slightly above it.[11]

Still, for all this grumbling, it seems to me that reporting Pell share is a very serviceable way of highlighting an institution's commitment to socioeconomic progress. Notwithstanding the assertions by Delisle and by Chetty and his colleagues, data from the College Board show that, for academic year 2015–2016, 58 percent of Pell recipients had family incomes below $30,000, and, for another 16 percent, between $30,000 and $40,000.[12] Yes, 14 percent had family incomes above $50,000, but they presumably qualified only because of their parents' sizable household expenditures.

Pell Recipient Graduation Rates
One must remember, of course, that Pell share only measures input, not outcomes. The fact that a school enrolls a significant

number of Pell recipients, by itself, tells us nothing about the quality of those students' experiences there and the extent to which that institution prepares them for a better life. As Anthony Jack chronicles in his acclaimed recent book, *The Privileged Poor*, students from disadvantaged backgrounds encounter enormous obstacles when thrust into a competitive higher-education environment.[13] And the drawbacks are even greater for what he calls the "non-privileged poor"—those who have none of the academic advantages of the "privileged poor," such as attendance at a private school or participation in college-preparatory programs.

One fairly basic way to evaluate how well a college supports its poorer students—whether privileged or not—is to compare the graduation rates of Pell students with non-Pell students. This is another statistic readily available from IPEDS and College Scorecard. Nationwide, there is a fairly sizable gap of about 9 percentage points between Pell and non-Pell graduation rates. Some elite schools have managed to shrink that gap. For example, at Anthony Jack's alma mater, Amherst College, the difference in six-year graduation rates in 2020 was about 4 percentage points (91 vs. 95), and at Notre Dame, the gap was only 2 points (95 vs. 97). But, in comparing Notre Dame's and Amherst's performances by this measure, one must keep in mind that only 9 percent of Notre Dame's students were receiving Pell grants, in contrast with Amherst's 24 percent.

Many people believe that selective schools can achieve a high Pell share only by admitting more students from less educationally privileged backgrounds, who, in turn, are more likely to struggle academically and thus less likely to finish on time. This attempt to be more inclusive could thus jeopardize a school's position in rankings that rely heavily on overall graduation rates. To account for this variation, several publications, led by Washington Monthly, have developed social-mobility measures that combined Pell shares with Pell graduation rates.

U.S. News ignored social mobility altogether until 2018, when it rather proudly proclaimed that it had modified its formula to include a measure based on Pell shares and the graduation rates of Pell recipients. This new component, however, counted for only 5 percent of a school's overall rating, prompting one commentator to dismiss the move as a "faux embrace" of social mobility.[14] This observer noted that Princeton remained at the top of the magazine's 2018 national universities category, notwithstanding the fact that 72 percent of its students came from the top quintile of family incomes and only 2 percent from the bottom quintile.

Nonetheless—and to its credit—U.S. News has tried to highlight social mobility by publishing a separate listing based on this criterion, using its Pell-related calculations.[15] In its 2021 edition, three University of California campuses (Irvine, Riverside, and Santa Cruz) as well as Rutgers University–Newark topped the roster of national universities. Among national liberal arts colleges, the College of Idaho, Lake Forest, Thomas Aquinas, and Spelman led the pack. Most of the winners in this particular contest are schools that admit high proportions of Pell students and manage to graduate them at rates nearly equivalent to those of their non-Pell students. The usual best-college chart-toppers—with their typically higher graduation rates but much lower Pell shares—are scattered far down the list.

RANKING BY STUDENT-LOAN DEBT

The alarming escalation of indebtedness incurred by college students and their families has propelled the issue of student loans to the foreground of political discourse in recent years. Not surprisingly, it also receives growing attention in measures of college affordability. The indicator of student debt most commonly used for this purpose is the average total amount of federally guaranteed loans incurred by a school's students between their matriculation and the time of their graduation or withdrawal. One can readily obtain such figures from College Scorecard and the IPEDS database. An alternative way to measure student indebtedness is to look at data on repayment rates. College Scorecard reports percentages of former students who, having entered the period of mandatory repayment, fall into its various categories, such as "paid in full," "deferment," "not making progress," or "defaulted." The most commonly used of these figures is the default rate.

IPEDS and College Scorecard data include just *federal* loans incurred by *the students themselves* (not their parents). Since only relatively lower-income students qualify for such loans, those measures do provide a reasonably good indicator of how well colleges and universities are serving that population. Nonetheless, those figures do not tell us how much the *parents* of such students are also borrowing to help support their children. Such indebtedness—often at much higher interest rates than federal student loans—can weigh heavily on families. And the prospect of having to take out large loans can surely lead some parents to discourage their children from attending certain high-cost colleges. In 2020, the DOE began to fill that information gap by releasing information about parental debt obtained through a federal loan program called "Parent PLUS."[16] Reliable information about private borrowing from banks and credit unions, however, is much harder to obtain.

Measures of student-debt loads, using federal data, have been creeping into the college rankings in recent years. Again, Money stands out, giving a 17 percent weight to various measures of federal student loans and Parent PLUS borrowing. It also features average student debt prominently on its online table. WSJ/THE has, for several years, assigned a 7 percent weight to an average debt figure. Washington Monthly, by contrast, utilizes a loan-repayment rate—both the actual rate and a performance number, which adjusts that rate for various characteristics of the student body and the institution.

In its 2021 issue, U.S. News finally joined the party by adding a student-debt measure to its formula. Its debt-load factor combined two variables: the median amount of federal student-loan borrowing by a school's graduates in the class of 2019 (worth a 3 percent weight), and the proportion of its total 2019 graduating class that had taken out such loans (a 2 percent weight). For each of those variables, the lower the number, the higher the score awarded to the school. In its methodology statement, the magazine explains that it seeks to reward institutions that minimize the aggregate debt burden borne by their graduates. A commendable ambition, to be sure. But there is a big problem with the U.S. News measure.

To see why, consider how a rich, elite school could score well on that metric. Admit mostly wealthy students who can pay their own way—thus not qualifying for, nor needing, federal loans—and then award very generous financial-aid grants to the few low-income students that you do admit. Sure enough, among national universities, Princeton came in 2nd on the U.S. News debt index, and Harvard, 3rd. According to the mobility-rate study discussed in the next section of this chapter, both schools enrolled negligible numbers of truly poor students but gave substantial fiscal assistance to them.

I would much prefer to see a debt measure that encourages wealthy schools to enroll larger numbers of low-income students and *then* help them graduate with low average debt loads. Among our profile schools, Berea is the perfect example.

INTERGENERATIONAL MOBILITY MEASURES

Affordability, Pell share, and debt-load measures provide, at best, a rough indication of how effectively each individual institution is assisting low-income students to achieve the American dream. A theoretically superior method would be to see whether, and how well, a school actually helps its students move up the economic ladder from the rung occupied by their parents. A couple of popular rankings use methodologies loosely based on this idea. For example, Washington Monthly's social mobility metric combines not only net cost, Pell share, and Pell graduation-rate data, but also the proportion of first-generation students, average earnings 10 years after graduation, and student-loan repayment. It then uses this formula to report regional "best bang for the buck" standings. Not surprisingly, by this measure, Berea College came in 1st in its region in the 2020 edition.

An outfit called CollegeNET computes a social mobility index (SMI), based on a mysterious algorithm that combines variables such as tuition, the percentage of students with incomes below the US median, graduation rates, endowment, and average earnings five years after graduation.[17] The five schools that received the highest scores in its 2020 SMI index included City College of New York–Baruch College and four California State campuses. All but two of the top 100 were public institutions. Of our profile schools, City College received a ranking of 24th. Spelman came in at 329th and Berea at 379th. The remaining five trailed far behind.

Mobility-Rate Scorecards

Probably the most ambitious—and transparent—effort at measuring how well higher educational institutions promote intergenerational mobility comes from Raj Chetty and his colleagues at Opportunity Insight. Using anonymized income information from the Internal Revenue Service, Chetty's team analyzed the impact of college attendance on the intergenerational economic mobility of every American born from 1980 to

1982.[18] By determining which school each member of that cohort went to, the researchers were able to compute income-mobility averages for over 2,000 identifiable institutions.

Their test for mobility compared the income earned by a person's parents at the time their child first enrolled in college (typically between 1997 and 2000) with the salary that student later earned in 2014 (i.e., roughly 10 years after completing college). The research team produced several different measures of mobility. The metric featured in most of their published results was what they sometimes called "Q1 to Q5 mobility"—that is, the percentage of students from families in the bottom quintile (Q1) of incomes who, 10 years post college, were earning incomes in the top quintile (Q5). Yet another, even more dramatic measure—which they called "upper-tail mobility"—computed the percentage of students from bottom-quintile families who ended up in the top 1 percent of the income distribution.

An interactive summary of their data that appeared in the *New York Times* displayed a somewhat different calculation: movement from the bottom two quintiles (Q1 or Q2) of family incomes to the top two quintiles (Q4 or Q5).[19] This measure seems to me to capture a broader picture of social mobility than the rags-to-riches versions discussed above. For that reason, I have utilized it to present mobility-rate data for our profile schools in table 20.3. (The table shows results for only seven of the eight schools because there apparently was insufficient information for Berea College.)

Using data such as those displayed on the first two columns of table 20.3, Chetty and his team computed a mobility rate (MR) for every institution in their sample. The mobility rate is the product of what the team called "access" (the percentage of a school's students who came from lower-income families), and "success rate" (the percentage of those students coming

TABLE 20.3.

Intergenerational mobility (for the 1980–1982 birth cohort)

College	Bottom 40% family income[a]	From bottom 40% to top 40%[b]	Mobility rate[c]
Amherst	10.2	71.1	7.3
Berea	N/A	N/A	N/A
City College	60.5	62.9	38.1
Michigan	8.1	69.5	5.6
Notre Dame	4.9	74.7	3.7
Penn	9.0	75.1	6.8
Reed	14.6	44.7	6.5
Spelman	25.2	58.5	14.7

Source: Chetty et al. (2017), accessed in Upshot (2017).

Note: Data reported for students who attended college in roughly 1997–2002.

N/A = not available.

[a] Percentage of enrolled students from families with incomes in the bottom 40 percent of the national income distribution at the time of college attendance.

[b] Percentage of students from families with incomes in the bottom 40 percent whose personal earnings in 2014 (at age 32–34) were in the top 40 percent of the national income distribution.

[c] Product of the previous two variables.

from lower-income families who ended up with higher-level salaries). The theory behind the MR measure echoes the sentiment I expressed at the end of the previous section of this chapter: colleges and universities should get the most credit for enrolling large shares of lower-income students *and* educating them in such a way that they can move up the economic ladder. That's why City College ends up looking so impressive among our profile schools. By contrast, the elite private institutions (exemplified by Notre Dame and Penn) get much lower marks. They are very successful at moving their low-income students into the top-income echelons, but they enroll and graduate so few of them.

The Chetty team's mobility rates seemingly provide a basis for ranking schools. And what happens when we do that? Arraying institutions in this way turns the prevailing prestige-based system on its head. By this measure, the top five schools, as reported by the *New York Times*, were Vaughn College of Aeronautics and Technology, City College of New York, Texas A&M International, CUNY's Lehman College, and CUNY's Bernard M. Baruch College. Among our profile schools, Spelman was ranked 369th; Amherst, 1,853rd; Penn, 1,918th; Reed, 1,959th; Michigan, 2,086th; and Notre Dame, 2,190th. These are not numbers that you are likely to see on their websites.

How Elite Colleges Could Increase Intergenerational Mobility

In a version of their research published in 2020, Chetty and his coauthors asked an intriguing and important question: what could the elite colleges do to improve their contribution to intergenerational mobility?[20] To answer that query, they conducted a kind of thought experiment. Actually, two thought experiments. First, what if those schools made *all* their admissions decisions solely on the basis of academic ability, with no advantage given to applicants with high family incomes? Second, what if they gave an admissions advantage to applicants from low-income families?

Chetty's team found that admitting students solely on the basis of academic potential would have the effect of modestly increasing the number of high-achieving poor students at selective schools—and, of course, commensurately reducing the number of rich ones. At schools classified by the authors in the middle-to-upper tiers of institutional selectivity, the numbers of low-income students would increase from about 7 percent of the student populations to nearly 9 percent. By contrast, at the very top tier of selectivity—the Ivy-plus schools—the proportion of students from families with incomes in the bottom quintile would barely budge. This suggested to the authors that these institutions were already admitting most of the available lowest-income applicants who met their elevated academic standards. But, significantly, in the Ivy-plus tier, there would be a large increase (from 28 to 38 percent) of applicants admitted from the second, third, and fourth family-income quintiles. In other words, an admissions strategy that looked at academic ability only, without regard to family wealth, would help restore the "missing middle class" to the elite schools.

The Chetty team's second thought experiment was to look at what would happen if elite institutions engaged in affirmative action for the poor. They operationalized this option by assuming that all applicants in the bottom quintile of income levels would be given an admissions boost equivalent to an extra 160 points on their combined SAT scores. The researchers chose this amount to be comparable to the boost typically given in other affirmative-action admissions programs—for example, those that favor certain recruited athletes, students of color, or children of alumni and donor prospects. Doing this, they concluded, would achieve an even larger impact on intergenerational mobility, however defined.

Over the past two generations, governmental agencies like the US Department of Education and researchers such as Raj Chetty and his colleagues have increasingly focused public attention on the extent to which selective institutions of higher education have responded to the glaring income inequalities that plague our society. They have fashioned multiple criteria—for example, the net cost of attendance, Pell share, Pell graduation rate, student-debt loads, and mobility scores—to judge the performances of individual schools. While each of these measures has its limitations, together they represent a salutary attempt to respond to President Kennedy's exhortation back in 1963.

And as we have also seen, the college rankings industry—including its dominant member, U.S. News—has slowly and fitfully responded by incorporating such metrics into their best-college formulas. But these organizations still give much more weight to measures that reward student selectivity, high levels of spending, and the accumulation of wealth than they accord to factors that reward schools for serving low-income students. In such a system, educational institutions know that they will pay, not only in dollars, but also in their ranking position, if they admit too many poor students. A college or university that enrolls more students from truly low-income families must substantially increase its financial-aid expenditures, most likely diverting resources from activities that could have helped that school improve its standing—such as reducing its student/faculty ratio, increasing the proportion of small classes, raising faculty salaries, or offering merit aid to wealthy students with high SAT scores. Moreover, to the extent that increasing the enrollment of poor students entails reducing the number of wealthy students, colleges could well experience a net loss of charitable giving from rich parents and alumni. This, in turn, could cause them to decrease their spending per student, a figure that also weighs heavily in most rankings.

If Kennedy were alive today, he would undoubtedly repeat his appeal to members of the higher-education establishment to match their responsibilities with their privilege. He might even applaud the tentative steps taken by the rankocrats to include measures of intergenerational mobility in their formulas. And he could concede that some progress has been made. But much more remains to be done.

CHAPTER 21

MAKING A LIFE

THE ART OF BEING HUMAN

In 2005, I published an essay entitled "Knowledge for Its Own Sake" in a volume edited by Lloyd Thacker.[1] As you may recall from chapter 5, Thacker was the rabble-rouser who, in 2007, tried to organize a boycott of the U.S. News peer-reputation survey. Like his boycott proposal, his book was a plea to restore some semblance of sanity and integrity to the frenzied world of rankings-polluted college admissions.

As the title of my essay suggests, I was making an argument that education is a process of "self-realization, through the cultivation, cherishing, and love of knowledge." I conceded that most people view education primarily in instrumental terms: as a means to achieve wealth, power, or prestige. But I expressed the hope that at least some of my readers would agree that "a life truly worth living is a life of inquiry and discovery—a life of pursuing knowledge for its own sake."[2]

The argument that higher education prepares one for making a life, not just making a living, is often repeated by educators, even though it so often falls on deaf ears. Christopher Nelson, former president of St. John's College, Annapolis, once said: "Measuring the value of an education in monetary terms fundamentally mischaracterizes the nature of higher education. The highest learning is no more a commodity than one's life is a commodity."[3] One might dismiss such a comment, coming as it did from the president of a "great books" college, but a similar sentiment was publicly expressed by Drew Faust while she was president of Harvard.[4] Likewise, Yale professor Anthony Kronman has written that higher education should foster the ideal that "there is an art to being human."[5]

Nice sentiments, most people might respond, but how would you measure them? After all, you can't have an ordinal listing without . . . ordinals!

Enter the murky world of attempts to quantify the noneconomic outcomes of higher education. Some of those metrics focus on the quality (rather than just the financial rewards) of post-graduate careers; some on various other indicators of professional success; and some on general well-being.

QUALITY OF JOB EXPERIENCES

PayScale asks its survey respondents whether their work "makes the world a better place" and reports the percentage of each institution's graduates that answer in the affirmative. Guess what? In its 2020–2021 edition, PayScale's top school by this measure was Bennett College, a financially struggling, historically Black, all-women's college in Greensboro, North Carolina. Among Bennett's graduates, 97 percent gave a positive reply. Almost all of the schools that received high scores on this criterion were either small religious colleges or health care schools, most of which are completely invisible to casual readers of college rankings.

By comparison, less than half of the graduates of the highest salary–producing institutions reported that their jobs made the world a better place. Among our eight profile schools, those whose graduates reported the highest levels of job satisfaction by this measure were Berea (57 percent), City College (57 percent), and Spelman (54 percent). Those with the lowest levels were Michigan (45 percent), Notre Dame (43 percent), and Penn (41 percent). The other revealing, though not surprising, finding was that graduates with only a baccalaureate degree reported lower levels of job satisfaction than those with an advanced degree (by an average of about 4 to 5 percentage points). So, if you want a job that will contribute to making the world a better place, go to City College or Berea—or a small religious or health care school—and then get a graduate degree!

Beginning in 2014, a collaboration among Gallup, the Lumina Foundation, and Purdue University has periodically published Gallup-Purdue Indexes that attempt to measure "the most important outcomes of higher education."[6] One of the outcome measures focuses on the degree to which college graduates experience "engagement" with their work. The 2014 index, based on interviews with some 30,000 graduates, rather depressingly found that only 39 percent found their work to be fulfilling.[7] Those who did report high levels of job satisfaction tended to give more-affirmative answers to questions about whether the institution they attended "prepared me well for life outside college," whether the school was "passionate about the long-term success of its students," or whether the respondent had a mentor or professor who cared about that person's "learning and success."

To date, almost none of the popular rankings have made any attempt to judge colleges by the quality of their graduates' career experiences. At one time, Money magazine used PayScale's "make the world a better place" percentage as a very small factor in its formula. But it dropped that criterion in its 2020 listings, conjecturing that schools can't be held responsible for the perceived social impact of their graduates' employment experiences. Really? If we can give institutions credit for the amount of money their graduates earn, it's not clear why we can't also give them credit for the amount of satisfaction their graduates receive from their work. But it *is* "Money" magazine, after all. U.S. News has never attempted to evaluate colleges by the degree to which they prepare their alumni for fulfilling careers. Significantly—and not surprisingly—a 2015 Gallup-Purdue survey found very little correlation between the position occupied by a school in the U.S. News rankings and its graduates' self-reported job satisfaction.[8]

PUBLIC AND COMMUNITY SERVICE

Most selective institutions of higher education today boast about their commitment to public service. They do this not only as partial justification for their tax exemptions or public subsidies, but also as a way to encourage their students to consider careers in the public and not-for-profit sectors. I don't question the sincerity of those exhortations. But, truth be told, so long as their rankings depend primarily on their wealth—including the earnings of their graduates—the competitive schools don't want *too many* of their alumni to go into less remunerative careers.

Among the publishers of popular collegiate ratings, Washington Monthly is the only one that has made a significant gesture in the direction of recognizing schools' contributions to public service. As in previous years, its 2021 edition devoted fully a third of its formula to criteria that attempt to measure the extent to which a college or university is engaged in "community and national service." To calculate this factor, it used a grab bag of measures, including the proportion of the student body enrolled in ROTC (Reserve Officer Training Corps) programs, the percentage of alumni serving in the Peace Corps, the share of federal work-study grant money spent on student community service projects, the amount of institutional support for students engaged in national service projects, and the degree of encouragement for electoral participation by students.

For most schools, the relative score awarded by Washington Monthly for public service deviated sharply from their overall score. For example, in our profile group, Penn received an overall ranking of 7th among national universities, but a service rating of only 130th. Conversely, Reed was 78th overall among liberal arts colleges, but 30th in service. Given the quirky choice of variables in Washington Monthly's service assessments, it's really hard to know how to interpret their results. But give the journal credit for at least making an effort to reward colleges and universities for their contributions to the common good, rather than just their accumulation of wealth and prestige.

CAREER ACHIEVEMENTS

Another approach to ranking institutions on nonpecuniary outcome measures is to focus on various kinds of praiseworthy career distinctions achieved by their graduates. This method makes a cameo appearance in a few of the popular publications. For example, in its 2020 formula, Forbes assigned a 15 percent weight to the proportion of a school's graduates that appear on the magazine's proprietary "American Leaders List." This methodology echoes an early ranking, mentioned in chapter 2, that graded institutions by the number of their graduates appearing in *Who's Who in America*.

Washington Monthly's approach is different. In addition to using the proportion of a school's graduates in the military and the Peace Corps as part of its "public-service" measure, it assigns some weight to the proportion of graduates who go on to obtain a doctoral degree as part of its research measure. Its PhD productivity measure was dear to my heart while I was president of Reed—proving that I was not averse to celebrating *some* rankings! According to data reported by the National Science Foundation, Reed always appeared among the top three or four undergraduate institutions when judged by the percentage of their students who obtain a doctoral degree within nine years of graduation.[9] This was, I used to say, an excellent proxy for Reed's intense focus on intellectual pursuits and attainment, and it set us apart from many schools that seemed more intent on feeding Wall Street than academia. Still, I had to concede that only about a fifth of our graduates earned PhDs. What about the rest? Well, they were scattered in dozens of professions and occupations. Were they somehow more socially valuable than the graduates of Amherst or Penn? The only quantitative—or even plausibly objective—measure we had was salary. And the salary data said no.

WELL-BEING AND QUALITY OF LIFE

If, as Anthony Kronman argues, higher education is truly designed to prepare people for the "all-embracing work of being human,"[10] is there evidence that going to college is good for the body and the soul? Yes, there is, but, as always in the empirical literature, the picture is muddy. In their survey of research findings, Mathew Mayhew and his colleagues devote an entire chapter to "quality of life after college."[11] Although research on the correlation between college attendance and subsequent "life satisfaction" (or happiness) was "inconclusive," they report clear evidence that college attendance was associated with better health status, increases in the welfare of one's children, and a higher level of political engagement.

In its 2014 index, Gallup-Purdue surveyed the respondents on five dimensions of well-being: sense of purpose, financial success, social engagement, community service, and physical health.[12] Although roughly half of those who replied said they were "thriving" in at least one of those categories, only 11 percent reported thriving in all five. As one would expect, job satisfaction strongly correlated with these various measures of contentment with one's life. Once again, those who indicated the highest levels of thriving also reported attending a school that provided strong mentoring and teaching, as well as career guidance.

Could colleges be ranked on the basis of similar measures of their graduates' well-being? In theory, anything is possible. Organizations like Gallup that already conduct periodic surveys of college graduates could compute, and compare, an average well-being score for the graduates of each institution attended. Or some college rankers—such as the WSJ/THE, Niche, or the Princeton Review—that already conduct large-scale surveys, could perhaps expand them to gather data on the participants' sense of well-being.

A more difficult question is whether it's appropriate to give schools credit (or blame) for the relative well-being of their graduates. Many people—Money magazine's staff surely among them—would dismiss such an idea out of hand. They might argue that well-being, however measured, is the product of far too many factors: genetic inheritance, family upbringing, physical environment, intimate relationships, social networks, personal habits, work history, and so on.

I suspect that this view explains why none of the comprehensive rankings have tried to enter this forbidding territory. But I dearly wish that someone would try. Higher education can be a powerful experience—for many, a four-year immersion in a distinctive culture and community, taking place at a transformative period in one's development as a human being. Students often form a lifelong association with the school they attend, providing a source of continuing bonds of friendship and a marker of professional and social recognition. While this period of one's life may not necessarily be, in author Paul Tough's phrase, "the years that matter most,"[13] it is certainly very consequential. Further, as the Gallup-Purdue surveys have shown, there is a strong correlation between the quality of the mentoring students received in college and their subsequent well-being.

So, those of us who believe that higher education is a preparation for a genuinely fulfilling life can only hope that someone, someday, will attempt to measure that connection more rigorously. And maybe somebody, at some point, will actually try to rank colleges accordingly. Washington Monthly shows us that using measures of public service can shake up the usual prestige-based hierarchy. I strongly suspect that judging schools by their contribution to quality of life would do the same. As I have tried to demonstrate throughout this book—an argument I will summarize in the final chapter—the long-term health of my chosen profession would be well served by shaking up the prestige-based order of things.

BREAKING THE RANKOCRACY'S GRIP

College rankings have become a fixture of America's higher educational landscape. They have withstood decades of dismissive commentary. Perhaps no amount of additional criticism, even a book-length critique like this, will change that.

The main reason they have assumed this place, especially in the selective portion of higher education, is that they serve as a powerful enabler of the sector's hypercompetitive culture. Why has higher education become so competitive? Some economists point to the declining costs of obtaining information about colleges and universities and the diminishing price of transportation to attend more-distant schools. As a result, they argue, colleges that used to compete for students with only a handful of regional institutions must now contend with hundreds of rivals all across the nation, and even the world.[1] Others assert that the shift in the American economy, from manufacturing-based to knowledge-based industries, has heightened the demand for college degrees—especially from the most selective institutions.[1] Still others point to a change in public attitudes. Postsecondary education was once viewed primarily as a "public good"—a means of fostering collective welfare through economic growth, social mobility, and democratic participation. Now, however, it is increasingly viewed as a private good—a passport to personal wealth and influence.

These factors are surely part of the explanation for the increasing competitiveness of higher education. But I don't think they fully account for its intensity. As I argued in chapter 7, even in supposedly post-aristocratic America, many people retain an unquenchable thirst for pedigree. The triumph of the meritocratic myth sends an unfortunate message that those who get admitted to, and graduate from, the top schools have superior worth and are therefore accorded the highest social status. The winners in this particular sport are the dukes and earls; the losers are the commoners.

So long as higher educational institutions are engaged in hand-to-hand combat, someone will step in to write the rule book for that combat, serve as the referee, and declare winners and losers. Hence the emergence of U.S. News and a succession of copycats and would-be competitors.

THE PERILS OF A RANKOCRACY

As I have documented throughout this book, since the publication of the first U.S. News best-college edition in 1983, the ranking industry has gradually become an unofficial ruling body—a rankocracy. In the process, it has quietly transformed higher education. Perfectly honorable educators have turned repeatedly to unseemly gaming strategies, including outright falsification, in a—usually hopeless—scramble to climb the ladder or to avoid getting knocked down several rungs. Comprehensive ratings have punished schools that try to maintain distinctive niches and missions, pressuring them relentlessly into a mind-dulling homogeneity or dumping them into a low-ranked purgatory.

The struggle to reach the top of the pecking order has

reinforced competitive tendencies to privilege SAT scores in college admissions, often at the expense of rewarding hard work and creativity or of promoting social mobility and ethnic diversity. Rankings-fueled competition to maximize per-student spending has pressured colleges and universities to favor the admission—and even subsidize the attendance—of wealthy early-decision applicants, children of alumni, and children of former and prospective major donors. Meanwhile, these ordinal listings have, in too many cases, pushed issues of educational practice, pedagogy, and student learning to the back burner and contributed to outcomes such as grade inflation and the withering of the humanities.

All this might well have happened in the absence of college rankings. After all, those publications didn't create the underlying conditions that feed higher education's competitive frenzy. They did not convert self-contained local and regional postsecondary markets into nationwide free-for-alls. They did not transform the US economy from one based on physical work to one based on mental labor. They did not alter political attitudes about government's responsibility for the education of its citizens. They did not create the classist yearning for prestige and pedigree.

But they did exacerbate all of these phenomena. By constructing comprehensive, one-size-fits-all formulas, they lumped together groups of widely divergent institutions into one competitive, undifferentiated mass. They gave privileged visibility to elite schools that prepare students for the highest-paying, but often least-fulfilling, careers. By building their assessment criteria around the perpetuation of wealth and privilege, they reinforced the idea that education serves primarily personal interests, rather than the collective welfare. And by trumpeting overall lists of "best colleges," they quenched the pedigree-seekers' thirst for status-signifying labels. In short, I cannot imagine that higher education would be afflicted with such intense competitive fever without college rankings.

THE EVOLUTION OF RANKINGS: SIGNS OF PROGRESS

Despite this litany of unfortunate consequences, it's important to recognize how the world of college rankings has evolved since U.S. News staked out its claim back in 1983. Some of the changes represent genuine progress. First, the number of publications has increased, reducing at least somewhat the monopolistic power exercised by U.S. News and diversifying the range of measures used to evaluate schools. At one time, the cost of entry into this business was sufficiently high to discourage competitors from challenging the hegemony of U.S. News. They had to replicate what it had done to gain its first-mover advantage—develop a formula, replete with quantitative variables and weightings; prepare and circulate detailed questionnaires to thousands of educators and convince them that it was worth their while to fill them out; collect and record their responses; plug the data into the formula and crank out scores; and publish the results in widely available magazines or booklets.

Now, anyone with a computer can harvest information from the US Department of Education's database or from the Common Data Set, manipulate those statistics according to an algorithm of one's own design, produce a ranking, and publish it on the web. Not a trivial undertaking, to be sure, but much less costly than it was back in the 1980s or 1990s. This has made the emergence of several alternatives possible, as well as a host of more-specialized listings. Today, one can readily find interschool comparisons based on criteria such as affordability, social mobility, diversity, revealed preference, research output, career earnings, and teaching quality. Likewise, one can find ratings for separate sectors of higher education, such as women's colleges, HBCUs, Catholic schools, work colleges, military academies, engineering schools, colleges in Ohio or Oklahoma or Oregon.

Second, the shift from publishing in hard-copy format to providing access on the web has unleashed a flood of additional information beyond mere numerical orderings. Most internet-based listings offer detailed descriptive profiles of the institutions, along with helpful links to their websites and other resources. Many publish periodic how-to articles for the frenzied college applicant. In addition, several permit their readers to re-rank colleges according to criteria or weightings of their choice. For example, students who sign up (for a fee) for the U.S. News "College Compass" feature can take a stab at compiling a list of schools that reflect their preferences and profiles. The WSJ/THE permits its online readers to adjust the weightings to be given to each of its four overall performance measures. In 2021, if you wanted to assess colleges entirely by "resources" (i.e., essentially, wealth), Caltech popped up at the top of the list. If you chose to order them solely by "environment," La Sierra University was number one. You are still stuck with the WSJ/THE's choice of subsidiary factors, measures, and weights, but you at least have some opportunity to put the stamp of your own personality and interests on the process.

THE EVOLUTION OF RANKINGS:
SIGNS OF STASIS AND REGRESSION

So, yes, there have been positive developments in college rankings over the past four decades. Undeniably so. But two things haven't changed. First, as the one-time monopolist and first mover, U.S. News continues to exert a disproportionate influence on the world of higher education. It has many competitors but still no genuine rivals. Early indications that national weekly magazines like *Time* and *Newsweek* might enter the fray dissipated, as they turned to publishing college guides instead.[2] The *New York Times* occasionally issues one-off comparisons of colleges, according to a single criterion. But the *Times* has, for whatever reason, never placed its formidable reputation and circulation behind a regular, annual, hierarchical assessment of America's colleges and universities. Nor has the *Washington Post*.

Even the *Wall Street Journal*, with its national circulation and prominence among members of the competitive-college demographic, has struggled to earn a large market share via its WSJ/THE publication. And, unfortunately, it has sought readership by essentially replicating U.S. News' prestige-plus-wealth approach. So has Forbes. Entities that have tried to offer a divergent style, such as Washington Monthly, with its "what colleges do for the country" method, or Money, with its "best value for the dollar" strategy, have thus far made only a small impact. One can be thankful for other specialized rankings from the likes of PayScale, Parchment, or CollegeNET. But these variants appear to have attracted only a limited following.

At one time, it appeared that the US government might try to enter the field, when President Obama and Education Secretary Arne Duncan floated the idea of creating a federal ranking of colleges. While most educators have generally—if grudgingly—applauded the entry of new private publications into the marketplace, they were understandably horrified at the prospect of an official, public-sector version. It would have combined the inevitable subjectivity and arbitrariness of one-size-fits-all listings with the imprimatur of the federal government. Fortunately, cooler heads prevailed. But not completely. The Department of Education's backup plan—College Scorecard—effectively created an "official" college guide, one whose choice of metrics and format reflects a similar homogenizing mentality.

Second, for all of the tinkering with their methodologies and the proliferation of their subsidiary ratings over the years, U.S. News and its competitors continue to rely on the preposterous "best-colleges" claim to grab viewers' attention (and generate thousands of derivative headlines). They still insist that they can compose a single list of schools, presented sequentially from best to worst, based on a multivariate formula that conceals massive arbitrariness under a veneer of statistical rigor.

In at least one way, the U.S. News assessments have gotten worse, not better, over time. Instead of assigning ordinal ranking numbers, as it once did, to only a limited number of institutions (25 or 50) and then grouping the rest alphabetically in tiers, it now purports to assign an exact numerical order to hundreds of institutions. The result is a ludicrous pretense that there is a 387th-ranked national university that is actually better than the 388th. And U.S. News's many clones have taken that ordinal obsession to ridiculous extremes. In 2021, Niche listed colleges all the way from 1st to 610th, and Money, from 1st to 739th. Yes, you read that last number correctly. According to Money magazine's number crunchers, Hampshire College, the famously rebellious school with its unique curriculum, was 729th; Dillard University, one of the nation's most prolific producers of future Black physicists, showed up as 731st; and the Berklee School of Music, a phenomenally successful school for musicians and music-industry professionals, almost hit rock bottom at 738th.

LIVING WITH COLLEGE RANKINGS: ADVICE TO STUDENTS

The fact that rankings are here to stay, and that the dominant listings glorify prestige and wealth, does not mean that they must exercise a stranglehold on either the consumers or the operators of higher education. Let's start with the consumers. Many critics of these types of publications have repeatedly advised students (and their parents, teachers, and counselors) to ignore the best-colleges siren song altogether. In my view, this is still the soundest advice. The seduction begins the moment you start to focus on those numbers. You may think that you can treat them just as a starting point, a gateway into deeper, more qualitative explorations. But the promise of being told exactly where each school fits into the prestige hierarchy is often irresistible.

To take an example I used in chapter 3, suppose you are considering applying to Berkeley and USC. You notice that U.S. News says that Berkeley is 22nd in its list of national universities, while USC is 24th. You then begin reading descriptions of the two schools and comparing them on multiple criteria of interest to you. But those numbers—22 versus 24—hover in your consciousness, poisoning your deeper exploration with their fake precision and false authority. Implicitly, they tell you that the higher educational landscape consists not of a horizontal distribution of multiple diverse schools, but, rather, a vertical hierarchy of relative values. And the numbers tell you where each institution belongs in that hierarchy. They are siren songs that most of us find very hard to resist. So if, like Ulysses, you can figuratively tie yourself to the mast, ignore the seductive lure of their siren song, and sail resolutely past those destructive shoals, do it!

I am enough of a realist to know that such advice is impractical for most prospective college applicants to heed. So I have some backup advice: take the rankings—not just U.S. News, but all of them—really seriously. Read at least five different evaluative publications, and preferably more. Study not only the best-college lists, but also several of the specialized listings that interest you. And pour over the methodology statements that typically accompany their assessments. View them for what they really are—opinions expressed by a bunch of amateurs, not authoritative pronouncements by professional educators. Review how each edition describes the colleges and universities that interest you. Read what several different guides say about those places. Surf the websites of these schools. In other words, approach the search for a collegiate destination in the same way you would conduct a scientific experiment or undertake a piece of historical research. Higher education is, after all, primarily about intellectual exploration and learning. Undertake your college quest in the same spirit.

Here's one way to do this. Formulate a tentative hypothesis about your personal preferences regarding higher education. What is it that you honestly want from the school you will attend? A way to achieve an impressive pedigree? A route to an economically rewarding career? Preparation for service to your community or your country? Guidance for a life replete with meaning and fulfillment? An opportunity to strengthen your general cognitive skills? A means of developing expertise in a particular field or subject matter? A vehicle for honing your social skills, so you can successfully navigate within an increasingly diverse society? Four years of fun and games away from the prying eyes of parents?

Set out with 100 points and allocate them among the various choices I have listed (or others of your own design), in a way that reflects their relative importance to you. Finally, using the leading college rankings and guidebooks, as well as other sources of data, such as the institutions' own websites and governmental databases, try to identify 10 schools that seem to offer the best match with your set of priorities. In selecting your list of candidates, you should, of course, choose those that seem to be within your reach, based on your credentials and financial resources. But you should also treat those factors as decidedly secondary considerations. After all, if you start your search by focusing on your limitations, you will miss possibilities. And higher education is all about possibilities.

What I have just described could well be the foundation of a high-school course offered in, say, the second semester of a student's junior year. If high schools want to treat the process of choosing a college—or even deciding whether to go at all—with the seriousness it deserves, they should address the subject through their formal curriculum, rather than treat it as a sidelight to be handled by their typically overworked college-counseling staff. By treating the methodology of this vital choice as an integral part of one's secondary education, high schools would not only make the process more transparent and systematic, but they would also reduce the frenzy that typically accompanies this search. And it might even save some anxious parents the thousands of dollars they now spend hiring college counselors.

QUESTIONING THE RANKINGS: ADVICE TO EDUCATORS

There is not much that prospective college students can do to influence the rankings. But there are steps that educators can take. After all, they have it within their power to cooperate with the rankings or ignore them, to publicly celebrate or inveigh against them, to use them as a blueprint for their efforts or pursue their distinctive missions relentlessly. In other words, educators can, by their actions, either bolster or undermine the legitimacy of such rankings.

Once again, the best advice is to ignore them. Start every work day remembering the unique character of your institution. Do not focus on where you stand, or wish you stood, in someone else's idea of a best-college pecking order.

Concentrate instead on the intentions of your institution's founders, the lessons of its history, and the possibilities of its future evolution. Ask yourself what the attainment of your school's mission really entails and what it truly requires. Then charge ahead in pursuit of that goal.

I realize, of course, that most educators will find it unrealistic—indeed probably impossible—to ignore the best-college seduction altogether. Like a bad penny, your institution's magic number will keep popping up in conversations with trustees, fellow administrators, alumni, donors, students, and perhaps even next-door neighbors. So my backup counsel to educators, like my advice to students, is to take the rankings extremely seriously. Delve into their methodologies and data sources, to understand what they are really measuring. And then ask yourself, honestly, whether those calculations include what you consider important, and whether they are worthy of the esteem that an honorable and intellectually demanding institution requires.

If you conclude, as we did at Reed, that most of the listings do not deserve your professional and institutional respect, then consider entering into what I call the four stages of rankings withdrawal.

Stage One:
Don't Fill Out Peer Reputation Surveys

The most modest act of withdrawal is simply to throw the U.S. News annual "peer-assessment" survey (and others like it from other rankocrats) into the wastebasket. As I discussed at length in chapter 8, educators need to be honest with themselves about the limits of their knowledge regarding other institutions. Unless you have employed methods comparable to those used by Consumer Reports to evaluate refrigerators, you should not pretend to know enough about a sufficient number of your supposed "peers" to assign them overall quality ratings. As a casual customer of various restaurants, you may feel perfectly comfortable giving one five stars and another only two. But, as a professional educator, enlisted to participate in a highly consequential assessment of institutions in your own industry, you should apply a much higher standard. And, by the way, don't fool yourself into thinking you can game the system by giving your closest peers a low rating. The survey industry has plenty of ways to detect and nullify that tactic.

Stage Two:
Don't Publicize Rankings You Consider Illegitimate

The second stage of withdrawal from any of the rankings that you don't respect is not to publicize how your school fares in them. As I mentioned in chapter 5, the presidents of 19 leading liberal arts colleges agreed in 2007 to not publicly celebrate how they fared in the latest U.S. News edition. I understand why those schools felt the need for collective action. When many competitors agree to such a position, it both generates greater publicity and also protects each signatory from being undercut by its rivals.

But collective action is not necessary. If a particular ranking, such as the one published by U.S. News, is fundamentally incompatible with your values, then don't brag about your score on it. Period. I realize that many people consider the annual release of best-college listings as newsworthy. A college or university that boasts about where it appears in, say, the latest U.S. News edition might argue that it is merely reporting on an important event in the world of higher education. Really? Schools have a choice of what items of consequence to mention on their website and which ones to ignore. Most higher educational institutions that publicize their improved ranking in one year remain curiously silent when it declines in the following cycle. Aren't both events equally newsworthy? Furthermore, by highlighting the results of a particular publication, you are implicitly endorsing its legitimacy. Suppose, for example, that your institution professes to be truly dedicated to promoting racial and ethnic diversity. If you celebrate your position on a listing, such as the one published by U.S. News, that gives zero weight to racial and ethnic diversity, aren't you undercutting your own professed values?

Stage Three:
Celebrate Rankings That Truly Reflect Your Values

My suggestion to refuse to publicize rankings you consider antithetical to your values does not necessarily mean that you have to boycott every one of them. If a particular assessment captures a quality that dovetails with your school's distinctive mission, go ahead and celebrate it. Just as Reed applauded a ranking of colleges based on future PhD productivity. Or, perhaps, as Spelman might draw attention to one featuring HBCUs and women's colleges; or Notre Dame, to one highlighting Catholic schools; or Berea or City College, to one lauding schools serving low-income students through excellent educational programs. As I experienced at Reed, doing so doesn't close you off from a national audience; it merely helps you emphasize what is truly distinctive about your institution. And, by backing up your professed values with concrete actions, you send a powerful message to a generation deeply cynical about the credibility of America's higher educational institutions.

Stage Four:
Give Everyone Equal Access to Your Data

Information is the lifeblood of education—the essential foundation for the discovery, understanding, and transmission of knowledge. So, too, must it be the vital factor in institutional choices for every would-be college student. Educators have a professional obligation to provide comprehensive, current information about their schools, including both favorable and unfavorable aspects of those institutions. Fortunately, today much of that data is required by the US Department of Education and is readily available on its websites. Beyond that baseline, colleges and universities should participate in the Common Data Set by annually filling out its questionnaire and making their submissions easily accessible on their web pages—not buried, as they too often are, under three or four layers of website architecture. And, of course, institutions should publish additional information specifically tailored to their distinctive missions.

All of this information should be freely and readily available to *everyone*, on an *equal* basis. The implications of that statement should be clear. Educators should *not* give anyone—including specific college rankings organizations—privileged access to all or even some portion of their data. To me, this means that they should not fill out the annual U.S. News statistical question-naire. If you don't hand deliver information to the editors at U.S. News, they will have to make the effort to dig it out, just as all the other commercial best-college publications and college guides do. If you make it easier for U.S. News to rank your school than, say, Money or Washington Monthly, you are implicitly saying that the former's methodology is more worthy.

The act of providing more information, or more-current information, to U.S. News rather than to the general public implicitly endorses its ranking. If you truly believe that insti-tutions of higher education should be arrayed in a uniform numerical hierarchy, from "best" to worst, based on criteria that primarily celebrate prestige and wealth, then go ahead and fill out their questionnaire. But if you adhere to what you say in your mission statement about the centrality of, say, intellectual excellence, or social mobility, or racial and ethnic justice, or the promotion of religious values, or preparation for a meaningful life, then don't legitimize assessments that are at odds with those purposes.

Refusing to hand over data to U.S. News—or, for that matter, to any similar commercial venture—will not spare your school from being graded. These publications will go ahead, with or without your cooperation or complicity, and rate you anyway. And, yes, they might even try to punish you, as U.S. News has done to the likes of Hampshire, Reed, St. John's, and Sarah Lawrence. Instead of fearing such treatment, you should see that "punishment" as a badge of honor—and publicly celebrate it. If a larger number of mainstream higher educational institutions ceased to cooperate with U.S. News, I suspect that the magazine would stop disciplining those who refuse to respond. It's one thing to penalize Hampshire College or St. John's. It would be quite another matter to do so for schools like Amherst or Notre Dame or Penn.

The fact that the number of non-respondents to U.S. News's annual beauty contest has lately risen to 15 percent gives me a sense of hope. So does the growing recognition of higher education's responsibility to address the grotesque levels of social and economic inequality in America. When the elite institutions stop celebrating prestige and wealth and truly roll up their sleeves to work at social justice, the rankings will cease to rule both them and us.

CELEBRATING INDIVIDUAL AND INSTITUTIONAL DIVERSITY

I end as I began in chapter 1, celebrating the rich diversity of needs and expectations of those who seek a postsecondary education, and the wide range of institutions that have evolved to satisfy those desires. My dream is that this profusion can and will survive the relentless homogenizing pressures exerted by the rankocracy. In my dream, Tyrell will choose Amherst, not because it shows up near the top of someone's annual best-college list, but because it meets his needs for a school that prizes social justice as an essential ingredient of academic excellence. Amanda will select Berea, because, even in the face of pressures for cultural conformity, it persists in providing a first-class liberal education for low-income students from her region. Carlos will attend City College, precisely because it still preserves its legacy as the "Harvard on the Hudson" for recent immigrants and working-class New Yorkers.

Chad will opt for Michigan, but not because of some number attached to it by self-appointed arbiters of institutional quality. Rather, he will go there because it continues to serve the academic aspirations of working-class students in his state, while shining as a beacon of excellence to the world. Maureen will decide on Notre Dame, because it has never surrendered its devotion to a power far greater than princes and provinces, even as it seeks to serve the secular world. Sarah will find in Penn the internationally distinguished center of learning that prepares its graduates for leadership in all aspects of our global society. Jonah will thrive in Reed's sanctuary for freethinking, iconoclastic intellectuals of uncompromising academic integrity. And, at Spelman, Tanya will receive what she was seeking—a superb education in the liberal arts and sciences, preparing young African American women for service in a society begging for their gifts.

If I could wave a magic wand, there would be no one-size-fits-all, pseudoscientific rankings to mislead anxious applicants and corrupt educators' values. In their place, one would find a wealth of information, curated by respected commentators with no obvious ax to grind. I have in mind examples such as the "Almanac," published annually by the

Chronicle of Higher Education, which is filled to the brim with tables, graphs, and data on dozens of institutional characteristics and attributes.

If there were college rankings, they would be multiple, equally credible ones, each addressing a particular educational style or goal. There would, of course, be one based on wealth, for those obsessed with the pursuit of prestige. But there would also be separate listings for those who truly care about social mobility, racial and ethnic diversity, academic rigor, teaching and learning excellence, affordability, admissions selectivity, earnings, returns on investment, religious and spiritual fulfillment, and preparation for a life of meaning. Reflecting the arbitrariness of the proxies needed to measure these attributes, institutions of higher education would not be ranked ordinally, but would, at most, be sorted into clusters.

Prospective college students, along with their advisors, mentors, and parents, would approach the choice of where to apply as an exercise in personal discovery and fulfillment. They would engage, first, in a process of self-examination to identify what criteria to look for. Second, and only then, would they engage in a search for schools to match those criteria. They would approach the task with the same sense of seriousness that characterizes the approach to academic research. And they would utilize the full range of informational resources so plentifully available to them, without the seductive distraction of some self-appointed "expert's" opinion about various institutions' relative positions in a contrived hierarchy.

Since I cannot wave a magic wand, I can only content myself with sharing lessons learned from a lifetime in academia—one that has included periods of both subjection to rankings and freedom from them. My hope is that these observations can guide participants in the world of higher education to free themselves from the grip of the rankocracy. In that way, perhaps students will be liberated to find the best path forward to a life of service and meaning. And educators will be liberated to achieve the loftiest ideals of their chosen profession.

EIGHT SCHOOLS,
A THOUSAND FLOWERS . . .

Throughout this book, I have made frequent reference to eight colleges and universities as exemplars of the 7,600 institutions that populate the American higher educational landscape. I have used these schools to illustrate, both graphically and descriptively, how different ways of ranking and evaluating institutions can produce very different implicit orderings, based on their comparative "quality." For those readers curious to know more about the eight schools, I provide a more detailed profile of each in this appendix.[1]

AMHERST COLLEGE

Amherst is the quintessential New England liberal arts college. It was founded in 1821, in large part to train young men for the ministry, most of whom were very poor. Although it was nonsectarian, for decades it had a conservative Calvinist character, reflected in rules banning card games and alcohol consumption, as well as in the periodic religious revivals held on campus. Only in the late nineteenth century did its modern secular character firmly take hold.

At one time Amherst, Williams, and Wesleyan were popularly called the "Little Three" schools, a kind of liberal arts equivalent to the Ivy League. In recent decades, however, Wesleyan has become somewhat less competitive, both academically and athletically, leaving Amherst and Williams at the top of the liberal arts pyramid, in the view of many. Amherst is a member of the Five College Consortium, along with

Until the middle of the twentieth century, Amherst was—like most institutions of higher education at the time—primarily a regional school that catered to students from the northeastern United States. Much of the credit for transforming Amherst into a national powerhouse belongs to Charles W. Cole, its president from 1946 to 1960. Under Cole, the college adopted the "New Curriculum" that required all freshmen to take yearlong courses in multiple disciplines. In 1967, however, the faculty scrapped this plan in favor of a relaxed distribution requirement, which, in turn, eventually gave way to the current "open curriculum."

its neighbors: Smith, Mount Holyoke, Hampshire College, and UMass Amherst. Through the consortium, students have access to over 6,000 courses, although relatively few of them stray from Amherst's campus for their classes, given the richness of the college's own offerings (over 850 courses in 40 majors).

While providing a full range of outstanding instruction in all major disciplines, Amherst has, at times, styled itself as a "writing college," reflecting its association with such illustrious poets as Emily Dickinson, Robert Frost, and Richard Wilbur, in addition to well-known novelists like Scott Turow, Dan Brown, and David Foster Wallace. In recent years, it has made major investments in the sciences, including a new geology building that houses its celebrated museum of natural history and a 230,000-square-foot integrated science center.

Amherst was all male until 1974, when the board of trustees voted to make the college coeducational, incurring the wrath of many alumni. It expanded enrollment and built new dormitories to accommodate women, who were barred from the fraternity houses. Greek life was an important aspect of college social life, from the founding of the first fraternity in 1837 until 1984. In that year, the board of trustees abolished the last of the remaining fraternities, provoking another outcry, and converted the houses into gracious dormitories.

In the 1980s, Amherst launched a major initiative to make the college more racially and ethnically diverse. Notwithstanding its location in an overwhelmingly White section of rural New England, its efforts met with considerable success. Then, in the early 2000s, the college launched another effort to increase the socioeconomic diversity of its student body, again with impressive results. In recent versions of its mission statement, Amherst has sought to differentiate itself from its peers by proclaiming its unique combination of high academic quality and student diversity.

The college offers a large selection of varsity and intramural sports. Amherst competes in the New England Small College Athletic Conference and Division III in the NCAA. In recent decades, its athletic program has produced many outstanding teams, competing for athletic bragging rights with archrival Williams.

For decades, its unofficial mascot was "Lord Jeff," derived from Lord Jeffrey Amherst, commander-in-chief of British forces during the French and Indian Wars, and the namesake for the town. But revulsion at Lord Jeffrey's reported attempts to infect his Indian foes with smallpox led to a decision to scrap him as the college mascot, to the displeasure of some old-timers. In Lord Jeff's place, the college chose to dub its athletic teams the Mammoths—a reference to a woolly mammoth skeleton excavated by an Amherst professor in the 1920s and exhibited in the school's natural history museum. Unlike its extinct mascot, however, Amherst has once again displayed its uncanny ability to adapt and thrive.

BEREA COLLEGE

Berea College is a small, zero-tuition "work college" located in the town of Berea, Kentucky, some 30 miles south of Lexington, on the northwestern edge of the Daniel Boone National Forest. It traces its roots to a school founded in 1855. Cassius Clay, a wealthy Kentucky landowner and leader in the movement for gradual emancipation, donated land to an abolitionist preacher named Rev. John Fee to establish a school and church to teach and preach the gospel of antislavery. In 1866, Fee started a college-level program, attracting a class of 96 Blacks and 91 Whites, both men and women. Relying on funds that Fee was able to raise, the school charged its students no tuition but required them to work at the college, both to enhance their educational experience and to keep the fledgling institution's expenses under control.

In 1904, Kentucky enacted the Day Law, which prohibited any school in the state from offering integrated education. Berea challenged the law, but it, unfortunately, was upheld by the US Supreme Court,[1] based on the doctrine of "separate but equal" announced a few years earlier in *Plessy v. Ferguson.*[2] In response, the governing board set up a separate institution to educate Black students. The school reintegrated after the Day Law was amended in 1950 to permit voluntary integration at the postsecondary level, just a few years before the Supreme Court overruled the *Plessy* doctrine in *Brown v. Board of Education.*[3]

Berea has always focused on educating the children of Appalachia. The trustees formalized that commitment in 1911, and it remains in place to this day. Some 70 percent of Berea's students come from the southern portion of the Appalachian Mountains. The college's emphasis, in the early twentieth century, on educating poor students of all races made it an attractive object of local philanthropy, including charitable bequests. In 1920, the trustees adopted a policy, still in effect, that all unrestricted bequests to the college should be invested in its endowment fund, a practice that has helped it to build a formidable portfolio worth over $1.2 billion, enough to provide roughly 75 percent of its operating revenues.

Berea is one of only nine American colleges certified under the 1992 Higher Education Act Amendments as a work college, qualifying it for designated federal funding. All students are required to work 10 to 15 hours per week in one of over 100 placements, many on campus, but some elsewhere. First- and second-year students mostly fill unskilled jobs, while third- and fourth-years typically perform tasks that require knowledge and expertise attained through their formal education.

The college nominally charges a tuition of roughly $45,000, but it grants each student a full-tuition scholarship, funded from its endowment income and gifts. Thus it can still offer an education that is effectively tuition free. It admits only students with financial need—that is, those whose families have earnings in the bottom 40 percent of the national income distribution. Although the college does charge students for room and board, plus some incidentals, it compensates them for their required work assignments, enabling them to offset some of those charges. As a result, over 40 percent of its students graduate debt free, and the average financial liability among those who have taken out loans is about $6,000.

Berea has strong Christian roots, still reflected in some of its practices. Its motto is "God has made of one blood all peoples of the earth," taken from the Book of Acts. Its "Great Commitments" statement declares that it was founded to "promote the cause of Christ." All students must take a course on Understandings of Christianity. But in most other respects, it is thoroughly secular. It offers a classic liberal arts educational program, leading to a BA or BS degree in 32 different majors.

For generations, Berea College has stood as an emphatic refutation to those who doubt that the pursuit of academic excellence can be combined with a genuine commitment to economic justice.

CITY COLLEGE OF NEW YORK

City College of New York was the first free public college established in the United States, and it is still viewed by many as the leading exemplar of the urban public university. Under the leadership of Horace Webster, a wealthy businessman, New York State established the Free Academy in 1847 as a public institution of secondary and postsecondary education. Its declared mission was to provide education, at no charge, to the children of immigrants and the working class in New York City, "based on academic merit only." In 1866, the academy became the College of the City of New York, subsequently (in 1929) renamed the City College of New York, and later (1961) absorbed into the City University of New York (CUNY) consortium.

Originally located in downtown Manhattan, City College moved to its current campus in the Manhattanville neighborhood, adjacent to Harlem, in 1907, after the erection of its landmark collegiate gothic buildings. In 1953, the college expanded by purchasing the campus of the Manhattanville College of the Sacred Heart, located on its southern border. It now occupies about 35 acres, with an additional Midtown outpost.

The heyday of City College was undoubtedly during the first half of the twentieth century. Sometimes labeled "Harvard on the Hudson," City College attracted many brilliant faculty members to teach equally gifted students. Some enrollees were drawn to the school in large part because of its free tuition. But many attended City College because they were effectively excluded from Ivy League universities because of their infamous Jewish quotas and anti-immigrant biases. During this period, the college's physics program became especially celebrated, attracting Albert Einstein to give his first American lectures and producing several physics Nobel laureates.

A men's school in its early years, City College admitted women to graduate programs in 1930, and as undergraduates in 1951. The composition of its student body and its uptown Manhattan location virtually guaranteed that it would become a hotbed of student activism. A Vietnam War–era protest led to an administrative decision to adopt open admissions in 1970, guaranteeing entrance to any New York City high-school graduate. Because of the extreme disparities in entering students' college readiness, however, the school was forced to begin offering remedial programs, which placed a strain on its available resources.

In 1976, City College began charging tuition, albeit at a very low level. The open-admissions policy was scrapped in 1999, with the adoption of minimum academic admissions standards. Henceforth, the governing body of the CUNY consortium designated its network of community colleges as the entry point for less-qualified students, who were given the option to later transfer to City or one of CUNY's other four-year institutions. City College is now considered by Barron's to be a "selective" college, with an acceptance rate of about 50 percent and a median combined SAT score a bit above 1100.

City College comprises eight separate schools, but most of the institution's undergraduate education occurs in its College of Liberal Arts and Sciences. All undergraduates are required to complete a general education program, called "Pathways," that includes a common core of four courses—two in English composition and one each in quantitative reasoning and science—plus a flexible common core of six courses selected from five categories. In 2001, City College created an honors program that provides free tuition and access to specially designed courses for a limited number of students dubbed "University Scholars."

Like most public institutions in America, City College has suffered from the long-term decline in state support for higher education, most especially after the 2008–2010 recession. A 2016 article in the *New York Times* described in graphic detail the impact of New York State's budget cuts on the CUNY system.[4] According to City College's 2019 strategic plan, it can count on state appropriations for only about a quarter of its $200 million annual budget. In response, the university has recently announced an ambitious goal to strengthen its academic programs through private fundraising and endowment building, an objective it will surely pursue with characteristic scrappiness and ingenuity.

THE UNIVERSITY OF MICHIGAN, ANN ARBOR

Michigan, as it is generally known, is the paradigmatic flagship state university. It actually traces its roots back to pre-statehood days, when a Native tribe ceded land, in what is now Detroit, to a group of Catholic priests to found a secondary school, on the condition that it would educate tribal children. Initially dubbed the "Catholepistiemiad" by the governor and judges of Michigan Territory, the school later began offering college-level instruction. After Michigan became a state in 1837, the legislature relocated the institution to a new campus in the town of Ann Arbor and re-chartered it as the University of Michigan. Four years later, the College of Literature, Science, and the Arts (LSA) became the university's first college, eventually to be joined by 18 other schools, 13 of which would offer undergraduate education. The expansion of the state's population and economy throughout the second half of the nineteenth century brought about the university's rapid growth in both scale and quality. The appointment of philosopher John Dewey to its faculty in 1884 exemplified its attraction to first-rate academics. As early as 1866, *Atlantic Monthly* had proclaimed that Michigan "offers to thousands, free of expense, the best education this continent affords." Around the turn of the century, admiring educators not infrequently referred to as "the Harvard of the West."

What academic prowess could not accomplish in attracting national attention, football could. Michigan won its first national championship in 1901 and, by 1927, was motivated to build a football-only stadium that seats over 100,000 and—at least until COVID-19 struck in 2020—routinely overflowed for every game. Michigan's varsity teams have one of the highest win-loss ratios in America, and one of the largest numbers of national championships.

Michigan has played an important role in the history of race in higher education. In 1863, its medical school ordered a Black student to leave "for the peace and harmony of the institution." Atoning for that action, the university later began welcoming Black students, and in 1925 the Negro-Caucasian Club became what is believed to be the first interracial student organization at an American institution of higher education.

Much later, in 2003, the university's aggressive attempts at affirmative-action admissions were tested in two landmark US Supreme Court cases. In one, *Gratz v. Bollinger*,[5] the court struck down a mathematical formula used in the university's undergraduate admissions process; in the other, *Grutter v. Bollinger*,[6] the court upheld a practice utilized by its law school to treat race as a "plus factor" in a "holistic" system of admissions selection. Three years later, the voters of Michigan approved Proposition 2, banning the use of race in public university admissions, a law later upheld by the US Supreme Court.[7]

LSA, the focal point for most undergraduate education at Michigan, offers a huge selection of academic courses, arranged into 75 academic units, 85 majors, and over 100 minors. Its curriculum includes required courses in first-year writing, upper-level writing, race and ethnicity, quantitative reasoning, and a foreign language. Students must also satisfy an area-distribution requirement that includes 10 courses in fields such as science, mathematics, social science, humanities, and creative expression.

Like all public universities, Michigan has experienced a long, slow, painful decline in state financial support. In its 2018–2019 budget, state appropriations contributed only $320 million toward its overall $4 billion academic budget. Nonetheless, Michigan has successfully adopted the private model of fundraising and endowment building. An early (1983) campaign achieved what was then an ambitious goal of $180 million. Much more recently (2018), Michigan completed a $5 billion campaign. Its endowment now stands at approximately $12 billion.

Michigan also exemplifies the recent shift among public universities from the low-tuition/low-aid model of student finance to the private sector's high-tuition/high-aid model. In 2020, tuition for in-state students (at about $15,600) was relatively costly for schools in the public sector. At the same time, Michigan was relying heavily on attracting out-of-state and foreign students, to whom it charged tuition at a level (over $51,000), approaching that of elite private schools. In recent years, Michigan's financial-aid budget has grown rapidly, both to help lower-income students pay its hefty tuition charges and to fund a merit-aid program to attract star students and athletes. As a model of productive public-private partnerships in service of education's highest aspirations, Michigan stands almost without peer.

THE UNIVERSITY OF NOTRE DAME

Notre Dame is surely one of the most prominent Catholic institutions of higher learning in America, if not the most prominent. Its website's home page describes the institution as "a place born of vision and defined by its Catholic character." It began in 1842, when Rev. Edward Sorin, CSC, a priest in the French missionary order of the Congregation of Holy Cross, established a secondary school in the wilds of northern Indiana. Two years later, it received a state charter to award college-level degrees. Governed until 1967 entirely by Holy Cross priests, Notre Dame is now led by a two-tiered board with both religious and lay trustees. Its president is always a priest belonging to the Holy Cross order.

Growing steadily in size and quality throughout the nineteenth century, Notre Dame attracted nationwide attention early in the twentieth century, primarily through football. From 1918 to 1930, head coach Knute Rockne led its football team to three national championships and a stunning 90 percent winning record. Roman Catholics from around the nation rooted for the Fighting Irish as they played schools with more-Protestant, sectarian roots. It is surely the only university able to claim that one of its students (the great football player George Gipp) was portrayed in a movie by a future US President (Ronald Reagan).

To this day, the origin of the Fighting Irish moniker is still contested. Most pundits believe it was meant as an ethnic slur, aimed by envious opponents at Notre Dame's many Irish-surnamed players. But, derogatory or not, the label had become so widely admired that Notre Dame's president formally adopted it in 1927. The school may be French in its origins and name, but it proudly boasts a feisty Irish spirit.

By now, Notre Dame is deservedly better known and respected for its academic excellence than for its athletic prowess. Most of the credit surely belongs to Rev. Theodore Hesburgh, CSC, president of Notre Dame from 1952 to 1987. On Hesburgh's watch, Notre Dame experienced a huge expansion in its academic programs and academic quality. When he started, the university's endowment was a mere $7 million. By relentlessly fundraising, he set the school on a path that has enabled its endowment to grow to an amount exceeding $11 billion. And by aggressively recruiting star Catholic high-school students, Hesburgh enabled it to become one of the most selective institutions in America today.

Notre Dame houses eight schools on its 1,260-acre campus. Six of them (schools of arts and letters, business, science, engineering, architecture, and global affairs) offer undergraduate education to some 8,700 students. Describing itself as "dedicated to religious belief no less than scientific knowledge," Notre Dame has a strong and integrated general education requirement. All undergraduates must follow a core curriculum, consisting of six courses in various liberal arts disciplines; four courses "exploring the Catholic dimension of liberal arts" (including at least two theology courses); two writing-intensive courses; and a two-semester "Moreau First Year Experience" that seeks to integrate academic, co-curricular, and residential-life experiences.

Beyond the classroom, the religious character of Notre Dame is unmistakable. Spiritual life is centered on the landmark Basilica of the Sacred Heart, but it is also clearly manifested in the 50 campus chapels, with more than 100 Masses celebrated each week and over 40 Holy Cross priests in residence. In a typical year, over 80 percent of its students identify as Catholic, a percentage higher than that of some of its nationally recognized Jesuit-school cousins, such as Georgetown and Boston College.

In all of these ways, Notre Dame stunningly demonstrates how a great university can combine academic rigor and athletic excellence with devotion to its religious roots.

THE UNIVERSITY OF PENNSYLVANIA

Known to almost everyone simply as Penn, the University of Pennsylvania traces a continuous history, beginning with its founding in colonial Philadelphia and going all the way to its current status as a world-class center of learning. Penn claims to be fourth oldest of the nine colonially chartered institutions of higher education. In a bit of competitive legerdemain, in 1899, Penn's trustees decreed that the institution had been founded in 1740—putting it just ahead of archrival Princeton, founded in 1746. Though its first building was erected in 1740, it was not until 1750 that Benjamin Franklin assembled a lay board of 24 trustees to establish a private, nonprofit secondary school. It embodied Franklin's then iconoclastic idea that education should be not only "ornamental" (preparing students for the ministry), but also "practical" (grooming them for positions in commerce, government, and the professions).

Penn's receipt of a charter in 1755 to provide college-level instruction ushered in a period of rapid expansion, with the addition of the nation's first medical school and the gradual ascendancy of "practical" instruction. In 1779, Penn dubbed itself a university—believed to be the first American institution thus described. In 1802, the school moved from cramped space near Independence Hall to the then suburban expanses of West Philadelphia, where it now sits on 302 very urban acres, shaped into a welcoming campus by the closure of several city streets.

Throughout the nineteenth and early twentieth centuries, Penn rode the rising commercial fortunes of its home city as it expanded and enriched its offerings. Its association with what are now the seven other Ivy League universities began primarily in the athletic realm, with the adoption of early agreements involving competition in sports such as rowing, wrestling, and basketball. Although the term "Ivy League" appears to date back to various media reports in the mid-1930s, it wasn't until 1945 that the presidents of the eight constituent institutions agreed to form an Ivy Group football league, expanded nine years later to all varsity sports. The "Ivy" label is often attributed to the popular nineteenth-century custom of planting ivy to grow on college buildings—and is embodied in a tradition at Penn called Ivy Day, which began in 1873.

The university offers undergraduate education in four schools: the College of Arts and Sciences (CAS), the School of Engineering and Applied Science, the School of Nursing, and the Wharton School. CAS, which enrolls about 60 percent of Penn's undergraduates, requires students to complete a general education program, consisting of "Foundational Approaches"—including one course each in composition, quantitative data analysis, formal reasoning, cross-cultural analysis, and US cultural diversity. Students must also complete a program called "Sectors of Knowledge," which requires them to enroll in one course each from seven academic disciplines. Taking full advantage of its eleven schools, all located on one central campus, Penn allows students to cross-register among its various undergraduate programs and offers a bewildering array of dual-degree programs. It also seeks to distinguish itself by the size and scale of its study-abroad programs.

Although Penn first built dormitories in 1894–1912, it was still primarily a commuter school until after World War II, when it began constructing a collection of modernist residence halls. One motivation was the steady deterioration and declining safety of the surrounding neighborhood, as Philadelphia's industrial base began to disintegrate in the 1930s. To attract undergraduate students to its somewhat gritty neighborhood, Penn relied for many years on the outsized reputation of the Wharton School, a leading American business school, to offer undergraduate as well as graduate degrees. This gave the university a reputation as a feeder to Wall Street that persists, albeit somewhat weakened, even today.

As a result of Penn's heavy investment in its West Philadelphia environs, and, more recently, of the rising economic fortunes of Philadelphia, the past several decades have witnessed a striking resurgence of Penn's popularity and eminence on all fronts. It is certainly no longer referred to as the "doormat of the Ivy League"—a term that could sometimes be heard on campus back in the 1980s but has long since vanished from the school's proud lexicon.

REED COLLEGE

Reed College is a small liberal arts school with a deserved reputation as an intellectual hothouse for academically ambitious undergraduates. The youngest of the schools profiled here, Reed was founded in 1908 from the proceeds of the estate of Amanda

Reed, widow of Portland entrepreneur and transportation magnate Simeon Reed. Her bequest called for creation of a Reed Institute to provide "enlightenment" to the people of Oregon, including public lectures and vocational education. But its founding board of trustees was determined to establish a school offering a classical liberal arts education. Inspired in part by the then-recently created University of Chicago, Reed's founders were insistent that the school be nonsectarian, coeducational, egalitarian, and exclusively academic. No football, no fraternities, no social clubs.

The book value of the college's founding endowment—consisting primarily of Portland real estate—was thought to have been large enough to support not only a college, but also a graduate school. The collapse of Portland's economy in the mid-1910s, however, forced Reed to abandon dreams of a graduate school. But the faculty never quite gave up on its aspiration to treat their students as if they were doctoral candidates in the making. Focusing its limited resources exclusively on its instructional mission, Reed offered minimal nonacademic student support. This posture conformed to its student-centered founding philosophy, according to which students were supposed to fill many of the necessary jobs on campus and organize their own extracurricular activities. They were also expected to comport themselves according to a non-codifiable Honor Principle.

Reed's student centrism is also embodied in the conference method of learning—a variant on the seminar method—in which students take responsibility for much of the discussion, with faculty often playing a facilitating or mediating role. Even today, when a faculty member calls in sick, students frequently conduct the class by themselves. The faculty is so protective of this instructional philosophy that the college has never laterally appointed a senior faculty member from another school to a position automatically carrying tenure, insisting that all faculty must prove themselves in the conference method before qualifying for tenure. (Until 2019, this prohibition on the lateral hiring of individuals with tenure even included the extramural recruitment of the college's presidents!)

Throughout most of its history, Reed has offered a classic liberal arts curriculum. First-year students must all take a required yearlong interdisciplinary humanities course. Students must also enroll in an introductory science course and complete credits in each of several academic disciplines. Departmental requirements for majors are so rigorous that double majors are very rare. Students must pass a junior-year qualifying examination in their major in order to proceed to their senior year. Every senior must write a thesis, involving a yearlong tutorial with a faculty member, often resulting in original research. Until very recently, the college maintained only traditional, single-discipline academic departments.

Notwithstanding the conservatism of its curriculum (or, perhaps ironically, because of it), Reed has historically attracted iconoclastic, freethinking, deeply intellectual students. Left by themselves outside the classroom to pursue their own interests, the students created and sustained a culture of rebellion, activism, experimentation, and whimsical traditions. Though the college administration has, in recent decades, greatly beefed up student-support services, the capriciousness and idiosyncrasies of Reed's student culture persist to this day in traditions such as the year-ending senior thesis parade, the Renn Fayre celebration, the January student-run Paideia course offerings, and the recurrent hunt for the school's unofficial mascot, the Doyle Owl.

Not surprisingly, given its academic and social culture, Reed graduates are more strongly drawn to academia than to Wall Street. Nonetheless, the financial successes of its many entrepreneurial graduates have provided a basis for increasingly successful fundraising efforts, such as its $200 million centennial campaign. With an endowment exceeding $600 million, the college is able to provide an impressive level of nonacademic support to students and research support for its faculty, both of which complement its historic passion for fostering intellectual growth and discovery.

SPELMAN COLLEGE

Spelman College is surely one of the most celebrated institutions among the 102 historically Black colleges and universities (HBCUs) in America, and it is one of the two sole members that serve only women. Spelman traces its roots to the Atlanta Baptist Female Seminary, founded in 1881 as part of an undertaking to establish elementary and secondary schools for the children of freed slaves. That effort attracted the attention of John D. Rockefeller, himself a devout Baptist, who agreed to give the school a donation of $250. Thus began an ongoing connection between the school and the Rockefeller family—particularly John's wife, Laura Spelman Rockefeller; her sister Lucy; and her parents, who had been active abolitionists. In recognition of the Rockefeller gifts, the founders changed the school's name to Spelman Seminary in 1884, and then to Spelman College in 1927.

As is true of most of our profile institutions, its evolution from a secondary school to a college occurred in stages. A college department opened in 1897, and postsecondary education existed side by side with secondary education until the discontinuation of the elementary school in 1928 and the high school in 1930. Shortly after it became a college, Spelman entered into a consortium agreement with its next-door neighbors, all-male Morehouse College and graduate-level

Atlanta University (now Clark Atlanta University), to form the Atlanta University Center.

Once designed to produce "refined young ladies" (in the words of alumna Marian Wright Edelman),[8] Spelman slowly transformed its academic offerings and student culture from an emphasis on traditional women's functions (such as homemaking, nursing, and teaching) to one embracing the entire range of occupational and professional roles fulfilled by women today. It offers its students 30 majors, as well as opportunities to take additional courses from over 30 other partner institutions. Like other single-sex colleges, it has had to deal with the issue of transgender and nonbinary sexual identity. In 2017, it agreed to admit transgender students who identify as female.

Spelman's core requirements include English composition, a foreign language, wellness and health, mathematics, the African diaspora, international and comparative women's studies, computer literacy, and a sophomore seminar. Spelman is especially strong in math and science—as evidenced by occasional large grants from NASA and the National Institutes of Health, an engineering partnership with Georgia Tech, and the large number of its graduates who go on to obtain advanced degrees in those fields.

Like all of the HBCUs, Spelman has struggled throughout its history to find the financial resources to match its ambitions. In the face of intense competitive challenges to attract academically talented African American women, the college has felt it necessary to devote a large amount of its financial-aid budget to merit-based grants, leaving its needy students to borrow heavily in order to finance the outstanding education they are offered. Still, in recent decades the fiscal picture has definitely brightened. The school's endowment received a large boost from a successful $111 million fundraising campaign in the 1980s and 1990s, led by President Johnetta Betsch Cole, that included a $37 million gift from the DeWitt Wallace/Readers Digest Fund. In the last few years, Spelman has received several multimillion-dollar gifts from philanthropists attracted to the unique mission of historically Black institutions.

As another sign of hope for Spelman and her brother and sister institutions, the federal government has lately shown an increasing willingness to provide financial assistance to HBCUs. The 1990s-era HBCU Capital Financing Program, which provided low-interest loans for debt refinancing and new capital projects, was recently reauthorized. Also, HBCUs, as a group, received two large injections of direct aid from omnibus relief acts adopted in response to the COVID-19 pandemic. These developments, plus the election of Vice President Kamala Harris—an HBCU

(Howard University) graduate—has generated optimism that this crucial sector will be restored to its rightful place in the educational firmament. When it is, Spelman will surely lead the way.

CATEGORIES, CONNECTIONS, AND DISTINCTIONS

Each of the eight institutions profiled here can be viewed as an illustration of the amazingly rich diversity of American higher education. As a prototype of the exclusive, generously endowed liberal arts college, Amherst belongs in the company of schools such as Carleton, Pomona, or Williams, as well as the elite private universities with which it competes for students, such as Brown, Cornell, and Dartmouth. Berea illustrates the "work college," both strictly defined and more broadly interpreted to include schools like Northeastern or Drexel Universities, which offer student co-op programs. Berea's focus on serving poor, academically underserved students also links it with many public institutions, such as City College and its sister schools in the CUNY consortium. As an HBCU, Spelman is naturally mentioned in the same breath as institutions like Morehouse College and Howard University. And, as a women's school, it belongs in the company of colleges such as Wellesley, Smith, and Mount Holyoke. Reed's brainy reputation positions it with schools for intellectuals, such as the University of Chicago, Swarthmore, and MIT, while its counterculture reputation sometimes evokes comparisons with schools like Hampshire, Antioch, and Bennington.

City College, Michigan, Notre Dame, and Penn illustrate the multidisciplinary research universities that came into full flower at the end of the nineteenth century, in emulation of the German university model. But, again, surface similarities conceal major differences. Penn is an archetype of the world-class private research university, solidly in the company of true Ivy Leaguers, such as Princeton and Yale, and Ivy-like universities, such as Duke, Johns Hopkins, and Vanderbilt. As a former "streetcar" university that has capitalized on the increasing appeal of attending college in buzzy urban settings, it also calls to mind schools like NYU and Boston University.

Michigan epitomizes the category of gradually privatizing elite state flagship universities, such as Berkeley, Virginia, and Wisconsin, as well as athletic powerhouses like Ohio State, Alabama, and Louisiana State University. Another one-time athletic powerhouse, Notre Dame, exemplifies the large class of Catholic universities, such as Georgetown, Boston College, and Santa Clara, as well as schools such as Brigham Young and Yeshiva Universities, which are affiliated with other religious traditions. Yet it also illustrates the category of private higher educational institutions outside the Ivy-plus group, like Emory, the University of Southern California, and Washington University, that have built powerful academic reputations in recent decades. City College personifies the urban public university sector, devoted to educating sons and daughters of immigrants, racial and ethnic minorities, and working-class families, a category that would include schools like Cal State–Los Angeles and the University of Illinois–Chicago.

So, yes, each of the eight institutions highlighted in this book can be viewed as illustrating important categories in the cosmology of American higher education. But, as I hope my brief profiles demonstrate, no category or label can ever fully capture the essential character, history, culture, and mission of these schools—or, indeed, any center of higher learning. These eight colleges and universities are, like the thousands of others for which they stand as exemplars, truly unique, and uniquely wonderful.

· · · · · · · · · · · · · · · ·

ACKNOWLEDGMENTS
· · · · · · · · · · · · · · · ·

This book reflects the invaluable lessons I have learned from the many dedicated professionals—far too many to list here—with whom I have had the good fortune to interact, both within and beyond the halls of academe. The many colleagues with whom I have shared experiences working in city and state government, consulting for federal agencies, and serving on foundation boards have helped shape my conviction that higher education must serve the goal of achieving social and racial justice in our radically unequal society. Working with hundreds of gifted educators, especially at Amherst and Reed, deepened my love for education in the liberal arts and my appreciation for its role in opening minds and hearts. Dozens of talented administrators at those schools, as well as Boston University and Penn, gave me an invaluable introduction to the mysterious worlds of college admissions, financial aid, student services, fundraising, budgeting, human resources, finance, real estate management, and public relations. I owe all of them my undying gratitude. Likewise, I want to express my deep appreciation to the thousands of students whom I have taught during my career for both inspiring and, at times, humbling me.

I would probably not have had the opportunity to share those lessons were it not for my editor at the Johns Hopkins University Press, Greg Britton. After discovering an article I had written back in 2005 about my liberation from college rankings as Reed's president, Greg contacted me out of the blue and suggested that I convert it into a book-length discussion. His steady hand has guided what I initially viewed as a rather quixotic venture into an illuminating and productive journey. I thank the Press for providing me with excellent copyediting assistance from Kathleen Capels and production assistance from its capable staff.

I am indebted to the dean of the Penn Law School, Ted Ruger, whose invitation to return to Penn in 2019 as a visiting professor gave me an ideal platform to conduct much of the research reflected in these pages, with considerable assistance from librarian Gabriela Femenia. That visit also enabled me to reconnect with Penn education professor Bob Zemsky, whose writings and sage advice over the years have deepened my understanding of the higher-education marketplace.

My most heartfelt gratitude goes to my wife, Joan, for her unflaggingly patient editorial assistance. As a published author herself, she brought to the undertaking a musical ear for language and a critical eye for logical flaws and organizational disorder that helped me convert a rather ungainly collection of thoughts into a coherent finished product.

NOTES

· · · · · · · · · · · · · · ·

PROLOGUE

1. See Diver 2005A.

CHAPTER 1. APPLES, ORANGES, AND REFRIGERATORS

1. Consumer Reports 2021.
2. College Board 2020, 18-19.
3. See chapter 20, table 20.1.
4. Wermund 2017.
5. IPEDS.
6. NCES, College Navigator.
7. College Scorecard.
8. College Affordability.
9. Carnegie Classification 2018.
10. Craig 2015, 8.
11. Hansmann 1999.
12. Sahlins 2020.

CHAPTER 2. MEET THE RANKING INDUSTRY'S 800-POUND GORILLA—AND ITS COUSINS

1. E.g., D. Webster 1986.
2. For helpful histories of college rankings, see Kelchen 2018; Mfume 2019.
3. Sanoff 2007.
4. For data on U.S. News rankings over the years, see Public University Honors 2020; Reiter 2021.
5. Washington Monthly 2020.
6. Princeton Review 2021B.
7. Shanghai Ranking 2020; THE 2020; QS 2020.
8. U.S. News 2020A.
9. See, e.g., Hazelkorn 2015; Shin, Toutkoushian, and Teichler 2011; Yudkovitch, Altbach, and Rumbley 2016.
10. Morse 2008.

CHAPTER 3. MAKING "BEST-COLLEGE STEW"

1. Morse and Brooks 2020.
2. Wall Street Journal 2020.
3. Forbes 2019; Washington Monthly 2020; Niche 2021.
4. Sanoff 2007.

5. T. Webster 2001.
6. Zemsky and Shaman 2017.
7. Griffiths and Rask 2005.
8. Luca and Smith 2013.
9. Gladwell 2011.

CHAPTER 4. WHO CARES ABOUT COLLEGE RANKINGS ANYWAY?
1. Harr 1984.
2. McDonough et al. 1998.
3. Hazelkorn 2015, 2.
4. Eagan et al. 2016.
5. Art & Science Group 2020.
6. McDonough et al. 1998.
7. E.g., Monks and Ehrenberg 1999.
8. E.g., Tutterow and Evans 2016.
9. Meredith 2004.
10. Bowman and Bastedo 2009.
11. Meyer, Hanson, and Hickman 2017.

CHAPTER 5. RESIST OR EMBRACE
1. Kuczynski 2001.
2. E.g., Nocera 2012; Tierney 2013.
3. Morphew and Swanson 2011.
4. Dichev 2001; Gnolek, Falciano, and Kuncl 2014.
5. Schmidt 2008.
6. Gnolek, Falciano, and Kuncl 2014.
7. E.g., Stecklow 1995, 1997.
8. Hoover 2007A.
9. Chronicle of Higher Education 1996.
10. Machung 1998.
11. Education Conservancy 2007.
12. Finder 2007.
13. Hoover 2007A.
14. Hoover 2007B.
15. Sanoff 2007.
16. Stecklow 1997.
17. Lydgate 2019; Quintana 2019.
18. Myers 2007.
19. See Anderson 2014.
20. Levin 2002.
21. Espeland and Sauder 2016.
22. E.g., Leiter 2018; Princeton Review 2021A.
23. Kutner 2014.
24. Zemsky 2009.
25. Sanoff 2007.
26. Luca 2015.
27. Morphew and Swanson 2011.

28. Diep 2020.
29. Chronicle of Higher Education 2007.
30. Espeland and Sauder 2016.

CHAPTER 6. GARBAGE IN?

1. Stecklow 1995.
2. Trachtenberg 2012.
3. Jaschik 2012.
4. Pérez-Peña and Slotnick 2012.
5. Brown 2013.
6. Longden 2011.
7. Brown 2013.
8. Lederman 2011.
9. Levenson 2019.
10. Jaschik 2018A.
11. Morse, Mason, and Brooks 2019.
12. Tamanaha 2012, 70–84.
13. Jaschik 2012.
14. Zahneis 2018.
15. Jaschik 2018A.
16. Jaschik 2012.
17. Morse, Mason, and Brooks 2019.
18. Jaschik 2013.
19. Morse, Mason, and Brooks 2019.
20. Sanoff 2007.
21. Diver 2005A.
22. Brown 2013.
23. Sachdev 2011.
24. Snyder and Arvedlund 2019.
25. Roebuck and Snyder 2021.
26. Snyder 2018.
27. Lederman 2011.

CHAPTER 7. CONFERRING PEDIGREE

1. McPhee 2011, 163.
2. Jefferson 1813.
3. Sandel 2020, 81.
4. Young 1958.
5. Markovits 2019, 17.
6. Veblen 1899.
7. Gutkin 2019, discussing Kronman 2019.
8. Guinier 2015.
9. Markovits 2019, 115.
10. Sandel 2020.
11. Rivera 2015.
12. Hirsch 1976.
13. Salinas-Jiménez, Artés, and Salinas-Jiménez 2011.

14. Frank and Cook 1995.
15. See, e.g., Sauder 2006.
16. Debrett's 2019.

CHAPTER 8. MEASURING PRESTIGE BY POPULARITY POLL

1. Baumann, Chu, and Anderton 2009.
2. Morse, Mason, and Brooks 2019.
3. Bastedo and Bowman 2010.
4. Gnolek, Falciano, and Kuncl 2014.
5. Bastedo and Bowman 2010; Stake 2006.

CHAPTER 9. THE WEALTH OF INSTITUTIONS

1. Kowarski 2020.
2. College Raptor 2021.
3. University of Notre Dame 2020.
4. Winston 1999.
5. Kaplan 2021.
6. Corradi and Schifrin 2019.
7. Kaplan 2021.
8. Golden 2019.
9. Arcidiacono, Kinsler, and Ransom 2019A.
10. See, e.g., Levitz and Korn 2020; Peretz 2019.
11. For a full, and very readable, account of the Varsity Blues scandal, see Levitz and Korn 2020.
12. Medina, Benner, and Taylor 2019.
13. Chetty et al. 2017.
14. Upshot 2017.
15. Schifrin and Tucker 2021.
16. Federal Student Aid 2020.
17. Zemsky, Shaman, and Baldridge 2020.
18. Edmit 2020.
19. Moody's 2020.

CHAPTER 10. THE SPENDING RAT RACE

1. Bureau of Labor Statistics 2021.
2. Baumol and Bowen 1966; Baumol and Blackman 1995.
3. Commonfund Institute 2020.
4. Clotfelter 1996; Martin and Hill 2013.
5. H. Bowen 1980.
6. Halliday 2016; Clotfelter 2017.
7. Winston 2000.
8. Hoxby 2009, 112.
9. NCES 2020.
10. Blom et al. 2020.
11. Selingo 2021.
12. See, e.g., Garthwaite et al. 2020.
13. Tough 2019, 182-199.
14. Chetty et al. 2017.

CHAPTER 11. THE BEST AND THE BRIGHTEST

1. Halberstam 1972.
2. Zwick 2017, 151-152.
3. Winston 1999.
4. See also Clotfelter 1996.
5. Hansmann 1999.
6. Barron's 2018.
7. GradeInflation.com 2020.
8. Arenson 2004.
9. Beckman 2018.
10. Rojstaczer and Healy 2012.
11. See, e.g., Johnson 2003.
12. Hurwitz and Lee 2018.
13. Hurwitz and Lee 2018.
14. See, e.g., Long, Saenz, and Tienda 2010.

CHAPTER 12. SAT

1. Lemann 1999.
2. E.g., Plomin and Spinath 2004.
3. E.g., Fullinwinder and Lichtenberg 2004.
4. Kuncel and Sackett 2018; Zwick 2017, 66.
5. See, e.g., Fullinwinder and Lichtenberg 2004.
6. E.g., Espenshade and Chung 2012; Hoover 2020B.
7. See, e.g., Zwick 2017.
8. Belkin 2019A.
9. Lemann 1999.
10. Belkin 2019A.
11. Belkin 2019B.
12. Elletson 2019.
13. College Board 2021.
14. College Board 2019A.
15. Morse and Brooks 2020.
16. Challenge Success 2018.
17. Mayhew et al. 2016, 96.
18. Mayhew et al. 2016, 111–112; see also Pike 2004.
19. Campbell, Jiminez, and Arrozal 2019.
20. J. Kim and Shim 2019, 951.

CHAPTER 13. CHASING HIGH SAT SCORES

1. Woo and Choy 2011.
2. Korn 2018.
3. Burd 2020.
4. Summarized in Dynarski 2008.
5. Cohodes and Goodman 2014.
6. Clotfelter, Hemelt, and Ladd 2018.
7. McPherson and Schapiro 1998.
8. College Board 2019B.

9. Stecklow 1995.
10. Morse and Brooks 2020.
11. Espenshade and Chung 2012.
12. Diver 2006.
13. See, e.g., Fullinwinder and Lichtenberg 2004, 123–129.
14. E.g., compare Soares 2012 with Buckley, Letukas, and Wildavsky 2018.
15. E.g., Hoover 2019 (re the University of Chicago).
16. Belasco, Rosinger, and Hearn 2014.
17. E.g., Hurwitz 2015; Hyman 2017.
18. Hoover 2020C.
19. Hoover 2015.
20. Hoover 2019.
21. Strauss 2020.
22. Hoover 2020A.
23. Watanabe 2021.
24. Hoover 2020C.
25. Morse and Brooks 2020.

CHAPTER 14. INTERCOLLEGIATE ADMISSIONS COMPETITION

1. FIDE 2021.
2. Avery et al. 2013.
3. Parchment 2020.
4. E.g., Bruni 2015; Selingo 2020; Steinberg 2002; Stevens 2007.
5. Lu and Tsotsong 2021.
6. Arcidiacono, Kinsler, and Ransom 2019B.
7. Avery et al. 2013.
8. Golden 2001.
9. Ivy Coach 2020.
10. Park and Eagan 2011.
11. Avery, Fairbanks, and Zeckhauser 2004.
12. Castro 2019.
13. M. Kim 2010.
14. Avery, Fairbanks, and Zeckhauser 2004, 9.
15. Jaschik 2011.
16. See Garthwaite et al. 2020.
17. Arcidiacono, Kinsler, and Ransom 2019A.

CHAPTER 15. AFFIRMATIVE INACTION

1. Guinier 2003; Massey et al. 2007.
2. NCES 2017, 237.
3. Carnevale and Strohl 2013.
4. Rothwell 2015A.
5. NCES 2019.
6. Nichols 2020.
7. Chace 2011.
8. *Regents of the University of California* 1978.
9. *Gratz* 2003; *Grutter* 2003; *Fisher* 2016.

10. NCES 2020.

11. Guiasu and Guiasu 2012.

12. Mayhew et al. 2016, 87–88, 283–284.

13. Mayhew et al. 2016, 282–283, 302–304

14. Sander 2004.

15. Sander and Taylor 2012.

16. Kidder 2013.

17. W. Bowen and Bok 2006.

18. For graduation rates, see Carnevale, Quinn, and Campbell, 2019; Rothwell 2015A. For post-graduate earnings, see Dale and Krueger 2014.

19. U.S. News 2020B.

20. Larkin 2020.

21. Graf 2019.

22. Mayhew et al. 2016, 154–155.

CHAPTER 16. INSIDE THE BLACK BOX
1. ACT 2020; Educational Testing Service 2020; CAE 2020.

2. CLA+ 2015, 2019.

3. Belkin 2017.

4. Arum and Roksa 2011.

5. NSSE 2020; CSEQ 2020.

6. Bowman 2010, 2011.

7. Mayhew et. al. 2016, 73–74.

8. Babcock and Marks 2010.

9. Arum and Roksa 2011.

CHAPTER 17. PROXIES FOR LEARNING OUTCOMES
1. ACTA 2020.

2. Zemsky 2009, 120.

3. E.g., Zull 2002.

4. AAC&U 2020; Lumina Foundation 2020; Chickering and Gamson 1990.

5. Campbell, Jiminez, and Arrozol 2019; J. Kim and Shim 2019.

6. Rocha 2018.

7. Mayhew et al. 2016, 116.

8. Princeton Review 2021.

9. RateMyProfessors 2020.

10. Porter 2011.

11. NCES 2020.

12. Morse and Brooks 2020.

13. Mayhew et al. 2016, 44–45.

14. Zemsky 2009, 179.

15. Stolzenberg et al. 2019, 42, 44.

CHAPTER 18. CROSSING THE FINISH LINE
1. Kelderman 2020.

2. Koropeckyj, Lafakis, and Ozimek 2017.

3. Dougherty et al. 2016.

4. Ginder, Kelly-Reid, and Mann 2018.
5. Mayhew et al. 2016, 145.
6. Kirp 2019.
7. Gardner 2019.
8. E.g., Denning, Eide, and Warnick 2019.
9. Dougherty et al. 2016, 168.
10. National Student Clearinghouse Research Center 2019.
11. Ginder, Kelly-Reid, and Mann 2018.
12. Kimbrough 2020.
13. Porter 2000.
14. W. Bowen, Chingos, and McPherson 2009.

CHAPTER 19. MAKING A LIVING
1. Tamanaha 2012, 70-84; see also Segal 2011.
2. Campos 2011.
3. Woodhouse 2015.
4. Fishman 2015.
5. PayScale 2020.
6. PayScale 2021.
7. Georgetown University 2019.
8. E.g., Hoxby 2019.
9. Dale and Kreuger 2002, 2014.
10. Chetty et al. 2020; Hoxby 2019.
11. E.g., Witteveen and Attewell 2017; Zhang 2005.
12. Kulkarni and Rothwell 2015.
13. Hershbein 2013.

CHAPTER 20. SOCIAL IMMOBILITY
1. Amherst College Documents 1963.
2. Amherst College Documents 1963.
3. Opportunity Insights 2020.
4. Rothwell 2015A.
5. Fry and Cilluffo 2019.
6. Chetty et al. 2017.
7. For overviews of the pricing and financing of higher education, see Goldrick-Rab 2016; Lieber 2021; Zaloom 2019.
8. Money 2020.
9. College Board 2019B.
10. Delisle 2017.
11. Tough 2019.
12. College Board 2019B.
13. Jack 2019.
14. Jaschik 2018B.
15. U.S. News 2021A.
16. See Fuller and Mitchell 2020.
17. CollegeNET 2020.
18. Chetty et al. 2017.

19. Upshot 2017.
20. Chetty et al. 2020.

CHAPTER 21. MAKING A LIFE

1. Diver 2005B.
2. Diver 2005B.
3. Nelson 2015.
4. See Akers 2013.
5. Kronman 2019, 22.
6. Purdue University 2021.
7. Gallup-Purdue Index 2014.
8. Gallup-Purdue Index 2015, 2.
9. Reed College 2020.
10. Kronman 2019, 62.
11. Mayhew et al. 2016, 487–522.
12. Gallup-Purdue Index 2014.
13. Tough 2019.

CONCLUSION

1. E.g., Hoxby 2009.
2. E.g., Sandel 2020, 197.
3. Honan 1996.

APPENDIX

1. Information in this appendix comes primarily from college websites.
2. *Berea College* 1908.
3. *Plessy* 1896.
4. *Brown* 1954.
5. Chen 2016.
6. *Gratz* 2003.
7. *Grutter* 2003.
8. *Schuette* 2014.
9. Edelman 2000.

BIBLIOGRAPHY

AAC&U (Association of American Colleges & Universities). 2020. "VALUE Rubrics." https://www.aacu.org/value-rubrics/. Accessed July 12, 2020.

ACT. 2020. "ACT Collegiate Assessment of Academic Proficiency." http://www.act.org/content/act/en/postsecondary-professionals.html. Accessed Aug. 21, 2020.

ACTA (American Council of Trustees and Alumni). 2020. "What Will They Learn?" https://www.goacta.org/initiatives/what-will-they-learn/. Accessed Aug. 18, 2020.

Akers, Beth. 2013. "Criticisms of College Scorecard Are Off the Mark." Brookings, Feb. 2, 2013, https://www.brookings.edu/research/criticisms-of-college-scorecard-are-off-the-mark/.

Amherst College Documents. 1963. "Text of President Kennedy's Convocation Address." https://www.amherst.edu/library/archives/exhibitions/kennedy/documents#Final/.a.

Anderson, Nick. 2014. "U.S. News College Rankings: Amid Predictability, Some Major Shifts." *Washington Post*, Sept. 8, 2014.

Arcidiacono, Peter, Josh Kinsler, and Tyler Ransom. 2019A. "Legacy and Athlete Preferences at Harvard." NBER Working Paper No. 26316, Sept. 2019. National Bureau of Economic Research, https://www.nber.org/papers/w26316/.

———. 2019B. "Recruit to Reject? Harvard and African American Applicants." NBER Working Paper No. 26456, Sept. 2019. National Bureau of Economic Research, https://www.nber.org/papers/w26456.ack/.

Arenson, Karen W. 2004. "Is It Grade Inflation, or Are Students Just Smarter?" *New York Times*, Apr. 18, 2004.

Art & Science Group. 2020. "Student Polls" 1(1) (1995); 2(4) (1997); 5(1) (2002); and 12(3) (2016). Can be found at https://www.artsci.com. Accessed June 24, 2020.

Arum, Richard, and Josipa Roksa. 2011. *Academically Adrift: Limited Learning on College Campuses*. Chicago: University of Chicago Press.

Avery, Christopher N., Andrew Fairbanks, and Richard Zeckhauser. 2004. *The Early Admission Game: Joining the Elite*. Cambridge, MA: Harvard University Press.

Avery, Christopher N., Mark E. Glickman, Caroline M. Hoxby, and Andrew Metrick. 2013. "A Revealed Preference Ranking of U.S. Colleges and Universities." *Quarterly Journal of Economics*, 128(1): 425-467.

Babcock, Philip, and Mindy Marks. 2010. "The Falling Time Cost of College: Evidence from Half a Century of Time Use Data." *Review of Economics and Statistics*, 93(2): 468-478.

Barron's. 2018. *Barron's Profiles of American Colleges, 2019*, 35th edition. Hauppauge, NY: Barron's Educational Series.

Bastedo, Michael N., and Nicholas A. Bowman. 2010. "U.S. News & World Report College Rankings: Modeling Institutional Effects on Organization Reputation." *American Journal of Education*, 116(2): 163-183.

Baumann, Robert W., David K. W. Chu, and Charles H. Anderton. 2009. "Religious Penalty in the U.S. News & World Report College Rankings." *Education Economics*, 17(4): 491-504.

Baumol, William J., and Sue Anne Batey Blackman. 1995. "How to Think about Rising College Costs." *Planning for Higher Education*, 3(summer): 1-7.

Baumol, William J., and William G. Bowen. 1966. *Performing Arts, the Economic Dilemma: A Study of Problems Common to Theater, Opera, Music, and Dance.* Cambridge, MA: MIT Press.

Beckman, Kate. 2018. "The Top 15 Universities with the Highest Average GPAs." Ripplematch, https://ripplematch.com/journal/article/the-top-15-universities-with-the-highest-average-gpas-4f4b544d/.

Belasco, Andrew S., Kelly Ochs Rosinger, and James C. Hearn. 2014. "The Test-Optional Movement at American's Selective Liberal Arts Colleges: A Boon for Equity or Something Else?" *Educational Evaluation and Policy Analysis*, 37(2): 206-223.

Belkin, Douglas. 2017. "Exclusive Test Data: Many Colleges Fail to Improve Critical-Thinking Skills." *Wall Street Journal*, June 5, 2017.

———. 2019A. "SAT to Give Students 'Adversity Score' to Capture Social and Economic Background." *Wall Street Journal*, May 16, 2019.

———. 2019B. "What Happens if SAT Scores Consider Adversity? Find Your School." *Wall Street Journal*, Nov. 26, 2019.

Berea College v. Kentucky, 211 U.S. 45 (1908).

Blom, Erica, Kelia Washington, Macy Rainer, and Carina Chien. 2020. "IPEDS Finance User Guide," version 1.0. Urban Institute, May 2020, https://www.urban.org/sites/default/files/publication/102227/ipeds-finance-user-guide_finalized_0.pdf.

Bowen, Howard R. 1980. *The Costs of Higher Education: How Much Do Colleges and Universities Spend per Student and How Much Should They Spend?* San Francisco: Jossey-Bass.

Bowen, William G., and Derek Bok. 2006. *The Shape of the River: Long-Term Consequences of Considering Race in College and University Admissions.* Princeton, NJ: Princeton University Press.

Bowen, William G., Matthew M. Chingos, and Michael S. McPherson. 2009. *Crossing the Finish Line: Completing College at America's Public Universities.* Princeton, NJ: Princeton University Press.

Bowman, Nicholas A. 2010. "Can First-Year Students Accurately Report Their Learning and Development?" *American Educational Research Journal*, 47(2): 466-496.

————. 2011. "Validity of College Self-Reported Gains at Diverse Institutions." *Education Researcher*, 40(1): 22-24.

Bowman, Nicholas A., and Michael N. Bastedo. 2009. "Getting on the Front Page: Organizational Reputation, Status Signals, and the Impact of U.S. News and World Report on Student Decisions." *Research in Higher Education*, 50(5): 415-436.

Brown, Abram. 2013. "Why Forbes Removed 4 Schools from Its America's Best Colleges Rankings." *Forbes*, Aug. 12, 2013.

Brown v. Board of Education, 347 U.S. 483 (1954).

Bruni, Frank. 2015. *Where You Go Is Not Who You'll Be: An Antidote to the College Admissions Mania*. New York: Grand Central.

Buckley, Jack, Lynn Letukas, and Ben Wildavsky, eds. 2018. *Measuring Success: Testing, Grades, and the Future of College Admissions*. Baltimore: Johns Hopkins University Press.

Burd, Stephen. 2020. "Crisis Point: How Enrollment Management and the Merit-Aid Arms Race Are Derailing Public Higher Education." New America, Feb. 13, 2020, https://www .newamerica.org/education-policy/reports/.

Bureau of Labor Statistics. 2021. "College Tuition and Fees in U.S. City Average, All Urban Consumers, Seasonally Adjusted," for time period 2001-2020. BLS Beta Labs, https://beta .bls.gov/dataViewer/view/timeseries/CUSR0000SEEB01/.

CAE (Council for Aid to Education). 2020. "Assessing Essential College and Career Skills Since 2002." https://cae.org/. Accessed Aug. 24, 2020.

Campbell, Corbin M., Marisol Jiminez, and Christine Arlene N. Arrozal. 2019. "Prestige or Education: College Teaching and Rigor of Courses." *Higher Education*, 77(4): 717-738.

Campos, Paul. 2011. "Served: How Law Schools Completely Misrepresent Their Job Numbers." *New Republic*, Apr. 25, 2011, https://newrepublic.com/article/87251/law-school -employment-harvard-yale-georgetown/.

Carnegie Classification of Institutions of Higher Education. 2018. "2018 Classification Update." https://www.carnegieclassifications.iu.edu.

Carnevale, Anthony P., C. Quinn, and Kathryn Peltier Campbell. 2019. "SAT-Only Admission: How Would It Change College Campuses?" Georgetown University Center on Education and the Workforce, https://cew.georgetown.edu/cew-reports/satonly/.

Carnevale, Anthony P., and Jeff Strohl. 2013. "Separate & Unequal: How Higher Education Reinforces the Intergenerational Reproduction of White Racial Privilege." Georgetown University Center on Education and the Workforce, July 2013, https://cew.georgetown.edu /wp-content/uploads/SeparateUnequal.FR_.pdf.

Castro, Abril. 2019. "Early Decision Harms Students of Color and Low-Income Students." Center for American Progress, Nov. 4, 2019, https://www.americanprogress.org.

Chace, William M. 2011. "Affirmative Inaction." *American Scholar*, Dec. 1, 2011, https:// theamericanscholar.org/affirmative-inaction/#.Xx2F5yo5Rp8/.

Challenge Success. 2018. "A 'Fit' Over Rankings." White Papers, Oct. 2018, https://www
.challengesuccess.org/resources/research/white-papers/.

Chen, David W. 2016. "Dreams Stall as CUNY, New York City's Engine of Mobility, Sputters."
New York Times, May 28, 2016.

Chetty, Raj., John N. Friedman, Emmanuel Saez, Nicholas Turner, and Danny Yagan. 2017.
"Mobility Report Cards: The Role of Colleges in Intergenerational Mobility." NBER
Working Paper No. 23618, revised version, Dec. 2017. Opportunity Insights, https://
opportunityinsights.org/paper/mobilityreportcards/.

———. 2020. "Income Segregation and Intergenerational Mobility across Colleges in the U.S."
Quarterly Journal of Economics, 135(3): 1567-1633.

Chickering, Arthur W., and Zelda F. Gamson, eds. 1990. *Applying the Seven Principles for
Good Practice in US Education: New Directions for Teaching and Learning*. San Francisco:
Jossey-Bass.

Chronicle of Higher Education. 1996. "Stanford Students Attack 'U.S. News' College Rankings."
Oct. 25, 1996.

———. 2007. "The $60,000 Question: Will Arizona State Rise in Magazine's Rankings?" Mar.
18, 2007.

CLA+ (Collegiate Learning Assessment). 2015. "Spring 2015 CLA+ Results: Institutional Report,
Kansas State University." Assessment of Student Learning, Kansas State University, https://
www.k-state.edu/assessment/surveys/cla/.

———. 2019. "Spring 2019 CLA+ Results: Institutional Report, St. Olaf College." https://
wp.stolaf.edu/ir-e/files/2019/09/Spring-2019-CLA-Institution-Report.pdf.

Clotfelter, Charles T. 1996. *Buying the Best: Cost Escalation in Elite Higher Education*. Princeton,
NJ: Princeton University Press.

———. 2017. *Unequal Colleges in the Age of Disparity*. Cambridge, MA: Belknap Press of the
Harvard University Press.

Clotfelter, Charles T., Steven W Hemelt, and Helen F Ladd. 2018. "Multifaceted Aid for Low-
Income Students and College Outcomes: Evidence from North Carolina." *Economic
Inquiry*, 56(1): 278-303.

Cohodes, Sarah, and Joshua Goodman. 2014. "Merit Aid, College Quality, and College
Completion: Massachusetts' Adams Scholarship as an In-Kind Subsidy." *American
Economic Journal: Applied Economics*, 6(4): 251-281.

College Affordability. See US Department of Education.

College Board. 2019A. "SAT: Understanding Scores 2019." https://web.archive.org/web
/20191211232552/https://collegereadiness.collegeboard.org/pdf/understanding-sat
-scores.pdf.

———. 2019B. "Trends in Student Aid 2019." Trends in Higher Education Series, https://
research.collegeboard.org/pdf/trends-student-aid-2019-full-report.pdf.

———. 2020. "Trends in College Pricing and Student Aid 2020." Trends in Higher Education Series, https://research.collegeboard.org/pdf/trends-college-pricing-student-aid-2020.pdf.

———. 2021. "Landscape: Consistent High School and Neighborhood Information for Colleges." https://pages.collegeboard.org/landscape/. Accessed Jan. 13, 2021.

CollegeNET. 2020. "2020 Social Mobility Index: Opportunity through U.S. Higher Education." https://www.socialmobilityindex.org.

College Raptor. 2021. "Endowment per Student for 2021." https://www.collegeraptor.com/college-rankings/details/EndomentPerStudent/.

College Scorecard. See US Department of Education.

Commonfund Institute. 2020. "Higher Education Price Index: 2020 Update." https://www.commonfund.org/hubfs/Institute/HEPI/Reports/2020-Commonfund-Higher-Education-Price-Index.pdf.

Consumer Reports. 2021. "Best Refrigerators of 2021." https://www.consumerreports.org/refrigerators/best-refrigerators-of-the-year/.

Corradi, Anna, and Matt Schifrin. 2019. "Grateful Grads 2019: Follow Alumni Love and Money into the Best Colleges." *Forbes*, Aug. 15, 2019.

Craig, Ryan. 2015. *College Disrupted: The Great Unbundling of Higher Education.* New York: St. Martin's.

CSEQ (College Student Experiences Questionnaire). 2020. "The College Student Experiences Questionnaire Assessment Program." cseq.indiana.edu/cseq_generalinfo.cfm. Accessed Aug. 23, 2020.

Dale, Stacy B., and Alan B. Krueger. 2002. "Estimating the Payoff to Attending a More Selective College: An Application of Selection on Observables and Unobservables." *Quarterly Journal of Economics*, 117(4): 1491-1527.

———. 2014. "Estimating the Effects of College Characteristics over the Career Using Administrative Earnings Data." *Journal of Human Resources*, 49(2): 323-358.

Debrett's. 2019. *Debrett's Peerage and Baronetage 2019.* London: Debrett's.

Delisle, Jason. 2017. "The Pell Grant Proxy: A Ubiquitous but Flawed Measure of Low-Income Student Enrollment." Brookings , Oct. 12, 2017, https://www.brookings.edu/research/the-pell-grant-proxy-a-ubiquitous-but-flawed-measure-of-low-income-student-enrollment/.

Denning, Jeffrey T., Eric R. Eide, and Merrill Warnick. 2019. "Why Have College Completion Rates Increased? An Analysis of Rising Grades." EdWorkingPaper No. 19-11, June 2019. Annenberg Institute at Brown University, https://edworkingpapers.org/index.php/authors/eric-r-eide/.

Dichev, Ilia D. 2001. "News or Noise? Estimating the Noise in the U.S. News University Rankings." *Research in Higher Education*, 42(3): 237-266.

Diep, Francie. 2020. "The Rules of the Game: How the U.S. News Rankings Helped Reshape One State's Public Colleges." *Chronicle of Higher Education*, Sept. 14, 2020.

Diver, Colin S. 2005A. "Is There Life after Rankings?" *Atlantic*, Nov. 2005, 136-139.

———. 2005B. "Knowledge for Its Own Sake." In Lloyd Thacker, ed., *College Unranked: Ending the College Admissions Frenzy*, 133-139. Cambridge. MA: Harvard University Press.

———. 2006. "Skip the Test, Betray the Cause." *New York Times*, Sept. 18, 2006.

Dougherty, Kevin, Sosanya M. Jones, Hana Lahr, Rebecca S. Natow, Lara Pheatt, and Vikash Reddy. 2016. *Performance Funding for Higher Education*. Baltimore: Johns Hopkins University Press.

Dynarski, Susan. 2008. "Building the Stock of College-Educated Labor." *Journal of Human Resources*, 4(3): 576-610.

Eagan, Kevin, Ellen Bara Stolzenberg, Abigail K. Bates, Melissa C. Aragon, Maria Ramirez Suchard, and Cecilia Rios-Aguilar. 2016. "The American Freshman: National Norms, Fall 2015." Cooperative Institutional Research Program, Higher Education Research Institute at UCLA, https://www.heri.ucla.edu/monographs/TheAmerican Freshman2015.pdf.

Edelman, Marian Wright. 2000. "Spelman College: A Safe Haven for a Young Black Woman." *Journal of Blacks in Higher Education*, 27(spring): 118-123.

Edmit. 2020. "Edmit College Search." https://www.edmit.me/browse/. Accessed Sep. 3, 2020.

Educational Testing Service. 2020. "ETS Proficiency Profile." https://www.ets.org /proficiencyprofile/about/. Accessed Aug. 21, 2020.

Education Conservancy, The. 2007. "Dear Colleague" letter, May 10, 2007, http://www .educationconservancy.org/presidents_letter.html.

Elletson, Grace. 2019. "Facing Criticism, College Board Backs Away from 'Adversity Score.'" *Chronicle of Higher Education*, Aug. 27, 2019.

Espeland, Wendy Nelson, and Michael Sauder. 2016. *Engines of Anxiety: Academic Rankings, Reputation, and Accountability*. New York: Russell Sage Foundation.

Espenshade, Thomas J., and Chang Young Chung. 2012. "Diversity Outcomes of Test-Optional Policies." In Joseph A. Soares, ed., *SAT Wars: The Case for Test-Optional College Admissions*, 177-200. New York: Teachers College Press.

Federal Student Aid. 2020. "Financial Responsibility Scores." https://www.studentaid.gov /data-center/school/composite-scores/. Accessed Sept. 3, 2020.

FIDE (International Chess Federation). 2021. "Top Chess Players." https://ratings.fide.com.

Finder, Alan. 2007. "Some Colleges to Drop Out of U.S. News Rankings." *New York Times*, June 20, 2007.

Fisher v. University of Texas, 136 S.Ct. 2198 (2016).

Fishman, Rachel. 2015. "Deciding to Go to College: 2015 College Decisions Survey; Part I."

New America, May 2015, https://www.luminafoundation.org/files/resources/deciding
-to-go-to-college.pdf.

Forbes. 2019. "America's Top Colleges 2019." https://www.forbes.com/top-college
/#4343c0811987/.

Frank, Robert H., and Philip J. Cook. 1995. *The Winner-Take-All Society*. New York: Free Press.

Fry, Richard, and Anthony Cilluffo. 2019. "A Rising Share of Undergraduates Are from Poor
Families." Pew Research Center, May 22, 2019, https://www.pewresearch.org/social
-trends/.

Fuller, Andrea, and Josh Mitchell. 2020. "Which Schools Leave Parents with the Most
College Loan Debt?" *Wall Street Journal*, Dec. 3, 2020.

Fullinwinder, Robert K., and Judith Lichtenberg. 2004. *Leveling the Playing Field: Justice,
Politics, and College Admissions*. Lanham, MD: Rowman & Littlefield.

Gallup-Purdue Index Report. 2014. "Great Jobs, Great Lives: The 2014 Gallup-Purdue Index
Report." https://www.gallup.com/services/176768/2014-gallup-purdue-index-report
.aspx.

———. 2015. " The Gallup-Purdue 2015 Report: The Relationship between Student Debt,
Experiences and Perceptions of College Worth." https://www.gallup.com/services/185924
/gallup-purdue-index-2015-report.aspx.

Gardner, Lee. 2019. "Students under Surveillance? Data Tracking Enters a Provocative New
Phase." *Chronicle of Higher Education*, Oct. 13, 2019.

Garthwaite, Craig, Jordan Keener, Matthew J. Notowidigdo, and Nicole F. Ozminkowski. 2020.
"Who Profits from Amateurism? Rent-Sharing in Modern College Sports." NBER Working
Paper 27734, Oct. 2020, National Bureau of Economic Research, https://www.nber.org
/system/files/working_papers/w27734/w27734.pdf.

Georgetown University Center on Education and the Workforce. 2019. "Ranking ROI of 4,500
US Colleges and Universities." https://cew.georgetown.edu/cew-reports/collegeroi/.

Ginder, Scott, Janice E. Kelly-Reid, and Farrah Mann. 2018. "Graduation Rates for Selected
Cohorts, 2009-14." NCES No. 2018-151, Dec. 2018. National Center for Education Statistics,
Institute of Education Sciences, https://nces.ed.gov/pubs2018/2018151.pdf.

Gladwell, Malcolm. 2011. "The Order of Things: What College Rankings Really Tell Us." *New
Yorker*, Feb. 14, 2011.

Gnolek, Shari L., Vincent T. Falciano, and Ralph W. Kuncl. 2014. "Modeling Change and
Variation in 'U.S. News & World Report' College Rankings: What Would It Really Take to
Be in the Top 20?" *Research in Higher Education*, 55(8): 761-779.

Golden, Daniel. 2001. "Glass Floor: How Colleges Reject the Top Applicants, Accepting Only
the Students Likely to Enroll." *Wall Street Journal*, May 29, 2001, https://www.wsj.com
/articles/SB991083160294634500/.

———. 2019. *The Price of Admission: How America's Ruling Class Buys Its Way into Elite Colleges— and Who Gets Left Outside the Gates*, updated edition. New York: Crown.

Goldrick-Rab, Sara. 2016. *Paying the Price: College Cost, Financial Aid, and the Betrayal of the American Dream.* Chicago: University of Chicago Press.

GradeInflation.com. 2020. "Grade Inflation at American Colleges and Universities." https:// gradeinflation.com. Accessed Dec. 14, 2020.

Graf, Nikki. 2019. "Most Americans Say Colleges Should Not Consider Race or Ethnicity in Admissions." Pew Research Center, Feb. 25, 2019, https://www.pewresearch.org/fact-tank/.

Gratz v. Bollinger, 539 U.S. 244 (2003).

Griffiths, Amanda, and Kevin Rask. 2005. "The Influence of the U.S. News and World Report Collegiate Rankings on the Matriculation Decisions of High-Ability Students: 1995-2004." CHERI Working Paper No. 76, Sept. 2005. Cornell Higher Education Research Institute, https://archive.ilr.cornell.edu/sites/default/files/WP76.pdf.

Grutter v. Bollinger, 539 U.S. 306 (2003).

Guiasu, Radu Cornel, and Silviu Guiasu. 2012. "The Weighted Gini-Simpson Index: Revitalizing an Old Index of Biodiversity." *International Journal of Ecology*, Feb. 16, 2012, https://doi.org /10.1155/2012/478728/.

Guinier, Lani. 2003. "The Supreme Court, 2002 Term—comment: Admissions Rituals as Political Acts; Guardians at the Gates of Our Democratic Ideals." *Harvard Law Review*, 117(1): 113-224.

———. 2015. *The Tyranny of the Meritocracy: Democratizing Higher Education in America*. Boston: Beacon Press.

Gutkin, Len. 2019. "Elite Schools Are National Treasures. Their Elitism Is What Makes Them Such." *Chronicle of Higher Education*, July 12, 2019.

Halberstam, David. 1972. *The Best and the Brightest*. New York: Random House.

Halliday, Daniel. 2016. "Private Education, Positional Goods, and the Arms Race Problem." *Politics, Philosophy, and Economics*, 15(2): 150-169.

Hansmann, Henry. 1999. "Higher Education as an Associative Good." Yale International Center for Finance Working Paper No. 99-13 and Yale Law School Program for Studies in Law, Economics, and Public Policy Working Paper No. 99-15. Social Sciences Research Network, http://papers.ssrn.com/paper.taf?abstract_id=192576/.

Harr, Jonathan. 1984. "The Admissions Circus." *New England Monthly*, Apr. 1984, 48, discussed in Clotfelter (2017), 166.

Hazelkorn, Ellen. 2015. *Rankings and the Reshaping of Higher Education: The Battle for World-Class Excellence*. London: Palgrave Macmillan.

Hershbein, Brad J. 2013. "Worker Signals among New College Graduates: The Role of Selectivity and GPA." Upjohn Institute Working Paper No. 13-190, Jan. 1. W. E. Upjohn Institute for Employment Research, https://research.upjohn.org.

Hirsch, Fred. 1976. *Social Limits to Growth*. Cambridge, MA: Harvard University Press.

Honan, William H. 1996. "Time and Newsweek Join Lucrative Fray for College Guides." *New York Times*, Aug. 4, 1996.

Hoover, Eric. 2007A. "College Rankings from 'U.S. News' Change Little, but Response Rate to Reputational Survey Drops." *Chronicle of Higher Education*, Aug. 17, 2007.

———. 2007B. "Presidents of 19 Top-Ranked Liberal-Arts Colleges Warn of 'Inevitable Biases' in College Rankings." *Chronicle of Higher Education*, Sept. 10, 2007.

———. 2015. "College Admissions, Frozen in Time." *Chronicle of Higher Education*, May 26, 2015.

———. 2019. "An Elite College Dropped the ACT/SAT: Then What?" *Chronicle of Higher Education*, July 19, 2019.

———. 2020A. "Golden State Blockbuster: U. of California Will Replace ACT and SAT with New Test—or None at All." *Chronicle of Higher Education*, May 21, 2020.

———. 2020B. "Here's Why a University of California Panel Recommends Keeping the ACT and SAT—for Now." *Chronicle of Higher Education*, Feb. 30, 2020.

———. 2020C. "'U.S. News' Will Start Ranking Test-Blind Colleges. But Will It Adjust Methodology for Test-Optional Ones?" *Chronicle of Higher Education*, June 17, 2020.

Hoxby, Caroline M. 2009. "The Changing Selectivity of American Colleges." *Journal of Economic Perspectives*, 23(4): 95-118.

———. 2019. "The Productivity of American Postsecondary Institutions." In Caroline M. Hoxby and Kevin Stange, eds., *Productivity in Higher Education*, 31-66. Chicago: University of Chicago Press.

Hurwitz, Michael. 2015. "The Maine Question: How Is 4-Year College Enrollment Affected by Mandatory College Entrance Exams?" *Economics of Education Review*, 37(1): 138-159.

Hurwitz, Michael, and Jason Lee. 2018. "Grade Inflation and the Role of Standardized Testing." In Jack Buckley, Lynn Letukas, and Ben Wildavsky, eds., *Measuring Success: Testing, Grades, and the Future of College Admissions*, ch. 3. Baltimore: Johns Hopkins University Press.

Hyman, Joshua. 2017. "ACT for All: The Effect of Mandatory College Entrance Exams on Postsecondary Attainment and Choice." *Education Finance and Policy*, 12(3), 281-311.

IPEDS (Integrated Postsecondary Education Data System). n.d. National Center for Education Statistics, https://nces.ed.gov/ipeds/.

Ivy Coach. 2020. "2023 Ivy League Admissions Statistics." ivycoach.com/2023-ivy-league -admissions-statistics/. Accessed Aug. 10, 2020.

Jack, Anthony Abraham. 2019. *The Privileged Poor: How Elite Colleges Are Failing Disadvantaged Students*. Cambridge, MA: Harvard University Press.

Jaschik, Scott. 2011. "Elite Universities Surrender to Early Admissions." *USA Today*, Feb. 25, 2011.

———. 2012. "Another Rankings Fabrication." Inside Higher Ed, Nov. 9, 2012, https://www .insidehighered.com/news/2012/11/09/george-washington-u-admits-submitting-false -data-class-rank/.

———. 2013. "Can You Verify That?" Inside Higher Ed, Feb. 6, 2013, https://www.insidehighered
.com/news/2013/02/06/wake-reports-false-data-us-news-considers-new-way-promote
-accuracy/.

———. 2018A. "8 More Colleges Submitted Incorrect Data for Rankings." Inside Higher Ed,
Aug. 27, 2018, https://www.insidehighered.com/admissions/article/2018/08/27/eight-more
-colleges-identified-submitting-incorrect-data-us-news/.

———. 2018B. "The 'U.S. News' Rankings' (Faux?) Embrace of Social Mobility." Inside Higher
Ed, Oct. 28, 2018, https://www.insidehighered.com/admissions/article/2018/09/10/us
-news-says-it-has-shifted-rankings-focus-social-mobility-has-it/.

Jefferson, Thomas. 1813. "Letter of Thomas Jefferson to John Adams, Oct. 28, 1813." In Lester J.
Cappon, ed., *The Adams-Jefferson Letters: The Complete Correspondence between Thomas
Jefferson and Abigail and John Adams*, vol. 2, 387. Chapel Hill: University of North Carolina
Press, 1988.

Johnson, Valen E. 2003. *Grade Inflation: A Crisis in College Education*. New York: Springer.

Kaplan, Ann E. 2021. "Voluntary Support of Education Key Findings 2019-20." Council for
Advancement and Support of Education, Feb. 9, 2021, https://www.case.org.

Kelchen, Robert. 2018. *Higher Education Accountability*. Baltimore: Johns Hopkins University
Press.

Kelderman, Eric. 2020. "Happy New Year, Higher Education: You've Missed Your Completion
Goal." *Chronicle of Higher Education*, Jan. 7, 2020.

Kidder, William. 2013. "A High Target for 'Mismatch': Bogus Arguments about Affirmative
Action." Los Angeles Review of Books, Feb. 7, 2013, https://lareviewofbooks.org/article
/a-high-target-for-mismatch-bogus-arguments-about-affirmative-action/.

Kim, Jeongeun, and Woo-Jeong Shim. 2019. "What Do Rankings Measure? The U.S. News
Rankings and Student Experiences at Liberal Arts Colleges." *Review of Higher Education*,
42(3): 933-964.

Kim, Matthew. 2010. "Early Decision and Financial Aid Competition among Need-Blind
Colleges and Universities." *Journal of Public Economics*, 94(5-6): 410-420.

Kimbrough, Walter M. 2020. "It's Time to Stop Calculating Graduation Rates." *Chronicle of
Higher Education*, Feb. 28, 2020.

Kirp, David. 2019. *The Dropout Scandal*. New York: Oxford University Press.

Korn, Melissa. 2018. "Prizes for Everyone: How Colleges Use Scholarships to Lure Students."
Wall Street Journal, Apr. 17, 2018.

Koropeckyj, Sophia, Chris Lafakis, and Adam Ozimek. 2017. "The Economic Impact of
Increasing College Completion." American Academy of Arts and Sciences Commission on
the Future of Undergraduate Education, https://www.amacad.org/publication/economic
-impact-increasing-college-completion/.

Kowarski, Ilana. 2020. "10 Universities with the Biggest Endowments." U.S. News & World

Report, Sept. 22, 2020, https://www.usnews.com/education/best-colleges/the-short
-list-college/articles/10-universities-with-the-biggest-endowments/.

Kronman, Anthony T. 2019. *The Assault on American Excellence*. New York: Free Press.

Kuczynski, Alex. 2001. "The Media Business, 'Best' List for Colleges by U.S. News Is under
Fire." *New York Times*, Aug. 20, 2001.

Kulkarni, Siddharth, and Jonathan Rothwell. 2015. "Beyond College Rankings: A Value-
Added Approach to Assessing Two- and Four-Year Schools." Brookings, Apr. 29, 2015,
https://www.brookings.edu/research/beyond-college-rankings-a-value-added
-approach-to-assessing-two-and-four-year-schools/.

Kuncel, Nathan, and Paul Sackett. 2018. "The Truth about the SAT and ACT." *Wall Street
Journal*, Mar. 8, 2018.

Kutner, Max. 2014. "How to Game the College Rankings." *Boston Magazine*, Aug. 26, 2014,
https://www.bostonmagazine.com/news/2014/08/26/how-northeastern-gamed-the
-college-rankings/.

Larkin, Max. 2020. "Under Financial Stress, Pine Manor College to Join Boston College."
WBUR, May 13, 2020, https://www.wbur.org/edify/2020/05/13/pine-manor-acquisition/.

Lederman, Doug. 2011. "Disingenuous Data." Inside Higher Ed, Nov. 9, 2011, https://www.
insidehighered.com/news/2011/11/09/iona-admits-ex-official-misreported-data
-outside-entities/.

Leiter, Brian. 2018. "Top 50 Law Schools Based on Scholarly Impact." Brian Leiter's Law
School Reports, Aug. 13, 2018, https://leiterlawschool.typepad.com/leiter/2018/08/top
-50-law-schools-based-on-scholarly-impact-2018.html.

Lemann, Nicholas. 1999. *The Big Test: The Secret History of the American Meritocracy*. New
York: Farrar, Straus & Giroux.

Levenson, Eric. 2019. "University of Oklahoma Gave False Data to U.S. News College
Rankings for 20 Years." CNN, May 24, 2019, https://www.cnn.com/2019/05/23/us/
university-oklahoma-best-colleges-ranking/index.html.

Levin, Daniel J. 2002. "The Uses and Abuses of the U.S. News Rankings." *Priorities*, 20(fall): 1-19.

Levitz, Jennifer, and Melissa Korn. 2020. *Unacceptable: Privilege, Deceit, and the Making of
the College Admissions Scandal*. New York: Portfolio/Penguin.

Lieber, Ron. 2021. *The Price You Pay for College: An Entirely New Road Map for the Biggest
Financial Decision Your Family Will Ever Make*. New York: Harper.

Long, Mark C., Victor B. Saenz, and Marta Tienda. 2010. "Policy Transparency and
College Enrollment: Did the Texas Top Ten Percent Law Broaden Access to the Public
Flagships?" *Annals of the American Academy of Political and Social Science*, 627(1): 82-105.

Longden, Bernard. 2011. "Ranking Indicators and Weights." In Jung Cheol Shin, Robert K.
Toutkoushian, and Ulrich Teichler, eds., *University Rankings: Theoretical Basis,
Methodology, and Impacts on Global Higher Education*, 73-104. New York: Springer.

Lu, Vivi E., and Dekyi T. Tsotsong. 2021. "Harvard College Accepts Record-Low 3.43% of Applicants to Class of 2025." *Harvard Crimson*, Apr. 7, 2021. https://www.thecrimson.com/article/2021/4/7/harvard-admissions-2025/.

Luca, Michael. 2015. "Strategic Disclosure: The Case of Business School Rankings." *Journal of Economic Behavior and Organization*, 112: 17-25.

Luca, Michael, and Jonathan Smith. 2013. "Salience in Quality Disclosure: Evidence from the U.S. News College Rankings." *Journal of Economics and Management Strategy*, 22(1): 58-77.

Lumina Foundation. 2020. "The Degree Qualifications Profile." https://www.luminafoundation.org/files/resources/dqp.pdf. Accessed July 15, 2020.

Lydgate, Chris. 2019. "Students Find Glaring Discrepancy in U.S. News Rankings." *Reed Magazine*, July 24, 2019, https://www.reed.edu/reed-magazine/articles/2019/usnews-discrepancy.html.

Machung, A. 1998. "Playing the Ranking Game." *Change*, 30(4): 12-16.

Markovits, Daniel. 2019. *The Meritocracy Trap: How America's Foundational Myth Feeds Inequality, Dismantles the Middle Class, and Devours the Elite*. New York: Penguin.

Martin, Robert, and Carter Hill. 2013. "Involuntary and Voluntary Cost Increase in Private Research Universities." SSRN, Apr. 20, 2013, https://ssrn.com/abstract=2254339/.

Massey, Douglas S., Margarita Mooney, Kimberly C. Torres, and Camille Z. Charles. 2007. "Black Immigrants and Black Natives Attending Selective Colleges and Universities in the United States" *American Journal of Education*, 113(2): 243-271.

Mayhew, Matthew J., Alyssa N. Rockenbach, Nicholas A. Bowman, Tricia A. D. Seifert, and Gregory C. Wolniak. 2016. *How College Affects Students: 21st Century Evidence That Higher Education Works*, vol. 3. San Francisco: Jossey-Bass.

McDonough, Patricia, Anthony Lising, Antonio Marybeth Walpole, and Leonor Xochitl Perez. 1998. "College Rankings: Democratized College Knowledge for Whom?" *Research in Higher Education*, 39(5): 513-537.

McPhee, John. 2011. *Giving Good Weight*. New York: Farrar, Straus & Giroux.

McPherson, Michael S., and Morton Owen Schapiro. 1998. *The Student Aid Game: Meeting Need and Rewarding Talent in American Higher Education*. Princeton, NJ: Princeton University Press.

Medina, Jennifer, Katie Benner, and Kate Taylor. 2019. "Actresses, Business Leaders and Other Wealthy Parents Charged in U.S. College Entry Fraud." *New York Times*, Mar. 12, 2019.

Meredith, Marc. 2004. "Why Do Universities Compete in the Rankings Game? An Empirical Analysis of the Effects of the U.S. News and World Report College Rankings." *Research in Higher Education*, 45(5): 443-461.

Meyer, Andrew G., Andrew R. Hanson, and Daniel C. Hickman. 2017. "Perceptions of Institutional Quality: Evidence of Limited Attention to Higher Education Rankings." *Journal of Economic Behavior and Organization*, 142(C): 241-258.

Mfume, Tiffany Beth. 2019. *The College Completion Glass—Half-Full or Half-Empty? Exploring the Value of Post-Secondary Education*. London: Rowman & Littlefield.

Money. 2020. "The Best Colleges in America, Ranked by Value," Aug. 25, 2020. https://money.com/best-colleges/.

Monks, James, and Ronald Ehrenberg. 1999. "U.S. News & World Report's College Rankings: Why Do They Matter?" *Change*, 31(6): 42-51.

Moody's. 2020. "Outlook for US Higher Education Sector Remains Negative in 2021 as Pandemic Effects Curtail Revenue." Moody's Investor Service, Dec. 8, 2020, https://www.moodys.com/research/Moodys-Outlook-for-US-higher-education-sector-remains-negative-in-PBM_1255981/.

Morphew, Christopher C., and Christopher Swanson. 2011. "On the Efficacy of Raising Your Rankings." In Jung Cheol Shin, Robert K. Toutkoushian, and Ulrich Teichler, eds., *University Rankings: Theoretical Basis, Methodology, and Impacts on Global Higher Education*, 185-199. New York: Springer.

Morse, Robert. 2008. "The Birth of the College Rankings." U.S. News & World Report, May 16, 2008, https://www.usnews.com/news/national/articles/2008/05/16/the-birth-of-college-rankings/.

Morse, Robert, and Eric Brooks. 2020. "How U.S. News Calculated the 2021 Best Colleges Rankings." Sept. 13, 2020, https://www.usnews.com/education/best-colleges/articles/how-us-news-calculated-the-rankings/.

Morse, Robert, Matt Mason, and Eric Brooks. 2019. "Updates to 5 Schools' 2019 Best College Rankings." U.S. News & World Report, July 25, 2019, https://www.usnews.com/education/blogs/college-rankings-blog/articles/2019-07-25/updates-to-5-schools-2019-best-colleges-rankings-data/.

Myers, Michele Tolela. 2007. "The Cost of Bucking the College Rankings." *Washington Post*, Mar. 11, 2007.

National Student Clearinghouse Research Center. 2019. "Snapshot Report: Yearly Success and Progress Rates (Fall 2012 Entering Cohort)," Spring 2019. https://nscresearchcenter.org/wp-content/uploads/SnapshotReport34.pdf.

NCES (National Center for Educational Statistics). 2017. "The Condition of Education 2017." https://nces.ed.gov/pubsearch/pubsinfo.asp?pubid=2017144/.

———. 2019. "The Condition of Education 2019." https://nces.ed.gov/pubsearch/pubsinfo.asp?pubid=2019144/.

———. 2020. "IPEDS 2020-21 Data Collection System." https://surveys.nces.ed.gov/ipeds/public/glossary/.

———. n.d. "College Navigator." https://nces.ed.gov/collegenavigator/.

Nelson, Christopher B. 2015. "Salary Isn't the Only Measure." Inside Higher Ed, Sept. 14, 2015, https://www.insidehighered.com/views/2015/09/14/essay-criticizes-obama-administrations-new-scorecard-colleges/.

Niche. 2021. "2021 Best Colleges in America." https://www.niche.com/colleges/search/best
-colleges/.

Nichols, Andrew Howard. 2020. "Segregation Forever? The Continued Underrepresentation
of Black and Latino Undergraduates at the Nation's 101 Most Selective Public Colleges
and Universities." Education Trust, July 21, 2020, https://edtrust.org/resource
/segregation-forever/. Accessed Aug. 24, 2020.

Nocera, Joe. 2012. "The College Rankings Racket." *New York Times*, Sept. 28, 2012.

NSSE (National Survey of Student Engagement). 2020. "Evidence-Based Improvement in
Higher Education." https://nsse.indiana.edu. Accessed July 24, 2020.

Opportunity Insights. 2020. "The American Dream Is Fading. Only Half of Children Today
Grow Up to Earn More Than Their Parents." https://opportunityinsights.org/national
_trends/. Accessed Aug. 17, 2020.

Parchment. 2020. "Parchment Student Choice College Rankings 2020." https://www
.parchment.com/c/college/college-rankings.php.

Park, Julie J., and M. Kevin Eagan. 2011. "Who Goes Early? A Multi-Level Analysis of
Enrolling via Early Action and Early Decision Admissions." *Teachers College Record*,
113(11): 2345-2373.

Payscale. 2020. "PayScale's 2020-21 College Salary Report." https://www.payscale.com
/college-salary-report/.

———. 2021."Best Value Colleges." https://payscale.com/college-roi/. Accessed Jan. 1, 2021.

Peretz, Evgenia. 2019. "To Cheat and Lie in L.A." *Vanity Fair*, Sept. 2019, https://archive.
vanityfair.com/article/2019/9/to-cheat-and-lie-in-la/.

Pérez-Peña, Richard, and Daniel E. Slotnick. 2012. "Gaming the College Rankings." *New York
Times*, Jan. 31, 2012.

Pike, Gary R. 2004. "Measuring Quality: A Comparison of the U.S. News Rankings and
NSSE Benchmarks." *Research in Higher Education*, 45(2): 193-208.

Plessy v. Ferguson, 163 U.S. 537 (1896).

Plomin, Robert, and Frank M. Spinath. 2004. "Intelligence: Genetics, Genes, and
Genomics." *Journal of Personality and Social Psychology*, 86(1): 112-129.

Porter, Stephen R. 2000. "The Robustness of the Graduate Rate Performance Indicator
Used in the U.S. News & World Report College Rankings." *CASE International Journal of
Educational Advancement*, 1(2): 145-164.

———. 2011. "Do College Student Surveys Have Any Validity?" *Review of Higher Education*,
35(1): 45-76.

Princeton Review. 2021A. "The Best Law Schools 2021." https://www.princetonreview.com
/law-school-rankings/best-law-schools/.

———. 2021B. "The Best 386 Colleges, 2021A." https://www.princetonreview.com/college
-rankings/best-colleges/.

Public University Honors. 2020. "Average U.S. News Rankings for 123 Universities: 2013-2021," Sept. 14, 2020, https://publicuniversityhonors.com/. [Similar summaries for earlier periods can also be found at this URL.]

Purdue University. 2021. "Gallup-Purdue Index: Measuring the Most Important Outcomes of Higher Education." https://www.purdue.edu/newsroom/gallup/. Accessed May 6, 2021.

QS (Quacquarelli Symonds). 2020. "QS World University Rankings 2020." https://www.topuniversities.com/university-rankings/world-university-rankings/2020/.

Quintana, Chris. 2019. "U.S. News & World Report Ranks America's 'Best' Colleges, but Is There Really a Way to Know?" *USA Today*, Aug. 7, 2019.

RateMyProfessors. 2020. https://www.ratemyprofessors.com. Accessed May 2, 2020.

Reed College. 2020. "Doctoral Degree Productivity 2005-2014." https://www.reed.edu/ir/phd.html. Accessed Aug. 17, 2020.

Regents of the University of California v. Bakke, 438 U.S. 265 (1978).

Reiter, Andrew G. 2021. "U.S. News & World Report Historical Liberal Arts College and University Rankings." Datasets, http://andyreiter.com/datasets/. Accessed Apr. 27, 2021.

Rivera, Lauren A. 2015. *Pedigree: How Elite Students Get Elite Jobs*. Princeton, NJ: Princeton University Press.

Rocha, Leon. 2018. "What's Inside the Times Higher Education World University Rankings' 'Academic Reputation Survey'?" USS Briefs No. 64, Nov. 25, 2018, https://ussbriefs.com/briefs/.

Roebuck, Jeremy, and Susan Snyder. 2021. "Ousted Temple Business School Dean Indicted on Fraud Charges Tied to College Rankings Scandal." *Philadelphia Inquirer*, Apr. 16, 2021.

Rojstaczer, Stuart, and Christopher Healy. 2012. "Where A Is Ordinary: The Evolution of American College and University Grading, 1940-2009." *Teachers College Record*, 114(7), https://gradeinflation.com/tcr2012grading.pdf.

Rothwell, Jonathan. 2015A. "The Stubborn Race and Class Gaps in College Quality." Brookings, Dec. 18, 2015, https://www.brookings.edu/research/the-stubborn-race-and-class-gaps-in-college-quality/.

——. 2015B. "Using Earnings Data to Rank Colleges: A Value-Added Approach Updated with College Scorecard Data." Brookings, Oct. 29, 2015, https://www.brookings.edu/research/using-earnings-data-to-rank-colleges-a-value-added-approach-updated-with-college-scorecard-data/.

Sachdev, Ameet. 2011. "University of Illinois Law School Under Review for False Admissions Data." *Chicago Tribune*, Oct. 7, 2011.

Sahlins, Marshall. 2020. "Lessons from Sonnenschein: Don't Alert Faculty to Your Plans." *Chicago Maroon*, Feb. 4, 2020, https://www.chicagomaroon.com/article/2020/2/4/lessons-sonnenschein-dont-alert-faculty-plans/.

Salinas-Jiménez, Maria del Mar, Joaquín Artés, and Javier Salinas-Jiménez. 2011. "Education as a Positional Good: A Life Satisfaction Approach." *Social Indicators Research*, 103(3): 409-426.

Sandel, Michael J. 2020. *The Tyranny of Merit: What's Become of the Common Good?* New York: Farrar, Straus & Giroux.

Sander, Richard. 2004. "A Systematic Analysis of Affirmative Action in American Law Schools." *Stanford Law Review*, 57(2): 367-483.

Sander, Richard, and Stuart Taylor Jr. 2012. *Mismatch: How Affirmative Action Hurts Students It's Intended to Help, and Why Universities Won't Admit It.* New York: Basic Books.

Sanoff, Alvin P. 2007. "The U.S. News College Rankings: A View from the Inside." In Institute for Higher Education Policy, ed., *College and University Ranking Systems: Global Perspectives and American Challenges*, 9-22, http://www.ihep.org.

Sauder, Michael. 2006. "Third Parties and Status Position: How the Characteristics of Status Systems Matter." *Theory and Society*, 35(3): 299-321.

Schifrin, Matt, and Hank Tucker. 2021. "College Financial Grades 2021: Will Your Alma Mater Survive Covid?" *Forbes*, Feb. 22, 2021.

Schmidt, Peter. 2008. "Most Colleges Chase Prestige on a Treadmill, Researchers Find." *Chronicle of Higher Education*, Nov. 10, 2008.

Schuette v. Coalition to Defend Affirmative Action, 572 U.S. 291 (2014).

Segal, David. 2011. "Is Law School a Losing Game?" *New York Times*, Jan. 8, 2011.

Selingo, Jeffrey. 2020. *Who Gets In and Why: A Year Inside College Admissions.* New York: Scribner.

———. 2021. "Harvard and Its Peers Should Be Embarrassed about How Few Students They Educate." *Washington Post*, Apr. 8, 2021.

Shanghai Ranking. 2020. "Academic Ranking of World Universities 2020." www.shanghairanking.com.

Shin, Jung Cheol, Robert K. Toutkoushian, and Ulrich Teichler, eds. 2011. *University Rankings: Theoretical Basis, Methodology, and Impacts on Global Higher Education.* New York: Springer.

Snyder, Susan. 2018. "Temple Pays More Than $5 Million to Settle Claims over False Reporting by Its Business School." *Philadelphia Inquirer*, Dec. 21, 2018.

Snyder, Susan, and Erin Arvedlund. 2019. "Ousted Temple Business Dean's Lawsuit Blames Administrators, Employees, and Oversight Group for Rankings Scandal." *Philadelphia Inquirer*, May 2, 2019.

Soares, Joseph A., ed. 2012. *SAT Wars: The Case for Test-Optional College Admissions.* New York: Teachers College Press.

Stake, Jeffrey Evans. 2006. "The Interplay between Law School Rankings, Reputations, and Resource Allocations: Ways Rankings Mislead." *Indiana Law Journal*, 81(1): 229-270.

Stecklow, Steve. 1995. "Cheat Sheets: Colleges Inflate SATs and Graduation Rates in Popular Guidebooks; Schools Say They Must Fib to U.S. News and Others to Compete Effectively; Moody's Requires the Truth." *Wall Street Journal*, Apr. 5, 1995.

——. 1997. "Real-Life Lessons vs. the Ivory Tower: Resistant to Academic Vogues, Reed Scores by Stressing Classics." *Wall Street Journal*, Mar. 7, 1997.

Steinberg, Jacques. 2002. *The Gatekeepers: Inside the Admission Process of a Premier College.* New York: Viking Penguin.

Stevens, Mitchell L. 2007. *Creating a Class: College Admissions and the Education of Elites.* Cambridge, MA: Harvard University Press.

Stolzenberg, Ellen Bara, Melissa C. Aragon, Edgar Romo, Victoria Couch, Destiny McLennan, M. Kevin Eagan, and Nathaniel Kang. 2019. "The American Freshman: National Norms Fall 2019." Higher Education Research Institute, UCLA, https://www .heri.ucla.edu/monographs/TheAmericanFreshman2019.pdf.

Strauss, Valerie. 2020. "Dozens of Colleges and Universities Are Dropping SAT/ACT Requirements for Fall 2021 Applicants, and Some for Longer." *Washington Post*, April 10, 2020.

Tamanaha, Brian. 2012. *Failing Law Schools.* Chicago: University of Chicago Press.

THE (Times Higher Education). 2020. "World University Rankings 2020," https://www .timeshighereducation.com/world-university-rankings/.

Tierney, John. 2013. "Your Annual Reminder to Ignore the U.S. News & World Report College Rankings." *Atlantic*, Sept. 10, 2013, https://www.theatlantic.com.

Tough, Paul. 2019. *The Years That Matter Most: How College Makes or Breaks Us.* New York: Houghton Mifflin Harcourt.

Trachtenberg, Stephen Joel. 2012. "The Limits of the College Rankings 'Racket.'" CNN, Feb. 9, 2012, https://www.cnn.com/2012/02/08/opinion/trachtenberg-college-rankings /index.html.

Tutterow, Craig, and James Evans. 2016. "Reconciling the Small Effect of Rankings on University Performance with the Transformational Cost of Conformity." *Research in the Sociology of Organizations*, 46:265-301.

University of Notre Dame Investment Office. 2020. "Endowment History." https://web .archive.org/web/20070831090327/http://investment.nd.edu/endowment/history .shtml. Accessed Aug. 10, 2020.

Upshot, The. 2017. "Economic Diversity and Student Outcomes at America's Colleges and Universities: Find Your College." *New York Times*, Jan. 18, 2017, https://www.nytimes .com/interactive/projects/college-mobility/.

US Department of Education. n.d. "College Affordability and Transparency List." https:// collegecost.ed.gov/affordability/.

——. n.d. "College Scorecard." https://collegescorecard.ed.gov.

U.S. News & World Report. 2020A. "Best Global Universities 2020." https://www.usnews.com/education/best-global-universities/.

———. 2020B. "Campus Ethnic Diversity." https://www.usnews.com/best-colleges/rankings/national-universities/campus-ethnic-diversity/. Accessed Aug. 25, 2020.

———. 2021A. "Top Performers on Social Mobility." https://premium.usnews.com/best-colleges/rankings/national-universities/social-mobility/.

———. 2021B. "U.S. News Best Colleges 2021." https://www.usnews.com/best-colleges/.

Veblen, Thorstein. 1899. *The Theory of the Leisure Class*. New York: Macmillan.

Wall Street Journal. 2020. "Best Colleges 2021: Explore the Full WSJ/THE College Ranking List," Sept. 17, 2020. https://www.wsj.com/articles/best-colleges-2021-explore-the-full-wsj-the-college-ranking-list-11600383830/.

Washington Monthly. 2020. "2020 College Guide and Rankings." https://washingtonmonthly.com/2020college-guide/.

Watanabe, Teresa. 2021. "UC Should Permanently Eliminate All Standardized Tests for Admissions, Experts Say." *Los Angeles Times*, Jan. 12, 2021.

Webster, David S. 1986. "Jack Gourman's Rankings of Colleges and Universities: A Guide to the Perplexed." *RQ*, 25(3): 323-331.

Webster, Thomas J. 2001. "A Principal Component Analysis of U.S. News & World Report Tier Rankings of Colleges and Universities." *Economics of Education Review*, 20(3): 235-244.

Wermund, Benjamin. 2017. "How U.S. News College Rankings Promote Economic Inequality on Campus." Politico, Sept. 13, 2017, https://www.politico.com/interactives/2017/top-college-rankings-list-2017-us-news-investigation/.

Winston, Gordon C. 1999. "Subsidies, Hierarchy and Peers: The Awkward Economics of Higher Education." *Journal of Economic Perspectives*, 13(1): 13-36.

———. 2000. "The Positional Arms Race in Higher Education." Williams Project on the Economics of Higher Education, Apr. 2000, https://www.econstor.eu/handle/10419/23501.

Witteveen, Dirk, and Paul Attewell. 2017. "The Earnings Payoff from Attending a Selective College." *Social Science Research*, 66: 154-169.

Woo, Jennie H., and Susan P. Choy. 2011. "Merit Aid for Undergraduates: Trends from 1995-96 to 2007-08." NCES No. 2012-160, Oct. 2011. Statistics in Brief, https://nces.ed.gov/pubs2012/2012160.pdf.

Woodhouse, Kellie. 2015. "ABA Tightens Rules on Employment Reporting." Inside Higher Ed, Aug. 4, 2015, https://www.insidehighered.com/quicktakes/2015/08/04/aba-tightens-rules-employment-reporting/.

Young, Michael Dunlop. 1958. *The Rise of the Meritocracy: An Essay on Education and Inequality*. London: Thames & Hudson.

Yudkovich, Maria, Philip G. Altbach, and Laura E. Rumbley, eds. 2016. *The Global Academic Rankings Game: Changing Institutional Policy, Practice, and Academic Life*. New York: Routledge.

Zahneis, Megan. 2018. "Temple U. Says Several Programs Submitted False Data to 'U.S. News.'" *Chronicle of Higher Education*, July 25, 2018.

Zaloom, Caitlin. 2019. *Indebted: How Families Make College Work at Any Cost*. Princeton, NJ: Princeton University Press.

Zemsky, Robert. 2009. *Making Reform Work: The Case for Transforming American Higher Education*. New Brunswick, NJ: Rutgers University Press.

Zemsky, Robert, and Susan Shaman. 2017. *The Market Imperative: Segmentation and Change in Higher Education*. Baltimore: Johns Hopkins University Press.

Zemsky, Robert, Susan Shaman, and Susan Campbell Baldridge. 2020. *The College Stress Test: Tracking Institutional Futures across a Crowded Market*. Baltimore: Johns Hopkins University Press.

Zhang, Liang. 2005. "Do Measures of College Quality Matter? The Effect of College Quality on Graduates' Earnings." *Review of Higher Education*, 28(4): 571-596.

Zull, James E. 2002. *The Art of Changing the Brain: Enriching the Practice of Teaching by Exploring the Biology of Learning*. Sterling, VA: Stylus.

Zwick, Rachel. 2017. *Who Gets In? Strategies for Fair and Effective College Admissions*. Cambridge, MA: Harvard University Press.

INDEX

163–64, 164t, 293; character and mission, 19, 292; cost of attendance, 234, 246t, 247; educational program, 293; finances, 94t, 96–87, 110t, 293–94; graduation rates, 218t, 220t, 223, 230; history, 174, 292–93; post-graduate outcomes, 231t, 234, 236–37, 263; racial and ethnic diversity, 182, 183; rankings, 28t, 29, 54; social mobility measures, 256, 258t, 258–59; socioeconomic diversity, 181, 249t, 250; student life, 293; wealth of, 94t, 103t

CLA (Collegiate Learning Assessment), 190–92

Claremont McKenna College, 65, 69

class-rank statistics, 125, 128–30

class-size metrics, 57, 209–10

Clemson University, 65

Clotfelter, Charles, 147

Cohodes, Sarah, 147

Cole, Charles W., 289

Cole, Johnetta Betsch, 301

Colgate University, 39

College Board, 11, 133, 136–37, 147, 251. *See also* standardized admissions tests

college guides, 16, 23, 46, 64, 124–25, 276–77

CollegeNet, 30, 256

college rankings: arguments against, 12–22; arguments in favor, 10–12; comprehensive ("best-colleges") rankings, 27–29, 41–42, 272–73, 276; eight profile schools, rankings of, 28t; fluctuations, year to year, 50, 58; history, 24–32, 274; personalized rankings, 27, 41–42, 275; global university rankings, 31–32; specialized rankings, 29–31, 274–75. *See also* ranking formulas; rankings' impacts

College Raptor, 94

College Scorecard, 15, 71, 125, 229–31, 254,

276–77

College Stress Test, The, 104–5

College Student Experiences Questionnaire (CSEQ), 194

Collegiate Assessment of Academic Proficiency (CAAP), 190

Collegiate Learning Assessment (CLA), 190–92

Columbia Law School, 156–57

commencement ceremonies, 212–13

Common Data Set, 16, 284

Commonfund, 107

Conant, James, 132

consumer preferences, diversity of, 13

consumer product ratings, 7–10

Consumer Reports, 9–10

Cooperative Institutional Research Program (CIRP), 44–45

cost of attendance. *See* affordability

Council for Advancement and Support of Education (CASE), 98

COVID-19 pandemic, impact of, 105, 153, 163, 294, 301

Crossing the Finish Line, 223

curricular structure and content, 198–200

Dale, Stacy, 237–38

Dartmouth College, 100, 157

Debrett's Peerage and Baronetage, 83

Delisle, Jason, 250–51

Dillard University, 222, 277

Diver, Benjamin and Ethleen, 77–79

Dropout Scandal, The, 217

Duncan, Arne, 276

Dynarski, Susan, 146

Early Admission Game, The, 167

early admissions. *See* admissions

selectivity and, 169; transfer students and, 219–21

Griffiths, Amanda, 39

Griswold, Erwin, 215, 216

Guinier, Lani, 81

Halberstam, David, 119

Hampshire College, 152–54, 277

Hansmann, Henry, 20–21, 121

Harvard Law School, 20–21, 40, 215

Harvard University: acceptance rate, 163; affirmative action lawsuit against, 101, 169, 181; curriculum, 200; early admissions, 167–68; fundraising, 98, 101; grade inflation, 127; pedigree-conferring role of, 77–78, 79; peer-effect learning and instructional costs at, 121; rankings, 28; student debt, 255

HBCUs (historically Black colleges and universities), 174, 222, 283, 300, 301–2

Hendrix College, 38

Hershbein, Brad, 239

higher education: complexity of the product, 12–13; consumers as producers of, 14; fulfilling life, as preparation for, 262–63, 268–69; long-term impacts of, 14–15; pedigree-conferring role of, 11, 78–84; as a "positional good," 82; as a private consumption good, 272; as a public-serving good, 271–72

higher education industry: classification of institutions in, 17–18; competitive structure of, 271–72; institutional diversity of, 17–20, 285–87; selective and nonselective tiers of, x, 174, 244–45

Higher Education Price Index (HEPI), 107

historically Black colleges and universities. See HBCUs

Holy Cross College, 77

How College Affects Students, 184

Hoxby, Caroline, 110–11, 113, 124, 238

Illinois, University of, Law School, 60, 66

instructional quality: curricular content and structure, 198–200; peer ratings of, 202–4; sound pedagogical practices and, 201; student ratings of, 204–6

instructional resources: class-size measures, 209–10; faculty compensation, 207; faculty credentials, 208; spending per student, 207–8; student-faculty ratio, 208

Iona College, 65, 69, 71

IPEDS (Integrated Postsecondary Education Data System). *See* US Department of Education

Ivy League, 21, 82, 113, 127, 166, 297–98, 302

"Ivy Plus" (or "expanded Ivies"), 26, 28, 244–45, 251, 259–60, 302

Jack, Anthony, 252

Jefferson, Thomas, 79

Jobs, Steve, 216

Johns Hopkins University, 98

Johnson, Lyndon B., 176

Johnson & Wales University, 66

Kelly, Brian, 67

Kennedy, John F., 119, 242–44, 261

Kidder, William, 180–81

Kim, Matthew, 167

Kimbrough, Walter, 222

Kirp, David, 217

Koblik, Steven, 1, 51

Kronman, Anthony, 81, 263, 267

Krueger, Alan, 237–38

Kutner, Max, 56–57

295–96; post-graduate outcomes, 231t, 263; racial and ethnic diversity, 182; rankings, 28t, 88, 159t; religious life, 297; social mobility measures, 258t, 258–59; socioeconomic diversity, 249t, 250; student-choice rankings, 159–61; wealth of, 94t, 95, 103t, 296

Obama, Barack, 213, 276

Oklahoma, University of, 65

Opportunity Insights, 31, 102, 256

Palin, Sarah, 12

Parchment student-choice rankings, 30, 159–62

parents of applicants and students, 46, 97, 100–103, 103t, 254

PayScale, 20, 72, 229, 231–33, 235, 237, 263–64

pedigree, 79–84, 272

peer assessment of colleges: anchoring effect of, 90; echo effect of, 90; gaming of, 57; lack of expertise by raters, 85–87; rankings and, 25, 27; response rate, 25, 88–89; standards for, 87–88; systematic biases in, 88

Pell grant program: eight profile schools, Pell data for, 249t; history, 249–50; Pell graduation rate, 36, 222, 251–53; "Pell share," 248–51

Penn (University of Pennsylvania): admissions, 139t, 163–64, 164t, 166; athletics, 297–98; character and mission, 19, 298; cost of attendance, 234, 246t, 247–48, 249t; educational program, 298; finances, 94t, 110t; financial aid, 144, 248; graduation rates, 218t, 220t, 223, 230; history, 297–98; post-graduate outcomes, 231t, 233–37, 264, 266; racial

and ethnic diversity, 182; rankings, 28t, 58, 60, 159t; social mobility measures, 258t, 258–59; socioeconomic diversity, 230, 249t, 250; student-choice rankings, 159–61; student life, 298; wealth of, 94t, 103t

Penn Law School, 2, 56, 156–57, 172, 212–13, 227, 255

Pérez, Angel, 114–15

Peterson's college guides, 16, 23, 46

Pine Manor College, 183

positional goods, 82–83, 108–9

post-graduate careers, 225–26, 263–65

post-graduate earnings: College Scorecard data on, 229, 231–34, 240; eight profile schools, data for, 231t; employment discrimination and, 233; employment rate of graduates, 66, 226–29; field of study and, 233–34; human capital explanation of, 236–39; PayScale data on, 231–33; selection bias explanation of, 236; signaling explanation of, 236–39. *See also* return on investment; social mobility

prestige: pedigree and, 11, 77–84; peer assessment of, 85–89; spending as proxy for, 106–16; wealth as proxy for, 92–103

Princeton Review, 29–30, 46–47, 71–72, 204–5, 297

Princeton University, 28, 40–41, 100, 127, 163, 168, 253, 255

Privileged Poor, The, 252

Profiles of American Colleges, 123

public universities: American dream and, 244; Collegiate Learning Assessment test scores at, 191; decline of state support for, 293–95; high-tuition/high-giving model of, 19, 146, 295; merit aid, use by, 146; performance funding of, 60–61, 214;

public universities (*cont.*)
  racial and ethnic diversity of, 175, 177;
  rankings' impact on, 26

Quinnipiac University, 54

racial and ethnic diversity: affirmative
  action and, 175–77, 180–81; curricular
  diversity, 179; educational justifications
  for, 178; interactive diversity, 178–79;
  national trends, 174–75; rankings and,
  173, 176, 182–85; remedial justification
  for, 175–76, 179–82
rankings formulas: changes over time, 26–
  27, 39–41; multicollinearity of variables
  in, 36–38; salience of ranking numbers
  in, 38–39; variables, choice of, 35–36;
  variables, weighting of, 36
rankings' impacts: college applicants,
  44–48; college self-promotion, 59–60;
  distortion of priorities, 60–61; educators'
  behavior, 49–63; institutional diversity,
  17–22; law schools, 55–56; performance
  evaluation of educators, 61–62;
  undergraduate programs, 56–58
rankings resistance: advice to educators,
  280–85; non-cooperation rate, 54;
  penalties for, 52–54; presidents' letter
  urging, 51–52; Reed College and, ix, 1–2,
  51, 52–53; Stanford University and, 51
"rankocracy," x, 2, 272
Rask, Kevin, 39
RateMyProfessors.com, 30, 205
Reed College: admissions, 139t, 157, 161–62,
  164t, 164, 168; character and mission,
  19, 298; commencement, 212–13; cost
  of attendance, 246t, 249t; educational
  program, 189–90, 197–99, 215, 299–300;

faculty, 299; finances, 94t, 95, 110t,
  299–300; financial aid, 144, 147, 248;
  grading policy, 126–27; graduation rates,
  215–16, 218t, 220t, 221; history, 298–99;
  post-graduate outcomes, 231t, 255–56,
  266–67; racial and ethnic diversity, 172,
  182; rankings, 28t; refusal to cooperate
  with rankings, 1–2, 51–54, 68–69;
  social mobility measures, 258t, 259;
  socioeconomic diversity, 249t; student-
  choice rankings, 159–62; student life, 168,
  299–300; wealth of, 94t, 103t
research productivity and rankings, 31, 207–9
return on investment (ROI), 234–36
revealed-preference rankings, 159t
Rivera, Lauren, 82
Rochester, University of, 50–51
Rodin, Judith, 58
Rojstaczer, Stuart, 127
Roksa, Josipa, 191, 195
Rothwell, Jonathan, 175

Sandel, Michael, 80, 81–82
Sander, Richard, 180–81
Sanoff, Alvin, 36, 52–53, 59
Sarah Lawrence College, 53, 152–53
SAT. *See* standardized admissions tests
Sauder, Michael, 55, 61
Schapiro, Morton, 147
Scripps College, 66, 99
Selingo, Jeffrey, 113
Shaman, Susan, 37
Shape of the River, The, 181
Simmons College, 78
Singer, Rick, 101–2
social mobility: eight profile schools, data
  for, 258t; higher education's role in
  promoting, 242–44; methods to increase,

academic quality, 170–71; as measure
of admissions success, 124, 162–64;
rankings, use in, 16
Young, Michael Dunlop, 80

Zemsky, Robert, 37, 58, 104–5, 210–11
Zimmer, Robert, 21
Zuckerman, Mortimer, 25